Praise for *My Journe*

*"I am honoured to provide a strong recommendation
to read Canon Andrew White's extraordinary book. I came to know and
respect Canon White when we worked in Iraq in the hectic days following
Saddam's overthrow. I now serve on the Board of his not-for-profit
organization which helps refugees and the underprivileged in the Middle East.
This well-written book is full of Andrew's light humour and deep Christian
faith. We learn of the rich spiritual life of his parents and then are taken on
the wonderful voyage of Andrew's own spiritual growth over the next forty
years. Andrew's lifelong struggle with health problems has only increased
his devotion and faith. The book is a fitting tribute to his lifelong faith and
continued work for the poor and the forgotten."*

Ambassador Paul Bremer, former Presidential Envoy to Iraq

*"Andrew White is the most extraordinary friend I have. His story so far is a
rollercoaster of a journey – and this is not fiction! This story will infuse
faith, hope and love."*

Revd Canon J.John

*"Abouna Andrew is for us in Iraq not just a spiritual
leader for the Christians: he is the spiritual leader of all of us Iraqis,
Sunni, Shia, and others. He has stood with us and been our supporter and
defender for nearly two decades. When people were too afraid even to come
to Iraq he stayed with us. He is like the Almighty: he will never leave us.
However hard the circumstances he is with us."*

Grand Ayatollah Hussein Al-Sadr, The Grand Ayatollah
of Khadameer, Baghdad

*"Canon Andrew White has devoted his life to the true mission
of religion – to assist, comfort and save lives of human beings in the most
difficult places of conflict. He is a messenger of divine peace in the world, and
a great friend of the Jewish people."*

Rabbi Melchior, Chief Rabbi of Norway, and former
Member of the Knesset

BY THE SAME AUTHOR:

Iraq: Searching for Hope (Continuum, 2007)
Suffer the Children (Continuum, 2010)
Faith Under Fire (Monarch Books, 2011)
Father, Forgive (Monarch Books, 2013)

THE VICAR OF BAGHDAD

MY JOURNEY SO FAR

AN AUTOBIOGRAPHY

ANDREW WHITE

Text copyright *The Vicar of Baghdad* © 2009 Andrew White
Text copyright *My Journey So Far* © 2015 Andrew White
This edition copyright © 2021 Lion Hudson IP Limited

Published by
Lion Hudson Limited
Prama House, 267 Banbury Road
Summertown, Oxford OX2 7HT, England
www.lionhudson.com

ISBN 978-0-74598-119-2
e-ISBN 978-0-74598-145-1

The Vicar of Baghdad first edition 2009
My Journey So Far first edition 2015

Acknowledgments
Unless otherwise stated, Scripture quotations taken from the Holy Bible, New
International Version Anglicised. Copyright 1979, 1984, 2011 Biblica, formerly
International Bible Society. Used by permission of Hodder & Stoughton Ltd, an
Hachette UK company. All rights reserved. "NIV" is a registered trademark of
Biblica. UK trademark number 1448790.

Scripture quotations marked NKJV taken from the New King James Version.
Copyright © 1982 by Thomas Nelson, Inc. Used by permission. All right reserved.

Scripture quotations marked KJV taken from the Authorized (King James) Version.
Rights in the Authorized Version are vested in the Crown. Reproduced by permission
of the Crown's patentee, Cambridge University Press.

Extract p. 196-98 taken from 'Charles Simeon: Pastor of a Generation' by Handley
Moule, published by Christian Focus Publications, Fearn, Ross-shire, Scotland
www.christianfocus.com

Extract p. 354 taken from *All of Us* by Raymond Carver, copyright © 1997 Raymond
Carver. Published by Harvill Press.

Every effort has been made to trace copyright holders and to obtain permission for
the use of copyright material. The publisher apologizes for any errors or omissions
and would be grateful to be notified of any corrections that should be incorporated in
future reprints of this book.

A catalogue record for this book is available from the British Library

Printed and bound in the United Kingdom, May 2021, LH29

I dedicate this book
to my mother, Pauline S. White;
Al, Alan, Jason, Jason and Peter
and all my friends at GardaWorld:
Jeff, Frank, John, Martin and Tank,
the ops managers, and our HQ team:
Del, Mick, Badger, Martin, Sean, Norrie,
Rollie and Taff and Natalie,
the international director.

Contents

PART 1

THE VICAR OF BAGHDAD

Acknowledgements

This book is about fighting for peace on the front line in some of the most difficult places in the world. It has itself been very difficult to write and edit. Here in Baghdad we do not even have proper internet access, but my editor, Huw Spanner, has persevered to the end and I would like to begin by thanking him.

Then, I would like to thank two of my closest co-workers for peace, both politicians, both men of faith, one a Jew and one a Muslim. Without Rabbi Michael Melchior in Israel and Dr Mowaffak al-Rubaie here in Iraq, there would have been no story to tell.

I would also like to thank all my staff, and especially those who are with me on the front line: in Iraq, the other two corners of "the Triangle", Samir Raheem al-Soodani and Essam al-Saadi, and in Israel/Palestine Hanna Ishaq.

I thank all my staff in Britain, my trustees and my two boards of advisers, on both sides of the Atlantic; but especially Rosie Watt, my project officer, who has overseen the writing of this book.

Everybody mentioned in these pages is part of the story and I thank them all. We pray that indeed, one day, peace and reconciliation will come to this region of the world.

Baghdad, 10 October 2008

Foreword

During my years at Canterbury I had the privilege of working with Andrew White on a number of occasions. A very special memory stands out when he enlisted my support to bring together the religious leaders of the Middle East region, in order to sign what would become The First Alexandria Declaration of the Religious Leaders of the Holy Land – a momentous document which owed a great deal to Andrew's tireless diplomacy.

Andrew is, truly, one of the most remarkable men I have ever encountered. With intelligence and exuberant energy, allied to a profound personal faith, he would be a force to be reckoned with in any walk of life. But what sets him apart is his capacity to love, and be loved. Children trust him. Crusty old clerics trust him. His staff esteem him. His words, often blunt, are always laced with humour and affection. If one gift above all sets him apart, it is that he is gifted in friendship.

The importance of this book is what it says about the centrality of religion in any discussion of the Middle East. In the secularized West politicians, diplomats and soldiers tend to discount, or underestimate, the importance of faith, but in countries like Iraq it simply cannot be ignored. Andrew White is trusted where few others can win confidence. A man of faith can speak to men of faith.

I wholeheartedly commend this book to your attention. It is an inspirational read.

LORD CAREY OF CLIFTON

(103rd Archbishop of Canterbury)

A Quite Unexpected Theatre

When I was young, I certainly had no intention of working in the Middle East. I remember when I was ten telling my teacher I wanted to work in anaesthetics and be a priest. She told me I could only do one thing and I was a Baptist and they didn't have priests. I had already read my first book on anaesthetics – I was a very strange child – and by the time I had finished my schooling seven years later my one desire was to go to St Thomas' Hospital in London and train as an "operating department practitioner".

And so I did, and I loved every minute of it. I had no desire ever to leave the medical world – to me it proved to be more wonderful than I had even imagined. But then, late one night, while I was on call for cardiac arrests, I went to pray in the hospital grounds, looking across the River Thames towards Big Ben. I had only recently qualified and I remember thanking God for all he had enabled me to achieve – passing my exams with distinction and getting the job I had always wanted at the hospital I'd always wanted to work at. I thought I should ask what I ought to do next – I hoped the Almighty would want me to just carry on with what I was doing. To my utter amazement, however, I felt very clearly that I was being called to go into the church – in fact, the Church of England.

I had no wish to be ordained, but I went to see Sir Nicholas Rivett-Carnac, the vicar of St Mark's, Kennington, the Anglican church that, like many of the hospital staff, I attended. He was one of the gentlest, wisest and most Spirit-filled men I have ever met, and he encouraged me. In due course, I embarked on the slow process that leads to ordination – and to my surprise found that things moved rather quickly. I also came to experience the glory of God as I never had done before. St Mark's was so alive, and so was the Christian Union at St Thomas'. When I went into the operating theatre early in the morning, the sense of God's presence was so real that often I felt I was in heaven. I spent my days singing his praises. As the weeks went by, my desire to go into the church increased almost by the hour and it wasn't long before all I wanted in life was to be ordained and serve God full-time. Eventually, I went to Ridley Hall, Cambridge and started my training for the Anglican ministry.

I didn't find my theological education easy. Spiritually, I would describe it as something of a "wilderness experience". Certainly, it was a good deal harder than my previous training at St Thomas' – at least, until I started studying Judaism under the inspirational professor Nicholas de Lange. This was a subject I felt passionate about. It had fascinated me ever since I was a child: my father had often talked to me about it, and it related to international affairs that had interested and enthused me since my last two years at school. The head of those years, Michael Amos, was one of the most inspiring people I have ever met. Not only did he teach me politics and economics, I would spend my lunch breaks in his study while he went through the serious newspapers with us and talked to us about the world. (I wasn't surprised when, many years later, his daughter became Leader of the House of Lords. In November 2007, when I was awarded the Woolf Institute's Pursuer of Peace Award at the Middle Temple in London, to my delight it was Baroness Amos who presented it to me, and in the presence of her father.)

Studying Judaism gave me the opportunity to take further my interest in international affairs, and in particular my interest in the Middle East. Crucial to the latter was a very English crisis at Cambridge. In 1988, members of the university's inter-collegiate Christian union (known as Ciccu) who were organizing its triennial mission decided to invite evangelists from Jews for Jesus to take part, to try to convert Jewish students. This caused a great deal of resentment among the practising Jews, who asked me to intervene. I was known to both sides and trusted and respected by both – by Ciccu's evangelicals because I was studying at a conservative evangelical college, and because the chair of their mission committee was a good friend of mine (indeed, in due course he was to be my best man!), and by the Jews because I regularly attended Cambridge's Orthodox synagogue and prayed there in Hebrew alongside them.

I told my fellow Christians that trying to persuade people to change their religion is a very dangerous undertaking, but in any event it can be done only if you form a relationship with them. The outcome was that Ciccu went ahead, very carefully, with its evangelistic meeting; but subsequently Jewish and Christian students got together to set up a society called Cambridge University Jews and Christians (or Cujac). This soon became a branch of the Council of Christians and Jews (CCJ), and it was only a matter of time before I found myself chairing the young leadership section of the International Council of Christians and Jews. I worked closely with Sir Sigmund Sternberg, the chair of the ICCJ, and learned a lot from him.

As part of my course at Cambridge, I spent some of my final year in Jerusalem, at the Hebrew University and an Ultra-Orthodox Jewish *yeshiva* or seminary. This was a life-shaping experience, totally different from anything else I had ever encountered. It was the first time I had engaged seriously with another faith tradition – a tradition, moreover, that was the foundation of my own religion. Originally, I had gone there to study the role of Israel – the people, the land and finally the state – in Christian thought; but I was challenged by seeing at first hand how these Jews practised their faith. So much of their religion was concerned with what they did rather than what they believed – quite the opposite from most Christianity. I had always been taught, by people who had very little understanding of it, that Judaism is all about legalism; but what I observed was that actually the 613 *mitzvot*, or commandments, had one purpose only: to please God.

At the same time, I also got to know well several Islamic leaders in Jerusalem, and so my study of Islam began.

On a second visit to Jerusalem, between my graduation from Cambridge and my ordination, I was instructed by an Ultra-Orthodox rabbi to go and see a woman known as Sister Ruth Heflin, who ran a very charismatic and rather American church called the Mount Zion Fellowship. She proved to be the most forceful person I have ever met. Indeed, I was scared of her. At the end of the first meeting I attended, in her house in East Jerusalem, she came up to me and started to prophesy over me. She had never met me before and knew nothing about me, but she declared that my calling in life was to "seek the peace of Jerusalem and the Middle East". At that stage, I couldn't make any sense of this (and I certainly had no inkling that "the Middle East" might include Iraq) but what I did understand was that her home was filled with the glory of God as I had never experienced it before.

Back in England, I was ordained in 1990 in a wonderful service at Southwark Cathedral and then started work as a curate, or assistant minister, at St Mark's Church, Battersea Rise in south London. It was at this time that I got married to the most wonderful – and most tolerant – woman I have ever met. I was preaching one day when I looked down from the pulpit and saw her for the first time. I liked what I saw so much that afterwards I went up to her and, even though I knew nothing about her, asked if she would help me to organize a mission. Six weeks later, I asked Caroline to marry me.

Our wedding was conducted by Donald Coggan, a former archbishop of Canterbury, who had become my mentor in life. Every time we met, he would say when we parted: "Don't take care, take risks!" I have never forgotten those words.

My involvement in Jewish-Christian relations continued. (So, indeed, did my work in anaesthetics, though now more as a hobby. Each week on my day off I went to St Thomas' to work as a volunteer. I doubt very much that that would be allowed today.) I regularly travelled overseas, and increasingly to the Middle East. I also deepened my acquaintance with Islam – initially in Africa, in Kenya and Nigeria for example, after the ICCJ had set up its Abrahamic Forum to promote interreligious dialogue between all three of the great monotheistic faiths. It was clear to me that if I was going to play a role in the Middle East I had to understand Islam as well as Judaism. To the surprise of my vicar, I had regular audiences with the Pope to brief him on my work, and we enjoyed a close relationship – I even took Caroline to meet him on one occasion. I liked him so much. As a Strict and Particular Baptist I had been brought up to think of the Vatican as the home of the Antichrist, but I had learned to respect Catholics for the certainty of their faith, and I had also come to believe that godliness matters more than doctrinal correctness (and not only in Christians).

After three years, I moved a mile down the road to become priest-in-charge of the Church of the Ascension, Balham Hill. The congregation was struggling, but it was a wonderful mix of black and white and rich and poor, and at times the glory of God came down there. I was very involved in the local community and eventually was voted onto Wandsworth Borough Council, where in due course I became chair of social services. Meanwhile, I was still chairing the young leadership section of the ICCJ, and by this stage we had also created an active branch of that section in the British CCJ, which was led by another great Jewish friend, Paul Mendel. I didn't know what God was preparing me for, and yet I was receiving an excellent grounding in the fundamentals of international relations and reconciliation.

At St Mark's, my vicar had told me off for being away so much, but now as a vicar myself I travelled all the more. I limited myself to being absent no more than one Sunday in six, but that still meant I could go abroad for almost two weeks at a time. I went back and forth to the Holy Land and the Holy See, and also became ever more involved in the Islamic world. In 1994, jointly with Lord Coggan, I was given the Sir Sigmund Sternberg Award for my "sustained contribution to the furtherance of interreligious understanding". I have won many other prizes since then, but none has meant as much to me as the one I shared with him.

Then, one day in 1998, having been at the Church of the Ascension for not quite five years, my bishop, Roy Williamson, suggested that I should apply for the job as canon in charge of international ministry at Coventry Cathedral. At the age of thirty-three I was barely old enough for such a senior position, but he encouraged me to apply anyway, and to my surprise

I was appointed and was soon installed. The cathedral of St Michael's, Coventry is a wonderful place, with an extraordinary history of taking risks for the sake of reconciliation. Moreover, I was succeeding Paul Oestreicher, a truly great man whom I had long admired from afar. Nonetheless, leaving the Church of the Ascension was one of the hardest things I have ever had to do. I loved those people so much, and when I had to tell them I was going I broke down in tears.

My enthusiasm for my new job was undiminished by the discovery that I had multiple sclerosis, a degenerative disease for which there is no known cure. I had gone to see my doctor because I was suffering from double vision and my balance was going. He put me in touch with the local hospital and they admitted me for five weeks. When they told me I had MS, I was upset, of course, but not for long, because my second son, Jacob, was born later that very day. (We called him Aaron at first, but we changed his name the next day. He didn't look like an Aaron.) I was aware of how great a handicap my condition might prove to be, but I am quite an optimist and my temperament as well as my faith averted any kind of spiritual crisis. My new employers didn't know whether I would be able to travel any more, but they realized that there was no point trying to tell me what to do. As for my doctor, he assured me: "The wonderful thing is, we have a hospice here especially for people with MS." That really made me laugh.

It soon was clear that if I and my new colleagues were really to help to bring peace to the world, we needed to deal with those who wielded power. Within months, I was forging links with politicians. With my predecessor's support, I also began to direct the work more towards the Middle East, in the belief that one of the greatest challenges that faced us now was the potential for conflict between the West and the Islamic world. This book is about the attempts I have made since then to build bridges between East and West. This work is so difficult, but it is now my life. Despite my deteriorating health, I have no plans to give it up. In recent years, my focus has moved from Israel, the West Bank and the Gaza Strip to Iraq. It may be the most dangerous place in the world, but it has the most wonderful people.

Though I spend most of my time engaging with diplomats and politicians, I do everything in the power and to the glory of the Almighty. I will never forget my experience of his glory at St Mark's, Kennington, when I was a student at St Thomas' Hospital, or my encounter with Ruth Heflin in Jerusalem. But I needed so much to have the presence of the glory of God with me constantly as my work in the Middle East developed, and so it was a great joy to me when a friend persuaded me to visit the congregation led by Mahesh and Bonnie Chavda in Charlotte, North Carolina. There, at All Nations Church, I found again the presence of the glory of God, and from that day on the Chavdas' church became my church, and their people my people. They pray for me faithfully. They pray that the presence of the glory of God – the almost physical manifestation of the Almighty that radically challenges and changes the "normal" world, which I see even in Baghdad – will be the thing that makes the impossible possible.

As my work has become ever more complex and difficult, it is only the presence of the glory of God that has enabled me to do what I have to do. With God, all things are possible. So, come with me on this seemingly impossible journey and maybe you, too, will see the glory of God making things possible.

CHAPTER 1

Declaration of Intent

One day, I shall tell the whole story of my involvement in the Holy Land (or, as I prefer to call it, the land of the Holy One). For the purposes of this book, I am going to recount two major developments in 2002 that I played a part in, both of which gave me invaluable experience that I was to use in Iraq in the years that followed.

For several years I had been going back and forth to Jerusalem, working hard with my colleagues on a number of grass-roots projects that brought Israelis and Palestinians together. We had also been trying to bring together Christians around the world. The church – not least, the Church of England – is still very divided over the Holy Land. Sadly, most Christians either love Israel and the Jews and disregard, or even despise, the Palestinians (including Palestinian Christians) or they love Palestinian Christians and hate Israel and the Jews. Usually, they seek to justify their position from scripture. I found this very disturbing – at the very heart of Jesus' teaching is the command to love your enemy, and yet so many of his followers today seemed readier to take sides than to seek reconciliation. I had endeavoured to bring unity to the church on this issue – for example, taking groups of British church leaders to Israel and the West Bank on behalf of the Anglo-Israel Association – and had had some success as people saw the pain and the need of both sides in the struggle; but in general I had failed.

Then came the year 2000, the so-called year of jubilee. Many millions of pilgrims were expected in the Holy Land, and many millions of dollars had been poured into repairing the infrastructure of both Israel and the West Bank. The most famous pilgrim of all was to be John Paul II. Hundreds of thousands flocked to see him, and Israeli television actually covered his whole tour live. It was an amazing time, and the Pope with great diplomacy managed to keep everyone happy, even the politicians. The image that remains in my mind most clearly is of his visit to the Western Wall. The plaza was empty as he slowly approached the ancient stones, accompanied by one other person: Michael Melchior, a government minister who was an Orthodox Jew and (as it happened) the Chief Rabbi of Norway. I didn't know it then, but Rabbi Melchior was soon to become one of my closest colleagues and friends.

Towards the end of that year, things started to go wrong politically. The fragile Oslo Accords were beginning to break down. President Bill Clinton had tried very hard at Camp David to forge an agreement on "final status" negotiations between Yasser Arafat, the President of the Palestinian Authority, and Ehud Barak, the Prime Minister of Israel, but without success. The two sides told very different stories about what had actually happened. Subsequently, Israeli areas came under attack – in particular, rockets and mortar shells were fired into Gilo, a new town (some would see it as a settlement) on the outskirts of Jerusalem, from the adjacent Palestinian town of Beit Jala. Next, massive rioting erupted after Ariel Sharon (then leader of the opposition in the Knesset) visited the Temple Mount. Within days, what was to become known as the al-Aqsa Intifada had been declared. Violence was escalating rapidly, scores of people were dead and everything was falling apart. I would often cry to God with the words of the psalmist: "How long, O Lord? How long?"

Hope evaporated – and, to make matters worse, the conflict seemed to be becoming increasingly religious in character. The very fact that this new *intifada*, or "shaking off", had been called "al-Aqsa", after one of the world's holiest Islamic shrines, seemed to suggest this. I continued travelling back and forth to Jerusalem, meeting with senior politicians, diplomats and religious leaders on both sides, searching for a way forward. Then, one day in 2001, over breakfast at the Mount Zion Hotel, everything changed. I was sitting with Gadi Golan, director of religious affairs in the Israeli Foreign Ministry, and he suggested that I should meet Rabbi Melchior, the man who had accompanied the Pope to the Western Wall. Now Deputy Foreign Minister, he was, Mr Golan said, a man who cared deeply about the role of religion in peacemaking. Like him, he had a vision to try to get all the religious leaders of the Holy Land to call for peace in this sacred place.

For the first time in a long while, I saw a chink of light. Maybe we could find peace again in the land of the Holy One. Maybe its religious leaders could play a positive role rather than a negative one. My meeting with Rabbi Melchior was very promising. We talked about the kinds of people we would need to involve and then discussed who should summon them all together. We decided it could not be either a Jew or a Muslim; it had to be a Christian. The Pope was too old and unwell for such an initiative, so we resolved that the person we had to approach was the Archbishop of Canterbury, George Carey, who had recently made a very successful visit to Israel and had also been to see Mr Arafat in Ramallah. Shimon Peres, then

Israel's Foreign Minister, concurred that he would be the right person, and I was to be the one to ask him.

Dr Carey is a kind and wise man with whom I get on very well, and he agreed to our proposal without any hesitation. That was the easy part. Now we had to find a suitable place where we could invite the religious leaders to come together. I decided that Egypt would be best, as a country where Jews, Christians and Muslims could safely meet in the Middle East. Next, we needed to speak to the key religious and political players there to get their support. I was assisted in Egypt by three exceptional people: Mounir Hanna, then Bishop of Egypt in the Episcopal Church in the Middle East; Dr Ali El Samman, a former diplomat who was now an adviser to the Grand Imam of al-Azhar, Sheikh Muhammad Sayed Tantawi; and the British ambassador to Egypt at the time, John Sawers. They devoted many hours to this endeavour and could not have been more helpful. Finally, we chose Alexandria as the venue, and specifically the exclusive Montazah Palace Hotel, which had its own extensive and very secure private grounds on the sea front. I made several visits to the city to make preparations and had many meetings with senior religious figures, from the Grand Imam to the head of the Coptic Church, Pope Shenouda III.

In Israel, the negotiations were intensive. We agreed that, if we wanted to be sure that this summit would be regarded as a success, it would have to issue a serious declaration. I wrote the first draft of this myself with my assistant, Tom Kay-Shuttleworth, and we would discuss it into the small hours with the various delegates on the planning committee we had formed. It took several weeks of this before they finally approved it. It was now nearly Christmas and I had to return home to Coventry for a week. The gathering had been scheduled for March 2002, but on Christmas Day Rabbi Melchior phoned me to say that it could not wait that long: the violence was escalating so sharply, and so little progress was being made on the peace process, that the declaration was needed as soon as possible. I told him he needed to speak to Dr Carey, which he did immediately. The following day, I travelled 160-odd miles down to Canterbury to see the Archbishop. He had listened to Rabbi Melchior and, after asking my advice, decided to bring the summit forward to January.

Some of his staff were not exactly pleased by this – it meant major changes to his diary, including the cancellation of a trip overseas. Within a few days, I was back in Jerusalem, trying to finalize details. It was a mammoth task. There was also the issue of money – the summit was not going to be cheap and we needed the funding quickly. To find $200,000 in a few days was not easy, and I don't think I have ever prayed so hard for money. I approached a friend of mine, Lady Susie Sainsbury, a committed Christian who chairs the Anglo-Israel Association, and she came up with more than half of what we needed from one of her trusts. Other funds came from the Church of Norway and the World Conference of Religions for Peace, which were both to send observers.

I did further work on the ground in Jerusalem and the West Bank, spending hours with Yasser Arafat, representatives of the Israeli government and various religious leaders. While the Israeli team was led by Rabbi Melchior, the Palestinian Muslims were led by the equally inspirational Sheikh Talal Sidr, who was a minister in the Palestinian Authority. The Christians were to be led in Alexandria by the Latin Patriarch of Jerusalem, Michel Sabbah. Tom and I would talk with them into the night at the Mount Zion Hotel as we worked on the final draft of the declaration. We also shuttled back and forth to Cairo, where we spent hours with Dr El Samman going through the document word by word to ensure that it was acceptable to the Grand Imam of al-Azhar, who as the highest authority in Sunni Islam was to be co-chair with Dr Carey of the gathering in Alexandria. In addition, we had regular sessions with the British ambassador, John Sawers, the Israeli ambassador and representatives of the Egyptian government. All of these meetings were very positive. So far, so good.

Then, on 19 January 2002, I returned to London to brief Dr Carey before our scheduled departure for the Holy Land the next day. Things there were now very difficult. Furthermore, the Israelis had decided that no foreigners were allowed to see Mr Arafat (though by now I had realized that such bans usually didn't apply to me). On my way into Lambeth Palace, I met a senior member of the archbishop's staff who politely informed me that we would not be going if he had anything to do with it. He didn't believe we would get access to either Mr Sharon (who was now Prime Minister) or Mr Arafat, let alone secure their support, and he thought I was just wasting Dr Carey's time. The two of us went in to see the archbishop, and this man gave him his advice. Calmly and quietly, Dr Carey said that nonetheless we were going.

Early next day, Tom and I made our way to the VIP lounge at Heathrow to meet Dr Carey. His wife, Eileen, was accompanying him – like him, a quite exceptional person – as well as two of his staff. With me, unusually, at Dr Carey's insistence, was my wife, Caroline. I briefed the Archbishop during the flight and in due course we landed in Tel Aviv, where we were met by Britain's ambassador to Israel, Sherard Cowper-Coles. He had been very helpful to us and now he gave us a warm welcome. In Jerusalem, we were met by the consul-general, Geoffrey Adams, who was responsible for Britain's relations with the Palestinians. He, too, had been very supportive.

After dinner with him and his wife, we were driven in armour-plated cars to see Yasser Arafat in his compound, the Muqata, less than ten miles away in Ramallah. We arrived there surrounded by Palestinian security vehicles with sirens screeching; but, despite the tension outside, it was a very pleasant meeting. Mr Arafat could not have been more positive. He told Dr Carey how important the gathering in Alexandria would be, as religious leaders from Israel and Palestine came together for the first time to search for peace. Also present at this meeting in Ramallah were Ahmed Qurei (also known as Abu Ala) and Mahmoud Abbas (or Abu Mazen), who were both to serve as prime minister of the Palestinian Authority the following year, and Mr Arafat's chief negotiator, Saeb Erakat. (Early on, I had had some heated arguments with Mr Erakat, but later he was to become a good friend.) We returned to Jerusalem feeling encouraged, to wait to hear whether we would be able to see Ariel Sharon.

As the sun rose the next day, things were looking hopeful, It seemed we would be able to meet Mr Sharon that very morning, before a Cabinet meeting. Accompanied by Mr Cowper-Coles, Dr Carey and I made our way to the rather spartan prime ministerial office, where we were joined by Rabbi Melchior and his immediate boss, Shimon Peres, who, always very supportive, now endorsed without reservation the declaration we had drafted. Mr Sharon was a different matter. On his desk, he had a copy of the Hebrew Bible (as he did for all meetings with religious leaders) and he reminded the archbishop of the words of Pope John Paul II: that to Christians this was the Holy Land, but to Jews it was the Promised Land. The message we got was: "Don't mess with our land!" Nonetheless, it was remarkable that both Mr Sharon and Mr Arafat, two people who would not talk to each other, approved our draft declaration. It was this agreement that we wanted to seal and share with the world.

It was at Ben Gurion Airport, where we were due to catch a specially chartered plane to Alexandria, that the problems really started. There were some forty-five people in our party in total, including the Archbishop (who had insisted on travelling with us rather than flying VIP, to show solidarity with the Palestinian dignitaries – who of course had no privileges at all). We had given everyone's name to the Israeli security services beforehand, and were also being accompanied on the flight by some agents from Mossad. However, while the Jews and Christians got through all the checks without difficulty, it was a very different matter for some of the Muslim delegates. The computers at passport control almost blew up! They could not allow these individuals onto an aircraft at Tel Aviv. For well over an hour we tried every argument and appeal we could think of to get them through. By now the whole party, archbishops, rabbis and all, was insisting that if our Muslim colleagues could not board the plane, none of us would.

At long last, we were all allowed through. Mr Cowper-Coles, who was still with us, had rung Danny Ayalon, Mr Sharon's senior foreign policy adviser, and some key people in Israeli intelligence, and this had done the trick. We were finally on our way to Alexandria. The plane landed very late, and then, surrounded by Egyptian police, we were driven to the Montazah Palace complex. My staff from Coventry Cathedral were already there and fortunately had removed from the bedrooms every painting that featured a naked woman, so that no offence would be caused to such senior religious leaders.

The summit began without further delay, at about 3 p.m. As Dr Carey opened the proceedings with a moment of silence, there was an air of great expectation in the room. We all knew we were on the verge of making history. The official language of the meeting was English, but there were interpreters on hand, provided by the Egyptian government, to translate to and from Hebrew and Arabic. The Israeli government had had the declaration we had written printed out on beautiful parchment paper, and I imagined that the signing was a mere formality before we got down to discussing our real business: how to put it into practice. To my horror, however, it became apparent that some of the Palestinian delegates would not sign it as it stood. The Christians had not really been involved in the weeks of preparation, and Patriarch Sabbah and the Anglican Bishop of Jerusalem and the Middle East, Riah Abu el-Assal, in particular, believed that the declaration did not adequately reflect their concerns. In my experience, Christians in Palestine often seem to feel they have to be even more Palestinian than the Muslims, to show how committed they are to the cause.[1] To be honest, this (as well as the rivalries and tensions between the different denominations) can make them very difficult.

Had all our work been in vain? When George Carey wrote his autobiography, *Know the Truth*, after his retirement as Archbishop of Canterbury, he said that this meeting was the hardest he had ever chaired. I don't doubt it. The delegates separated to work through the issues, with Bishop Riah and Archbishop Boutrous Mu'alem sitting with the six Israeli delegates, as they were entitled to, in the hope that they could influence them. The sticking points were not theological but political, the principal issues being whether the statement should mention the Israeli occupation of the West Bank and Gaza and whether as it

---

1. Of the five Christian delegates, Patriarch Sabbah, Bishop Riah, and the Melkite Archbishop of the Galilee, Boutrous Mu'alem, are all Palestinians holding Israeli citizenship. Archbishop Aristichos, who was representing the Greek Patriarch, is a Greek Cypriot, though he has lived in Jerusalem now for over forty years. The late Archbishop Chinchinian, who was representing the Armenian Patriarch, was a Syrian living in Egypt.

stood it implied that Palestinians were largely responsible for the bloodshed. The Palestinians made it clear that they thought the Israelis were primarily to blame. If the declaration was to condemn violence, they insisted, it must condemn the violence that had been committed against their people. The issue of the right of Palestinian refugees to return to their land in what is now Israel also came into the dispute.

Much of the discussion was conducted in separate groups, but periodically we all came together and then there was a great deal of shouting on both sides. It was obvious that all the delegates felt strongly that they must not undermine their own politicians or betray the interests of their people. At first, no one was willing to move an inch – and in any negotiation when this happens it generates anger and frustration. I had to keep my opinions and emotions to myself – my role was to go back and forth between one group and the other to try to find a form of words acceptable to both. In the end, it was the Israeli rabbis who proved to be more prepared to give ground, though not on major issues such as the status of Jerusalem.[2] The only man on the Palestinian side who was ready to make compromises was a Muslim, Sheikh Talal. He had moved a considerable distance in his own life, from being one of the founders of Hamas to serving as a minister in Yasser Arafat's administration.

Typically, only the most senior Muslim delegates – Sheikh Talal and the chief justice of the Palestinian *shari'a* courts, Sheikh Taysir al-Tamimi – actually took part in the debate at all. The other two, the muftis of Bethlehem and of the Palestinian armed

---

2. Apart from Rabbi Melchior, the Jewish delegates were Eliyahu Bakshi-Doron, the Sephardi Chief Rabbi; David Rosen, a former chief rabbi of Ireland who was now head of the American Jewish Committee's department of interreligious affairs; Menachem Froman, the Orthodox rabbi of the West Bank settlement of Tekoa, who has pioneered interfaith dialogue with leaders of the PLO and Hamas; and two influential members of the Chief Rabbinical Council, David Brodman and Yitzak Ralbag.

forces, did not say a word. (In fact, after the summit was over, the latter went to live in Britain and, to my knowledge, never returned to the West Bank.) As for me, when I wasn't needed by the various delegates I sat with Dr Carey and the Grand Imam, who were not involved in the minutiae of the discussions. The latter had a long conversation with the Sephardi Chief Rabbi, Eliyahu Bakshi-Doron, which in itself was quite historic.

At midnight, Dr Carey retired to bed, after instructing me that the problems must all be sorted out by the morning. Into the small hours the delegates argued in their separate groups, battling to find a resolution. I moved constantly between the Palestinians and the Israelis, but found them both so fixed in their positions that I began to despair. How could we move forward in the face of such intransigence? At 5 a.m., I went to bed. It had certainly been the most difficult meeting I had yet taken part in, and I was almost in tears as I went back to my room. I woke my wife and we prayed, but it all seemed hopeless. Night after night we had worked. We had all seemed to be moving in the same direction, we had gone so far and got so close, yet it looked as if now we were going to lose everything. Probably for the first time ever, I asked myself the question: Why were we failing? My past experience of conflict resolution had taught me that people can change their minds very suddenly – but in the Middle East, it seemed, Western techniques simply did not work. I lay awake thinking about my calling to be a minister of the gospel. Was this really what it was about? I longed to be back in my old parish in London, where the people loved me and I loved them; but I knew deep down that that was no longer my calling. My true vocation was what I was doing now.

Three hours later, I got up to go and tell Dr Carey that we had not succeeded. When I spoke to Tom, however, he actually encouraged me. "We mustn't give up," he said. He had been with me from the beginning of this process, an outstanding assistant, and he had deep faith. He, too, knew that God had called us to this and he was not going to quit. That morning, we were joined once again by John Sawers. He is a wise man and he, too, was not going to let this historic endeavour founder.

After breakfast, the Archbishop of Canterbury called everyone together. He was very firm and very fair. He told us we had until lunchtime to deliver; otherwise, he was going to tell the world's media that the religious leaders of the region had failed to come to an agreement. We went on working in small groups. I was with Mr Sawers, going through those issues that were proving particularly problematic. A crucial advance was his suggestion: the insertion in the declaration of a call, as a necessary "first step", for the implementation of the recent recommendations of two American envoys, George Mitchell and George Tenet, who had looked for ways to build on the Oslo Accords. In particular, they had urged the Israelis to lift restrictions on the Palestinians in the West Bank and Gaza and to admit other Arab nations, such as the Syrians and the Saudis, into the negotiations.

By lunchtime, we were almost there. Dr Carey allowed us a little more time, and after another two hours we came to a satisfactory conclusion. It was now three o'clock. Now all we needed to do was to get the assent of Ariel Sharon and Yasser Arafat, since the religious leaders on both sides needed political support. A press conference had been arranged at another, more accessible hotel nearby for 5.30 p.m. We had just over two hours. Mr Sharon readily agreed with the compromises the Israeli delegation had made, but getting the approval of Mr Arafat was not so easy. His most senior aide, Nabil Abu Rudeinah, was adamant: the President always slept in the afternoon and could not be woken under any circumstances. Sheikh Talal took the phone from me and tried to talk him round. Finally, Nabil Abu Rudeinah agreed to wake the President on condition that I promised never to ask such a thing again. I promised. Mr Arafat was duly woken, and was happy to endorse the declaration.

At this juncture, one of the Palestinian Christians came to me and asked if we could add a reference to "the end of occupation". By now I was exhausted and I also knew that adding even one word would have brought the whole process to a halt, so I nodded as if to say yes and didn't change a thing.

This is the wording that was finally to be signed, on 21 January 2002:

In the name of God who is Almighty, Merciful and Compassionate, we, who have gathered as religious leaders from the Muslim, Christian and Jewish communities, pray for true peace in Jerusalem and the Holy Land, and declare our commitment to ending the violence and bloodshed that denies the right of life and dignity.

According to our faith traditions, killing innocents in the name of God is a desecration of His Holy Name, and defames religion in the world. The violence in the Holy Land is an evil which must be opposed by all people of good faith. We seek to live together as neighbors respecting the integrity of each other's historical and religious inheritance. We call upon all to oppose incitement, hatred and misrepresentation of the other.

1. The Holy Land is holy to all three of our faiths. Therefore, followers of the divine religions must respect its sanctity, and bloodshed must not be allowed to pollute it. The sanctity and integrity of the holy places must be preserved, and freedom of religious worship must be ensured for all.

2. Palestinians and Israelis must respect the divinely ordained purposes of the Creator by whose grace they live in the same land that is called holy.

3. We call on the political leaders of both peoples to work for a just, secure and durable solution in the spirit of the words of the Almighty and the Prophets.

4. As a first step now, we call for a religiously sanctioned cease-fire, respected and observed on all sides, and for the implementation of the Mitchell and Tenet recommendations, including the lifting of restrictions and return to negotiations.

5. We seek to help create an atmosphere where present and future generations will co-exist with mutual respect and trust in the other. We call on all to refrain from incitement and demonization, and to educate our future generations accordingly.

6. As religious leaders, we pledge ourselves to continue a joint quest for a just peace that leads to reconciliation in Jerusalem and the Holy Land, for the common good of all our peoples.

7. We announce the establishment of a permanent joint committee to carry out the recommendations of this declaration, and to engage with our respective political leadership accordingly.

Now it had come to the point when we had to print out this definitive version, we found that the printer had stopped working. My PA, Sue Cutter, got it typed up in Arabic, Hebrew and English, and Tom taped it all together – one of the most important documents in religious history – and blew it up on the photocopier so there would be room for all the signatures. Finally, we took it in to the delegates and suddenly the anguish of the past three months gave way to elation. *"Al-hamdu li'llahi"* ("Thank God!" in Arabic) shouted the Palestinians. *"Baruch ha'shem!"* (the same in Hebrew) shouted the Israelis. They hugged and kissed each other, and then stood together to put their names to this statement that affirmed that killing innocent people was a desecration of the name of God – a point on which both Israelis and Palestinians very strongly agreed. The First Alexandria Declaration of the Religious Leaders of the Holy Land had been signed at last, and signed with joy.

I rang Lady Sainsbury and said simply: "We've done it!" I knew that she and others had been praying for these secret discussions, and without those prayers I don't think we would ever have made it. Like most achievements of real worth, it had not been easy. For me, the pain it had involved had been almost physical. I have said as much as I can about how it was accomplished – I doubt that the whole story will ever be told. It was only a beginning, of course, but it *was* a beginning: for the first time ever, leaders of the three great faiths of the Holy Land had said with one voice that violence in the name of God had to stop. Moreover, they acknowledged that the declaration was only a beginning – they spoke of the need to continue to work together to see this initiative through.

The press conference was very positive: nobody spoke of the pain that had been involved in getting this far, and there was unity in our diversity. The following day, we all flew to Cairo on a chartered plane to meet President Hosni Mubarak and present him with the declaration. By the time the Israelis and Palestinians returned to Jerusalem, yet another bomb had gone off; but this time there was real empathy among all the delegates. They had started out as strangers to each other, but they had ended up as friends.

Back in Cairo, Caroline, Tom and I had lunch with the Careys and John Sawers before returning to London via Rome, where I stopped off to brief the British ambassador to the Holy See. As we left Egypt, Tom turned to me and said: "I've just been part of what will probably be the most important event of my life and I'm only twenty-four!" It was probably true – and without his organization and encouragement the whole thing would not have happened. In the Israeli and Arab press, the Alexandria Declaration was big news for days, but the Western media barely mentioned it. The major lesson we had learned was that often the most important steps we take are the most painful.

We set up a permanent committee for the implementation of the declaration, and at first this met almost every month – twice with Dr Carey present. After a year, we decided to hold a meeting at Lambeth Palace, a week before he was to step down as archbishop. There are very few people who would have even attempted such a crucial meeting a week before retirement! The day before we convened, a very important event took place at Coventry Cathedral, where the Coventry International Prize for Peace and Reconciliation was presented to the three protagonists of the Alexandria Process: Rabbi Michael Melchior, Patriarch Michel Sabbah, and Sheikh Talal Sidr. It was a highly emotional occasion. There in the ruins of the old cathedral, on the sixty-third anniversary of its destruction by German bombs, three key leaders of their people accepted this notable honour. For the sheikh, it was particularly significant. Here was one of the founders and former leaders of Hamas, a radical organization committed to the destruction of the state of Israel, receiving a prize for peace. Ken Taylor, at the end of his term as Lord Mayor of Coventry, described this day as the most moving and memorable of his year in office.

The next day, before our meeting at Lambeth Palace, something occurred that will stay in my memory forever. A Jewish businessman hosted a lunch in London for Rabbi Melchior, Sheikh Talal, and me. There were many journalists present, and one of them, an Arab, shouted at the sheikh: "How can you sit with this evil Zionist?" The sheikh paused and then, taking the rabbi's hand, he declared: "This man is my brother and we will walk this long and difficult road of reconciliation together until we find peace." "What do you think you're doing?" someone called out. Sheikh Talal replied: "I am pulling up thorns and planting flowers." Suddenly, I realized that this was indeed the work God had called us to. A former advocate of violence was doing what the Prince of Peace calls us all to do. Whenever I am losing hope – which is often – it is this exchange I think of, and it enables me to keep going for another day.

Seven years after the signing of the Alexandria Declaration, the violence and bloodshed in Israel, the West Bank, and Gaza continue. Nonetheless, I believe it has made an important difference. The process that produced it has given birth to a large number of other initiatives. Many grass-roots projects have been established by the delegates that involve both Israelis and Palestinians – arranging exchanges and encounters between schools, for example, and training up people to go and teach students of Orthodox Judaism and Islam about the other faith and its adherents. There is now an interreligious council that brings together the key Jewish, Christian, and Muslim leaders. There is an Israeli and Palestinian Institute of Peace, with centres in Gaza, Jerusalem and, in the north of Israel, Kafr Kassem, where in 1956 Israeli border police had shot dead forty-nine Israeli Arabs, including eleven children. Furthermore, behind the scenes we are talking with some of the more radical Palestinian leaders who advocate or condone killing in the name of God.

New people have become involved. Sheikh Talal Sidr sadly died in August 2007, but in some ways his role has been filled by Sheikh Abdullah Nimr Darwish, who was the founder of the Islamist movement in Israel. He didn't come to Alexandria because he didn't think the summit would achieve anything – and he told me so in front of Yasser Arafat. Today, he is a key member of the permanent committee for the implementation of the Alexandria Declaration. He is a great man of peace.

So, we accomplished much. Even so, the work had only just begun.

CHAPTER 2

A Painful Delivery

This is the most traumatic chapter of this book to write. It tells the story of the 39-day siege of the Church of the Nativity in Bethlehem, the birthplace of our Lord, a siege that affected not only the people trapped in the church but all the inhabitants of the city and the neighbouring towns of Beit Jala and Beit Sahour. For most of that time I was a witness to their sufferings, all day and every day. By the end, I was exhausted physically, emotionally, and spiritually. I remember that I finally went home in tears.

The story began for me on 2 April 2002. I was in hospital in Coventry, being given steroids intravenously after a relapse in my multiple sclerosis. I was in a private room so I could have my five mobile phones switched on, and suddenly one of them rang. The voice at the other end of the line informed me that the *Ra'is* – the president, in Arabic – wanted to speak to me. As soon as Yasser Arafat came on the line, I could tell he was distressed. "They've taken our church!" he blurted out. "We need you quickly!" As he explained what was happening, I realized I was already watching it live on the news. More than 200 Palestinians – a mixture of heavily armed gunmen, policemen and civilians – had sought refuge in the Church of the Nativity from the troops of the Israeli Defense Forces, which had invaded Bethlehem in strength in search of wanted militants. Now, along with some sixty priests, monks, and nuns, they were surrounded by highly trained paratroopers backed up by tanks.

I said I was a little tied up at the moment but I would get there as soon as I could. Reluctantly, Mr Arafat accepted that assurance. Ten minutes later, my phone rang again. This time, it was the Deputy Foreign Minister of Israel, Rabbi Michael Melchior. Although he is a friend of mine, his manner was not quite as cordial as Mr Arafat's had been. "I told you that if you left, something like this would happen. Get back here quickly!" he said. Only half in jest, I replied: "So, it's all my fault, is it?" I told him I was in hospital, and I will never forget his response: "Who do you work for?" For a moment, I was speechless. He knew I worked for God and he believed that, however poorly I felt, God would get me to Bethlehem soon.

I got a sense of the enormity of the crisis when the Archbishop of Canterbury, George Carey, called me. He was, however, just as concerned about me as about the situation at the church and didn't want me to discharge myself from hospital prematurely. So, I waited patiently for another day and finished my course of treatment while my project officer, Alex Chance, got us on to the earliest possible flight to Tel Aviv. He was an outstanding assistant and his help with my often hectic schedule was always invaluable.

When Alex and I arrived in Jerusalem, we began quickly to assess the situation. It was bad – probably the worst I had ever known it. A military operation called Defensive Shield was well under way throughout the West Bank and much of the territory was under siege, including the Muqata in Ramallah (where the men who had assassinated Rehavam Ze'evi, the Israeli Minister of Tourism, in Jerusalem in October 2001 were said to have taken refuge). At the Church of the Nativity, an Israeli sniper had already shot the bell-ringer dead, thinking he might be a suicide bomber. The people inside the church compound had little to eat or drink, and were ill equipped to negotiate with their besiegers or deal with their persistent demands and threats. There was an oppressive atmosphere of fear.

Our first task was to see Dr Emil Jarjoui, a wonderful paediatrician and the only Christian on the PLO executive. Alex and I went to his home in Jerusalem many times to discuss exhaustively what could be done. At the same time, we were going back and forth between the Palestinians and the Israelis as unofficial intermediaries, but it was impossible even to get them to agree on who should do the negotiating. The Israelis refused to deal directly with the gunmen inside the church, as the Palestinians wanted, because they regarded them as terrorists. It wasn't long before the world's media discovered that I was involved, and requests for interviews began to pour in.

During this period, I made frequent excursions into the West Bank to visit Bethlehem, just a few miles across the border from Jerusalem. What I saw when I passed through the checkpoint was quite unbelievable. The only vehicles on the roads were either Israeli tanks, armoured personnel carriers and military trucks or the cars and vans of international television. Along the main streets, Israeli armour had bulldozed the lamp posts and smashed the frontages of houses, shops, and hotels. The reek of burnt-out cars and buildings enveloped the whole city in the stench of senseless destruction. I had been in Bethlehem, Beit Jala, and Beit Sahour many times, but had never seen them in such a state before. In recent months, the situation had deteriorated drastically. Beit Jala, a predominantly Christian town, is barely 500 yards across the valley from the new Jewish town of Gilo, and Palestinian fighters had been forcing their way into houses that overlooked it to send a constant stream of rockets and mortar shells into that unfortunate place. As expected, the Israelis had responded by sending Apache helicopters to destroy the homes from which the missiles were fired. Once again, Christians were caught in the middle. Later, I learned that the militants involved were among the leaders of the group that then took refuge in the Church of the Nativity. The havoc they caused was to have dreadful consequences.

The negotiations about negotiations continued, and I spent my days talking to politicians and Christian, Muslim, and Jewish leaders. I also gave scores of interviews to the international media at the request of the British consulate in Jerusalem, which was concerned by the exaggerations being broadcast by both the Palestinians and the Israelis. Geoffrey Adams, the consul-general, was a fine man who was greatly respected by Dr Carey, and he proved to be an excellent person to work with. With the help of a local member of my Coventry staff, Hanna Ishaq, I was also devoting an increasing amount of time and money to helping the people of Bethlehem and the two neighbouring towns to obtain food and medicine. Whenever we took supplies in, we would at once be surrounded by children desperate for something to eat. It was becoming obvious that the crisis was affecting not just the people inside the Church of the Nativity, but all the inhabitants of Bethlehem, Beit Jala, and Beit Sahour as well.

One afternoon, I was contacted by an English woman living in Bethlehem. She had heard that a local man called Edmond Nasser, who had recently been to Jordan to have open-heart surgery, was in dire need. He lived on the edge of Manger Square, in the centre of the city, which was now completely cut off. Out of curiosity, I asked how she had got hold of me and she explained that the British consulate (knowing of my medical training) had told her to contact me. I took that as a divine directive that I had to try to help this man. Accordingly, I rang the local Israeli commander, with whom I had quickly become good friends. Shmueli Hamburger was a colonel in the reservists, a jovial and generally very obliging older man who worked in the Ministry of Religious Affairs with oversight of the Christian communities of Israel and the occupied territories. Now, everything in Bethlehem went through him. I told him I had to go into the city to help someone who was seriously ill, but he insisted that it was far too dangerous – there was too much shooting. It was obvious I was not going to get in through the front door.

I got word that Mr Nasser's condition was deteriorating. Clearly, we had to get to him as a matter of urgency. Hanna told me of a back route into Bethlehem: into Beit Jala by car and then on foot over some barren, broken ground where surveillance would be minimal. He drove us at speed to Beit Jala and then, with my medical bag in my hand, I clambered over the rocks with Alex at my side. Even then there was still another two miles to go, so we shouted for a car. It was wishful thinking – there was a curfew and the streets were completely empty – and yet within seconds a man came running towards us. He said his name was Mustafa, and it turned out that he had a vehicle, covered in TV network signs but with Israeli plates. I knew it was almost certainly stolen, but there was no time to worry about ethics.

When we told him where we needed to go, Mustafa laughed and said there was no way he could get us there. So, we asked him to take us back to Beit Jala, to the King Hussein Hospital, and on the way I rang Shmueli. He was amazed that we had managed to get so far, and promised to meet us at the hospital in his armoured car. Now he was willing to escort us into Bethlehem, and so it was not long before we reached the very heart of that beleaguered city. One of the most sacred places in the world, it was now a theatre of war. There were tanks everywhere; searchlights pierced the darkening sky, and from a crane hung a huge loudspeaker blasting out noise in a psychological assault on the gunmen trapped inside the church.

Finally, we arrived at the home of Edmond Nasser. Mustafa waited outside in his car while Alex and I ran in, not knowing what we would find. Mr Nasser was in a bad way. The incision from his operation was badly infected and showing signs of septicaemia, and it didn't help that he was clearly malnourished. He could not believe that someone had simply shown up with the very medication he so desperately needed. As a Christian, he was overjoyed that God had sent a priest to his aid. But I am not only a priest, and at times like this my medical training takes over. Once more an operating department practitioner, I swabbed his wound.

We gave him the provisions we had brought and talked with him for a while, and then we had to go. Shmueli warned us to drive slowly and follow his vehicle closely as we made our way through the stricken city. So we did – until suddenly, without a word of warning or explanation, Mustafa hit the accelerator. Driving like a madman, he sped away from our escort and recklessly turned into a side road. The ring of my mobile phone cut through our shock. It was Shmueli, angry and very alarmed. I asked Mustafa what he thought he was doing, but he didn't reply. Shmueli ordered us to proceed directly to a nearby military base. "We could be in big trouble now," Alex commented drily, as perfectly composed as ever. When we arrived at the base, however, the colonel leapt out of his armoured car and, running towards us, threw his arms around me. When I asked him why his mood had suddenly changed, his answer appalled us. Just after he had rung me, someone had thrown a small bomb at Shmueli's vehicle which had landed just behind it. If we had still been following him, we would have all been killed. Mustafa never gave us an explanation for what he did, and I never saw him again. I have often wondered since whether he was, in fact, an angel – one with a Muslim name and a stolen Israeli car! Now at Christmas when I sing about angels in Bethlehem, I cannot help but think of him.

The next morning, we carried on with our laborious negotiations about negotiations. Mr Adams told me I should work with Alastair Crooke, who (he informed me) had been seconded from the Foreign Office to the European Union as a security adviser to Javier Solana, in effect the EU's foreign minister. I made contact with him and over the next month we spent most of our time working with him. He was a quiet man in his fifties, obviously very intelligent. He had a deep understanding of the Palestinians and could always see their point of view We got on very well.

The Israelis made it clear they didn't want any religious leaders to take part in the actual negotiations, but when eventually they and Yasser Arafat's office came up with their respective lists of people they wished to be involved, both of them included my name. I went back to the Israelis and asked them how come I was on their list. They laughed and told me I wasn't a religious leader. I didn't know what to make of that.

By now two men had been killed inside the church by Israeli snipers, who believed they were armed. We were told that their bodies were being kept in the grotto where Jesus is said to have been born. They were already decomposing, and there were ever more insistent threats from the besieged gunmen that, if we didn't remove them soon, they would bury them in the church.

This raised the very real risk that this Christian shrine could become the burial place for Muslim martyrs. I spent many hours with the Greek Orthodox Patriarchate trying to work out how we could retrieve the bodies and get them back to their families. The Israelis did not want anyone to go into the church, and apparently the militants did not want anyone to come out. It would take another ten days before this problem was resolved.

It was now 14 April. The siege was almost two weeks old but still no real negotiations had begun. It was on this day that the Israeli Prime Minister, Ariel Sharon, informed the world of his government's position: the Palestinian fighters in the church could either surrender and be tried by an Israeli military court or go into permanent exile. Yasser Arafat responded with his own announcement: There would be no trial in Israel and no exile. The dispute between the two men was very public – though, as he himself was under siege in the Muqata, Mr Arafat was not actually in any position to influence events.

Talks were still not under way six days later when we were told that there was no food or water left in the church. We were now meeting with other people who had been named as negotiators. Alastair Crooke was by now with me and Alex all the time, and it was decided that we would be based mainly with the Palestinian team in Beit Jala, at the home of the Palestinian Minister of Tourism, Mitri Abu Aita. With Shmueli's co-operation, Hanna was able to drive the three of us into Bethlehem. Day after day, we were told that face-to-face talks were about to begin, but they never did. The Israelis did not seem to be in any hurry.

At last, on 23 April, over three weeks after the siege of the church began, negotiations got under way. The Israeli team was composed entirely of military personnel, led by a very professional and pragmatic lieutenant-colonel called Lior; the Palestinian team was led by Salah Tamari, a former PLO commander (and a very good friend of mine) who was now a member of the Palestinian Legislative Assembly. At this point I thought the crisis would soon be over, but that was far too optimistic. The talks took place in the evenings under heavy security in the Peace Center in Manger Square. They were conducted in English, though only Palestinians and Israelis were present, and Lt-Col Lior followed a strict agenda. A crucial participant was a highly respected Christian lawyer called Tony Salman, who was a member of Bethlehem's municipal council. He was actually one of those who had taken refuge in the church, and was the only one that both the gunmen and the Israelis would allow to go in and out. He was our sole contact with the militants, and our principal source of information about what was going on inside the compound.

During the day – day after day – Alastair, Alex, and I sat with the Palestinians at the minister's house, discussing negotiating tactics with them in a room full of tension and blue with cigarette smoke. The minister's wife made us wonderful food to maintain our energy levels as the three of us spent hours talking to the Israelis on the phone or simply waiting. Salah would often be heard shouting angrily down the line to Yasser Arafat, who, like Ariel Sharon, was not willing to make any compromises. Alex and I were working with Alastair to try to find solutions to the impasse – I was to learn a great deal from him about hostage negotiations. By now it had become obvious to us both that he was not your average diplomat, and I could well believe the rumours that he worked not for the Foreign Office but for the Secret Intelligence Service, MI6, and had been engaged in covert operations from Colombia to Afghanistan.

Perhaps this explained why he wouldn't deal with the media. In fact, there was always a large number of reporters outside the gates of Mitri Abu Aita's house. I had got to know many of them well, but now we were actually engaged in negotiations we had to try to keep as low a profile as possible. This was easier said than done. The minister had a twelve-year-old son who had made friends with many of the reporters and we often saw him holding their cameras or microphones. Sometimes he even brought them into the house, and then all the talking had to stop.

On 24 April, on only the second day of formal negotiations, we finally saw some progress – despite the fact that two more Palestinians inside the church compound had been hit by Israeli snipers. (One of them, a policeman, was to die later.) By now we had realized that the situation in the church was in effect a double siege: many of the people inside the compound were trapped there by fear as much of the gunmen as of the Israelis outside. (The foreign religious had said they were staying as "voluntary hostages", to show solidarity with the Palestinians and to try to deter any more bloodshed.) However, the militants now agreed that nine teenagers could leave the church and could bring the two badly decayed bodies out with them. The following day they emerged, carrying their burden in makeshift coffins. They were questioned by the Israelis, and one of them was detained on the suspicion that he had been involved in planting explosives in Jerusalem. The two dead men were identified as policemen.

Things were becoming increasingly desperate in Bethlehem, Beit Jal, and Beit Sahour. Shmueli kept us informed of the more urgent needs he was aware of, and one day he came and told us that the Ethiopians hadn't had any food for three weeks. I hadn't even been aware that there were Ethiopian monks in Bethlehem. It turned out that they lived very close to Manger Square, which meant we couldn't get to them ourselves, so I sent Hanna out to find as much food as he could and we entrusted it – bags and bags of it – to Shmueli. When he returned a couple of hours later, I asked him: "Well? Were they happy with the food?" His answer astonished me. "No! You forgot to include any lemons!" To this day, I have never again forgotten the lemons.

Alex and Hanna and I spent hours every day just driving around obtaining and delivering food and medicine. I was becoming concerned that we were running out of funds – the needs were so great and our resources were so small. The Archbishop of Canterbury regularly rang me to ask about the humanitarian situation, and in time he sent a very considerable amount of money. It was certainly very welcome.

The atmosphere in the house of Mitri Abu Aita grew more and more tense. Salah was still shouting down the phone to Mr Arafat, and the bitter fog of cigarette smoke grew ever thicker. The Israelis were adamant that those men in the church whom they regarded as terrorists would have to be deported, and one of my principal concerns was to find somewhere they could go. My primary contact was a man in Italian intelligence called Aldo. One possibility we were investigating was to send some of the militants to the Arsenal of Peace in Turin, a former weapons factory that was now a Roman Catholic monastery and peace centre. I also spent many hours with the three patriarchs of Jerusalem – the Greek, the Armenian, and the Latin – who shared control of the Church of the Nativity; and in addition I was seeing both the senior Franciscan in Jerusalem, the Custos of the Holy Land, and the papal nuncio, Archbishop Pietro Sambi.

On 27 April, Alastair went with some of the Palestinian team to see Yasser Arafat in Ramallah, but I wasn't surprised to learn when they got back that they had achieved nothing. The outcome of meetings with Mr Arafat often depended on his mood. On this occasion he had clearly not been having a good day, and while they tried to talk with him he just continued signing a pile of paperwork in his customary red ink.

We were getting reports that the situation in the church

compound was now very serious indeed and people had been reduced to eating the boiled leaves of the lemon trees that grew in the courtyard. Salah kept offering to go in to try to get the civilians out in return for provisions for those who remained. Time and again, however, the leaders of the various groups of gunmen in the church refused to accept this offer. The Israelis were insisting that any food that was taken in must be supplied by them, and the militants knew that they would make political capital out of their supposed magnanimity. It was all part of the game the Israelis were playing.

On 29 April, the siege of Mr Arafat's bunker in Ramallah was finally lifted when the four men accused of killing Rehavam Ze'evi were tried and sentenced by a hastily convened Palestinian military tribunal. Briefly we believed that a similar deal might be possible in Bethlehem, but the Israelis soon made it clear that that was out of the question. They had withdrawn their forces surrounding the Muqata only under intense pressure from the Americans and regarded that as something of a humiliation, and they felt they could not afford to show any leniency in Bethlehem. In fact, that same day another Palestinian was shot by an Israeli sniper. Nidal Abayat had been one of the leaders in the church. The Israelis regarded him as a serious threat and he was on their "most wanted" list – it was he and some of his relatives who had been responsible for firing rockets and mortar shells into Gilo from Beit Jala. Now he was dead.

The next day, twenty-four more people were allowed to leave the church – but the provisions that were meant to be sent in in exchange for them were never delivered. Lt-Col Lior admitted that the Israelis were now concentrating not on negotiating an end to the siege but on "increasing the pressure" on those inside the compound, and he was no longer sure that he had the authority to send in food. By now we were all very tired and becoming very frustrated with the lack of any real progress. After so many strenuous days and sleepless nights, we seemed to be going nowhere. Then we were informed by Lt-Col Lior that the Israelis were going to allow Salah and Alastair into the church to get the names of everyone inside. Up until this point, we didn't even know how many people were in there, let alone who they all were. The Israelis were just as eager to find out as we were, though they still made out that they were doing us a favour.

An agent of Shin Bet, Israel's domestic security agency, then told Salah and Alastair that this was to be the last part they would play in proceedings, as the Palestinian and Israeli negotiating teams were both to be disbanded. This was a real surprise to me. Nothing of any great significance had yet been accomplished. What was going to happen now? We knew that President George Bush had been under immense pressure to intervene. The behaviour of its close ally Israel was damaging America's relations with the Arabs. The *intifada* was already compromising the "war against terror", and any further complications could undermine the attempt to build a consensus for action against Saddam Hussein. Now, it seemed, the Americans were going to get involved in Bethlehem. Exhausted and exasperated, Alastair and I returned with Hanna and Alex to Jerusalem, with no idea of what the future held. We went to a café for lunch, and then managed a couple of hours' sleep before we were informed that there would be a meeting that afternoon at the King David Hotel (famous as the location in 1946 of the Zionist bombing of the British military headquarters in mandatory Palestine). When we arrived, we found that the Americans were represented by two CIA men, the Israelis by some agents of Shin Bet and the Palestinians by Muhammad Rashid, Mr Arafat's Iraqi-born Kurdish adviser.

The four of us were told exactly what was required, of us and of others. Of course we were happy to co-operate in any way we could, but I couldn't see that the new plan was very different from anything we had already suggested. What *was* clear, however, was that the Americans expected things to happen and to happen right away. The plan was quite bold, requiring that some of the gunmen, whom the Israelis and the international community alike regarded as terrorists, should be put on trial at the International Court of Justice at The Hague. This was not at all what Mr Arafat wanted, though Mr Rashid agreed to it and he was one of the most powerful members of the Palestinian National Authority. (After this meeting Mr Rashid disappeared and to this day I have not seen him again, though I heard once that he was in Egypt. I suspect he felt that in consenting to this plan he had destroyed his credibility with ordinary Palestinians.)

The final outcome, however, was rather different. It was decided that the thirteen militants who were on Israel's "most wanted" list were simply to be sent into permanent exile abroad and another twenty-six would be removed to Gaza, to stand trial in Palestinian courts for seizing the church and for other alleged crimes against Israel. This all sounded fairly simple, but we still didn't know for certain where the thirteen could go. We had been talking to the Italians, but at that stage we had thought that only seven men were going to be expelled.

On 2 May, a group of peace activists from the International Solidarity Movement somehow managed to get into the church with some food – I have no idea how – to add yet another complication to an already complex situation. Nonetheless, by the following day nearly all the arrangements had been made and Alastair, Alex, Hanna, and I were instructed to go to Beit Jala to meet a new Palestinian negotiating team, led this time by one of the president's relatives, a man with a face badly scarred by burns, who also was called Arafat. He had presided over the trial of Mr Ze'evi's killers in Ramallah and, as his court had managed to try, convict, and sentence them all in a single morning, we knew he was a man of decision. Nonetheless, he and his colleagues had been trapped inside the Muqata for a month and they had only a very limited idea of what had been going on in Bethlehem.

The CIA then showed up, four big men who spoke perfect Arabic and drove identical SUVs. Neither Alastair nor I were fluent in Arabic, so we asked Hanna to eavesdrop on them for us, which he did very well. (Afterwards, he told us that these had been the best days of his life!) Next, we had to get hold of a floor plan of the church, to find somewhere where the thirteen "senior terrorists" (as the Israelis called them) could be locked up for a couple of weeks, once the siege had been lifted, while arrangements were made for their expulsion. It did not prove easy. I asked the Mayor of Bethlehem whether he had the plans, but he told me that as the church was much older than the municipality, he did not. Eventually, however, I did locate them. It turned out that a friend of mine in Jerusalem, Dr Petra Heldt, knew the person who had them – as it happened, at Oxford University.

The end seemed to be in sight, when I received a phone call from the same English woman who had alerted me to Edmond Nasser's plight. Now she was speaking on behalf of the peace activists inside the church. Apparently, they had decided that they would leave the building only on two conditions: that Yasser Arafat told them to and that they knew what was going to happen to them. It was now three in the afternoon, the hour when Mr Arafat always took a nap. I phoned Nabil Abu Rudeinah and asked him if he could possibly wake the *Ra'is* with this new, urgent request. He reminded me that earlier in the year I had had Mr Arafat woken with regard to the Alexandria Declaration and told me I simply could not expect to do it again. So, the activists stayed where they were.

There was a further obstacle. Now the Italians knew how many men were going to be expelled, they not only were adamant that they would not take thirteen of them, they insisted they had never been asked to take even one. We had been talking to Rome about this critical issue for weeks, yet everything now was denied. It was a stunning blow. All we could do was to carry on frantically looking for a country that was willing to accept these most unwanted men. At least we now had the help of the EU's special envoy to the Middle East, the Spanish diplomat Miguel Ángel Moratinos. Alex and I had met him at the Spanish consulate in Jerusalem and we knew him well and counted him as a friend. He had also worked with Alastair before.

By 9 May, we seemed at last to have a workable plan. The thirteen men were to be flown to Cyprus and held there in detention in the Flamingo Hotel until the members of the EU had decided where they should finally go. Quickly, all the arrangements were made, right down to the metal detectors to scan everyone as they came out of the church. Midnight came and all we were waiting for was the coaches the CIA had promised to provide, to take the thirteen to Ben Gurion Airport and the other twenty-six militants to Gaza. As I watched from a rooftop overlooking Manger Square, I listened to the many reporters talking to camera around me. As usual, none of them got their facts right. Among them was Michael Georgy, an Egyptian-American Christian who worked for Reuters. He had always been very persistent in trying to extract information from me about the negotiations – though without success – and I must admit I had become rather fond of him. Tonight, however, the principal thing on his mind was not the end of the siege but the BBC's Middle East correspondent Orla Guerin. He confessed to me that he wanted to marry her. I told him he was stupid: she was too sensible for him.

The promised coaches did not materialize – we never found out why – and at 7 a.m. I finally gave up and went back to Mitri Abu Aita's house. Another night wasted! I wanted to get back to Jerusalem, but Hanna fell asleep so deeply that nobody could wake him, though everyone tried. The following night, we returned to Manger Square to wait for the coaches, and this time they appeared. In the early hours of Saturday 11 May, the thirty-nine surviving gunmen who had taken refuge in the Church of the Nativity finally emerged, weak but defiant. As agreed, two-thirds of them were taken to Gaza while the thirteen Israelis regarded as the most dangerous, accompanied by Alastair, were put on an RAF Hercules transport plane to Cyprus. As I watched them go, I cried with relief. The whole thing had been so traumatic and so protracted – and in those days I wasn't used to that. I little imagined how much harder things could be – and, in Iraq, were to be. I was utterly exhausted. I made my way to the airport and after five gruelling weeks was very glad when I landed in England.

Eleven days later, EU negotiators announced that of the thirteen exiles being held in Cyprus, three would be permitted to live in Italy, three in Spain, two in Greece, two in Ireland, one in Portugal and one in Belgium. The last, who had been Yasser Arafat's chief of intelligence in Bethlehem and was viewed by the Israelis as the worst of all, was eventually accepted by Mauritania six months later. The twenty-six militants who had been removed to Gaza were set free as soon as they arrived there and never did stand trial.

I didn't see Michael Georgy again until 2003, when I bumped into him outside the Palestine Hotel in Baghdad after the liberation of Iraq. He told me he'd been looking everywhere for me. I asked him why and he said, "I want you to marry us." I asked him who he was marrying and he said: "Orla, of course!" I didn't believe him, so I gave him my phone number and told him to get her to call me. Eventually, she rang me to assure me that it was true, and would I officiate at their wedding. A few months later, I married them in Ireland. This was the one good thing that resulted from the siege of the Church of the Nativity: that the worst journalist in the world got to marry the best. And yes, I did say that at the wedding!

CHAPTER 3

From Darkness to Darkness

I have told the story of how I first became involved in Iraq in my earlier book, *Iraq: Searching for Hope* (Continuum, 2007), whose second edition took the narrative up to 2006. Those who have read that book may want to skip this chapter. Here I will tell the tale again, more briefly – though with the benefit of a little hindsight.

In the autumn of 1998, when I took over from Canon Paul Oestreicher as director of international ministry in Coventry, I had to decide where in the world our work of reconciliation was most urgently needed. It was obvious to me that our top priority had to be engaging with the Islamic world. One area of particular concern was Israel/Palestine, where I had been a regular visitor. Another was a country I had never been to: Iraq. We were beginning to hear of the terrible impact on its people of the Gulf War of 1991 and the sanctions that were afterwards imposed by the United Nations to try to prevent Saddam Hussein from rebuilding his military machine. America, Britain, and France had also enforced no-fly zones in the north and south of the country to protect its Kurdish and Shia populations from attack by his forces. Finally, in December 1998, President Bill Clinton ordered major air strikes on Baghdad.

I tried several times to get a visa to enter Iraq, but I was always told that our help was not needed. Finally, in March 1999, I assembled my team in the cathedral and together we prayed that we would get permission to go there without more delay. The next day, a fax arrived from Tariq Aziz, the Deputy Prime Minister of Iraq, asking me to meet him in his office in Baghdad the following week. As Archbishop William Temple once said: "When you pray, coincidences happen and when you don't, they don't." I flew first to Amman in Jordan, and from there I was driven across the desert to the Iraqi capital. It was a hard, thirteen-hour slog that was soon to be a regular part of my life. The highway inland from the border was very good, but in Baghdad everything was extremely shabby. I was taken to my hotel, al-Rashid, where I met the secret policeman who was to be my companion throughout my stay. My room looked dirty – in fact, I couldn't imagine that a hotel bedroom could look worse. Ten years later, there *is* a hotel whose rooms are even worse – it's al-Rashid.

I soon began to learn about the nature of Iraq. There was no prospect of doing what I wanted to do, or even seeing what I wanted to see. I was taken to meet a wide variety of political and religious leaders, Sunni, Shia, and Christian. With me at all times were my minders from Iraqi intelligence, the Mukhabarat. Everyone I met said the same thing: the country was being crippled by the sanctions and by the depleted uranium that had been used so liberally by the Allies in their munitions in the 1991 war. Everyone was frightened of my minders, though it was a long time before I realized this – but that didn't make what they were all telling me any less true. I was taken to a hospital where ward after ward was full of children dying either from malnutrition or from malignancies caused by uranium dust. It was a very disturbing experience, as it was meant to be.

That evening, I went to see the cigar-smoking Mr Aziz – the first of many such meetings. He made a very significant request: he wanted me to return soon with some bishops and other church leaders. I assured him I would do my best. The next day, I found I was both relieved and sad to leave Iraq. I was aware of the tension and fear that oppressed this country, but in a strange way I felt I was falling in love with its people, even though at that stage I really knew nothing about them. On the interminable drive back to Jordan, all I could think of was those words from Psalm 137:

By the rivers of Babylon we sat and wept...

I returned just seven weeks later, by the same exhausting route, with four others: Colin Bennetts, my bishop in Coventry; Peter Price, then Bishop of Kingston, my old diocese; Clive Handford, then Bishop of Cyprus and the Gulf, whose diocese included Iraq; and Patrick Sookhdeo, the international director of Barnabas Fund, which at the time was helping me and my colleagues with our work for reconciliation among Muslims in the Middle East. Once again, this visit was very productive. Most of our meetings were with people I had met before, but there were two people new to me who would make a big impact on my life. One was Margaret Hassan, the local director of the humanitarian organization Care International. Five years later, she would be the first good friend of mine to be taken hostage in the chaos that engulfed the country, though she was married to an Iraqi and had herself become a Muslim. I and my team would be involved in the harrowing effort to rescue her, but without success. The other was Georges Sada, the president of the Protestant Churches of Iraq, a passionate Christian who had been an air vice-marshal in the Iraqi air force before he retired in 1986. He quickly became my indispensable right-hand man, and was to remain so until 2005, when he was headhunted by the Americans to run Iraq's new Ministry of Defence.

Mr Aziz was delighted that I had returned so quickly with my trio of bishops. Now he had a new request: he wanted us to take a delegation of Iraqi religious leaders not only to Britain but also to America. I told him I thought America would be impossible, but Mr Aziz had the answer: Ask Billy Graham! He can do it, he said – and he was right. With Dr Graham's strong support, it did indeed happen, in September 1999. The three delegates chosen by the Iraqi government – one Shia, one Sunni, one Christian – were all very senior people. Two of them I had met before: Ayatollah Hussein al-Sadr – like all ayatollahs, a direct descendant of Imam Ali, Muhammad's son-in-law and the founder of Shia Islam – and Mar Raphael I Bidawid, the Chaldean Catholic Patriarch. The third, however, was new to me. Sheikh Dr Abdel Latif Humayem was in effect Saddam's personal imam; he had made the pilgrimage to Mecca on his behalf and was said to have written out a copy of the Qur'an in the dictator's blood. He was also the principal preacher on Iraqi television every Friday, for which the CIA report described him as "the Billy Graham of Baghdad".

For five days, these three dignitaries had to wait in Amman while the American embassy there refused to give them visas. Finally they were allowed into America, to meet Dr Graham and the former president Jimmy Carter (and to see the Niagara Falls), but only after they had been photographed and fingerprinted like criminals. In Britain, on the other hand, they were received as VIPs. In Coventry, Bishop Colin proved to be a wonderful host. The programme was very intensive, but two meetings were especially memorable. The first was a warm and frank discussion with the Archbishop of Canterbury, George Carey. I had no idea that a few years later he would be a colleague of mine, and a very close friend.

The second took place at the Royal Institute of International Affairs at Chatham House. Towards the end of the evening, some people from the Al-Khoi Foundation stood up. They unrolled a huge scroll with over 200 faces pictured on it and asked the ayatollah to tell everyone who these people were. He knew there were informers in the room, and so the only answer he would give was a quotation from the Qur'an. In the end, one of his questioners told the audience himself that they were members of the ayatollah's own family who had been killed by Saddam's regime or had otherwise disappeared. At the back of the auditorium stood a man who did not speak to the ayatollah but simply looked at him with tears running down his cheeks. It was only years later that I discovered that he was one of Ayatollah al-Sadr's closest friends, though they hadn't seen each other since he had fled to London in 1979. In Britain he was known as Mow Baker, a neurologist; but after the war he went back to his own country and resumed his old name, Mowaffak al-Rubaie. He was then soon appointed to the new, 25-strong Iraqi Governing Council, and later was given a five-year contract as National Security Adviser by the country's American administrator, Paul Bremer. Today, he is one of my closest friends and advisers.

These few days forged some crucial friendships, and sealed my relationship with the Christian, Shia, and Sunni communities of Iraq. The patriarch sadly passed away only two months after the liberation of his country, but ten years on I still count Ayatollah al-Sadr and Sheikh Dr Abdel Latif among my closest allies as they work with me to try to heal the sectarian division in their nation. The ayatollah is a man of great holiness and wisdom, whom I consult over everything I do in Iraq. The sheikh is a delightful man. Remarkably, they have developed a strong affection and respect for each other.

One other man I have to mention is Fadel Alfatlawi, a postgraduate student in Coventry who acted as our interpreter throughout this visit by his countrymen. When he returned to Iraq after the fall of Saddam, I invited him to become a member of my team. Just over a year later, he would succeed Georges Sada as secretary general of the new Iraqi Institute of Peace.

After this, I visited Iraq several times a year. I always went to see Mr Aziz, at his insistence, and often took him a bottle of his favourite brown sauce – for which the British media accused me of "playing with the Devil'. I was forever on Iraqi television condemning the sanctions. With Georges beside me, I was involved in many projects concerned with both opening channels of communication and relieving suffering – not least, helping to set up Iraq's first-ever bone marrow transplant centre and bringing its medical team to Britain for training. I met most of Saddam's ministers many times (though I never met Saddam himself). I continued to deepen my relationships with the various religious leaders I knew. My only concern was to bring relief and promote reconciliation – though it left an unpleasant taste when I was obliged to have dinner with Saddam's two odious sons and they thanked me for all I was doing.

I was sitting in my study in Coventry on 11 September 2001 preparing to leave for Iraq the next day when news broke of the attacks on the World Trade Center and the Pentagon. It was obvious that nothing was ever going to be the same again. It was also obvious that I was not going to get to Baghdad the next day. I did make it a few days later, however, and the first thing Tariq Aziz said – or shouted – when I met him was, "*Abuna*

["Father"] Andrew, tell them we had nothing to do with it! We are revolutionaries, not terrorists." I replied without thinking: "Your Excellency, it doesn't matter whether you are terrorists or revolutionaries, they are still coming to get you." And it was true. Suddenly, the CIA wanted to talk to me about Saddam's weapons of mass destruction – I was no longer just a nuisance. I assured them that those weapons existed. I still insist that I know this for a fact. They were never found because they were moved out of the country before the UN's weapons inspectors arrived. (In his 2006 book *Saddam's Secrets*, Georges was more explicit: there were chemical weapons in Iraq as late as the summer of 2002, which were then spirited away to Syria.)

When I went to Baghdad in October 2002, I knew it would be the last time before it came under inevitable attack. I had started out trying to work for reconciliation between Iraq and the West and I had failed, as I was acutely aware – but I no longer believed that this was what the Iraqis needed. Now I felt strongly that the Ba'thist regime had to be removed. I was no longer opposed to the very idea of war. Everywhere, people would tell me quietly that someone had to set them free from Saddam's tyranny. They knew there was nothing they could do themselves. Late on my last night in Baghdad, I escaped my minders and went for a walk with Georges. I asked him: "How can you keep going when everything seems so dreadful?" He quoted some words from the prophet Habakkuk:

> *Though the fig tree does not bud*
> *and there are no grapes on the vines,*
> *though the olive crop fails*
> *and the fields produce no food,*
> *though there are no sheep in the pen*
> *and no cattle in the stalls,*

yet I will rejoice in the LORD,
I will be joyful in God my Saviour.

In the years that followed, these have been words that strengthened me and enabled me to persevere.

I was in Cambridge, writing a short book on a fellowship from Clare College, when the war began. Saddam was given forty-eight hours to leave Iraq, and when the deadline expired on 20 March cruise missiles and bombs began to rain down on the city and the people I loved. I could see no alternative, but the emotional pain I felt was still intense. The collapse of the Ba'thist regime was very quick, however, and it wasn't long before we were watching Saddam's Minister of Information, Muhammad Sayed al-Sahaf (whom I knew and liked), insisting on television, "I triple guarantee you, there are no American soldiers in Baghdad" even as an Abrams tank was visible over his shoulder entering the city. Hours later, the whole world saw the huge statue of the dictator in al-Ferdos ("Paradise") Square being hauled down by the Americans and stamped on by Iraqis. (Today, the top half of that statue is in Dr Mowaffak's living room.)

Now that people in Iraq could talk freely at last, I was appalled to discover that in all the years I had been visiting their country even those close to me had been too afraid to tell me of the true horror they lived under. It was only now, for example, that Georges admitted that he had been imprisoned for nine months in 1991 for refusing to kill prisoners of war. My driver, Nashwan, told me that his own father, a general, had had an eye gouged out after he refused to obey a brutal order. Both he and Georges were reckoned to have got off lightly.

I lost no time in going to see Ayatollah al-Sadr at his home in Baghdad, and there I learned from his disciples how cruelly the regime had tortured this old man. Others told me of their own suffering. One man had been buried for several days inside a coffin. Another had been a day late in returning from a trip to Syria. The Mukhabarat took him to his home, where they were already holding his family prisoner. First they raped his wife in front of him, and then they picked his three-year-old son up by his ankles and smashed his head against the wall. Finally, they shot the rest of his family dead before they left. That was the nature of Saddam's regime.

It soon became clear that the tragedy of Iraq was not over, however. The Coalition made some very serious errors. Its troops had stood by while all the hospitals, museums, universities and libraries, and all the ministries except the Ministry of Oil, were comprehensively looted – but this was not its most catastrophic mistake. First, it failed to secure the country's borders. The first time I drove from Amman to Baghdad after the war, the border control consisted of one smiling American soldier chewing gum, and the only question he asked was "Where are you guys from?" Soon, Iraq was being infiltrated both by militant Shia from Syria and Iran and by al-Qa'ida and other Sunni radicals. I encountered three young British Asians on the border with Jordan who told me they had come "to fight the Coalition'.

I had already warned the British and American governments of the likelihood of sectarian conflict and I had urged them to engage with Iraq's religious and tribal leaders as a matter of urgency, but they thought that as a priest I was just beating my own drum. I still have the dismissive letter I received from the Foreign Office at the start of 2003 telling me that religious issues would have to wait until the water and electricity supplies had been sorted out. Today, as I write this in October 2008, water and electricity are still scarce. The ignorance of the Americans especially was sometimes quite disturbing. They had no real understanding of Iraqi society and assured me that it was essentially secular. They even proposed to set up a national religious council in Baghdad after the war whose twelve members would include six women – and not one cleric! The British were more knowledgeable, but they were simply ignored. Neither government seemed to me to have any real plan for the peace.

I have read Rajiv Chandrasekaran's book about the American administration of Iraq after the war, *Imperial Life in the Emerald City*, and I have to say that the picture it paints is very accurate. The Coalition Provisional Authority was a well-meaning shambles. There were so many hundreds of experts – but they were experts in setting up systems that work in America. And not everyone was even that: the man who was given the job of reviving the Baghdad stock exchange was a junior soldier who had never worked in finance! Paul Bremer, who took over the reins from the ex-general Jay Garner and his very short-lived Office of Reconstruction and Humanitarian Aid, was a splendid man but he knew absolutely nothing about the Arab world. His previous experience, as ambassador to the Netherlands and "ambassador-at-large for counterterrorism" under Ronald Reagan, did not qualify him for overseeing one of the most complex societies in the world. It was reportedly his unilateral decision to dismiss every last man in the Iraqi army and police. Clearly, some people had to go, but the result of sacking everyone was the anger and anarchy that engulfed the whole country. Suddenly, hundreds of thousands of men trained to fight (and still in possession of their weapons) had no job, no income, no status, and every reason to revolt. In the

CPA headquarters in Saddam's huge Republican Palace, the Ministry of Justice was located underneath a flight of stairs.

A new darkness descended on the land. The very day after Saddam's statue was pulled down, my friend Abdel Majid al-Khoi was hacked to death by a mob in the holy city of Najaf. Only a few days before, at a conference on religion and violence at Windsor Castle, I had sat at dinner with him and Prince Philip. This young ayatollah, still only forty years old, had told me that the Americans wanted him to return to Iraq from his exile as soon as possible to help with the task of reconstruction, and he asked me to go with him. I said I thought it was still too soon to go, but he went and now he was dead. No one knows who ordered his killing, though an Iraqi judge later issued a warrant for the arrest of another Shia cleric, Muqtada al-Sadr, the fiery young nephew of Ayatollah al-Sadr whose militia, the Mehdi Army, was to become such a challenge to the Coalition.

The murder of Ayatollah al-Khoi can be blamed on the struggle for power between rival Shia factions, but that was not the only source of conflict. I have already mentioned the rapid infiltration of Iraq by militant Shia and Sunna, who hated the West and also hated each other. Neighbouring countries such as Syria and Iran got involved, partly to hurt America and partly because they felt threatened by the prospect of a democracy next door to them. Many of the insurgents were former supporters of Saddam who had lost money, prestige, and power as a result of his fall. Others were simply taking advantage of the chaos to settle old scores or to turn to crime. There were people who had naively imagined that a free Iraq would become like one of the Gulf states overnight and were furious that it hadn't. In the few weeks after the war when I could still walk in the streets of Baghdad, I once found myself faced by a vast crowd shouting both "Death to Saddam!" and "Death to America!" Further anger would be provoked later in 2004 by the shocking abuses in Abu Ghraib and the bloody assault on Falluja (which took place during Ramadan), and by incidents – fortunately rare, but still dreadful – such as the massacre by US Marines at Haditha in 2005. And, finally, there were tens of thousands of young men without jobs who were willing simply to hire out their services as fighters.

Violent death soon became a feature of everyday life in Baghdad. The International, or "Green", Zone was now surrounded by blast-proof barricades and coils of razor wire. The hotels outside it, in what came to be known as the Red Zone, were more like prisons – except that prisons do not usually come under rocket attack. Two atrocities in particular in August 2003 announced Iraq's descent into bloody chaos. A huge car bomb outside the Jordanian embassy killed fourteen people and injured forty others. Twelve days later, the country's first suicide bomber detonated a colossal explosion that tore apart the UN headquarters in the old Canal Hotel. The head of the UN mission, Sergio Vieira de Mello, another friend of mine, was among the twenty-three dead. Someone had finally got revenge for all the years of sanctions.

Since then, I have lost count of the friends and colleagues who have been killed. Samir, my new driver, and one of my project officers had a narrow escape when a 1,000 lb car bomb went off outside the Palace while I was preaching at chapel inside. The heat was so intense that car doors were welded shut and people were burnt to death inside their vehicles. On many occasions, I have come very close to being shot or blown up. Hundreds of religious leaders, hundreds of politicians, have died. Nobody ever even tried to keep count of how many ordinary Iraqis were being slaughtered. There was a brief lull in the bloodshed when Saddam was captured at the end of 2003, but it didn't last. Many times over the next four years I would write in the regular "spiritual updates" I send to my supporters: "Every time I think the violence cannot get any worse, it does."

As soon as the war had ended, I had been invited by the American State Department to become involved in the reconstruction of Iraq. At the very beginning I was dealing with Britain's "special representative", John Sawers, my old friend from Alexandria, and our most senior soldier in Iraq, Major General Tim Cross. The latter had gained solid experience in Kosovo four years before – but it was he who suggested that I wait for a week or two before returning to Baghdad, "when the situation will be under control". Britain's "head of mission" in Baghdad was Christopher Segar, a seasoned diplomat fluent in Arabic who quickly became a crucial ally. It was with and through him that our real search for peace began. He regularly met the various religious leaders I was engaging with, and he secured funding from the Foreign Office for our work. Today he is one of the trustees of my foundation. Paul Bremer was also very supportive, as was his British deputy, Sir Jeremy Greenstock. Day after day, Georges and I did the rounds of the key players, British, American and Iraqi. Everyone was interested in Ayatollah al-Sadr's idea for an Institute of Religious Tolerance, though Prince Hassan of Jordan, a friend of Lord Carey, whose family had once ruled Iraq, told me that "tolerance" was not enough – what was needed was mutual respect. Of course, he was right.

Sheikh Dr Abdel Latif had fled the country, but we finally tracked him down in Amman and from exile he did all he could to help us. Among the Sunna, his name alone was useful. My first meeting with Sheikh Dr Abdel Qadir al-Ani in Baghdad was going very badly, for example – he even accused me of working for the CIA – until I thought to mention that Sheikh

Dr Abdel Latif was my friend. By the time our meeting ended, I had a firm commitment from him to work with us for peace. Other meetings proved equally tricky, but many of these had positive outcomes.

On 24 February 2004, after months of negotiation, we succeeded in bringing together many of the country's more influential religious leaders at the Babylon Hotel. Ayatollah al-Sadr and Sheikh Dr Abdel Qadir sat side by side at the head of the table – two of Baghdad's most eminent Muslims, meeting for the first time. Most of the country's faiths and sects were represented, though the Christian archbishops only turned up the following day to sign it – they felt very vulnerable in the new Iraq, and were afraid of being caught in the crossfire between the Shia and the Sunna. The Baghdad Religious Accord was based on the Alexandria Declaration (though we could never admit that). It affirmed that "killing innocents in the name of God is a desecration of the laws of heaven', condemned sectarianism and committed its signatories "to doing all in [their] power to ensure the ending of all acts of violence and bloodshed that deny the right to life, freedom and dignity'. In the end, it was signed by thirty-nine religious leaders. There was a sense of triumph – it was a historic achievement, though it was only a start.

Four months later, the Dokan Religious Accord was signed by leaders in the Kurdish-dominated north of Iraq. The only difference in the wording was that, out of deference to the religious minority the Yazidi, it did not say that acts of corruption, violence, and destruction "are the work of the Devil'.

We had so much hope in those early days. We really thought we could make a difference. We worked hard, day and night, to implement the accords, and in particular to establish the Iraqi Centre for Dialogue – everyone had agreed that "dialogue" must be in the title – Reconciliation and Peace. We set up six working parties to address the different aspects of our task:

- women, religion, and democracy
- youth and young people
- the media
- religious freedom and human rights
- interreligious dialogue
- conflict prevention and resolution.

Dr Mowaffak became the first chair of the ICDRP (soon to be renamed the Iraqi Institute of Peace), and for its headquarters in Baghdad we used a wonderful house on the banks of the Tigris that belonged to his wife. It soon became known simply as "the Centre". It was in al-Khadamiya, which is very much a Shia neighbourhood, and yet in those days everyone felt able to come there – though at its opening I counted thirty-nine guards with sub-machine guns in the grounds. Sadly, however, our optimism was shattered one day when a relative of Saddam was brought to us so that we could turn him in. I rang the American embassy to ask them to collect him, and the Iraqi prime minister's office to let them know what was happening. Eventually, four US Navy Seals arrived and discreetly took him away – and forty-five minutes later the Centre was surrounded by over a hundred plain-clothes police from the new Ministry of Interior, who beat me and threatened to shoot me, ransacked the house and stole our computers and over $20,000 in cash. It was a lesson in how divided and untrustworthy the new Iraqi government was. The next day, the British embassy asked me to move inside the Green Zone for my own safety.

Thereafter, we got used to these two extremes, of elation and despair. Whichever state you were in at the moment, you knew that the other was not far away. The progressive new temporary constitution was published in March 2004 on International Women's Day, and I shall never forget the sight of women dancing and singing and weeping on the streets of Baghdad. Yet it was less than a week before that a concerted series of attacks by al-Qa'ida had slaughtered at least 178 Shia worshippers, and injured at least 500 more, on their holy day of Ashura. The handover of sovereignty from the CPA to the Iraqi Interim Government on 28 June was marked by another spike of violence. As the date approached for the country's first democratic election, for a transitional assembly, the insurgents threatened to kill anyone who cast a vote; and yet on 30 January 2005 nearly 8.5 million people did so, and for a while the country was full of pride. Almost a year later, when the election for Iraq's new, permanent parliament, the Council of Representatives, took place, over 12 million people voted, a turnout of almost 80 per cent. All the while, however, the killing continued, and in fact it got worse.

One particular area in which we experienced both joy and grief – though, sadly, far more often the latter – was in negotiating for the release of hostages, which increasingly occupied my time after April 2004. Kidnapping had become an epidemic in the new Iraq. Most of the people responsible were petty criminals out to make some quick money, and the vast majority of the people they abducted were middle-class Iraqis or their children. However, if they managed to get a foreigner they would usually sell them on to terrorists, and then it was a different matter. British and American nationals commanded much the highest prices – and were the most reported in the Western media, which generally ignored (for example) the poor Filippino truck drivers who were seized and in the end brutally murdered, often on camera. Through the IIP, I and my team became involved in many of these cases, and over time we acquired a lot of expertise. Often, the negotiations were very complex, uncertain and protracted, and they were always very fraught. Some of the Iraqis in my team were killed.

When I was appointed as director of international ministry at Coventry Cathedral in 1998, it was supposed to be for a term of five years. I finally left in July 2005, to continue the work that Ruth Heflin had foreseen for me, seeking "the peace of Jerusalem and the Middle East'. I had already set up my own foundation with Lord Carey, and most of the key people who had worked for me while I was at the International Centre for Reconciliation in Coventry – Fadel and Samir in Baghdad, Hanna in Jerusalem – continued to work for me in my new capacity.

CHAPTER 4

A Measure of Progress

At the end of August 2008, I was sitting in a room in Beirut with four of Iraq's most senior religious leaders when one of them remarked that "nothing had happened in 2006 and 2007". None of us asked him what he meant. We all knew. They had been such difficult years. We had continued with our work, but as the fight for peace continued, so did the kidnapping and the killing. We had hoped for change, but it seemed so slow in coming. The carnage just went on and on and on. In just one day in November 2006, for example, 215 people were killed in Sadr City, the poor Shia suburb of Baghdad, by mortar fire and car bombs. I wrote then: "In [2005,] I could still speak about specific acts of violence and individual tragedies, but now the slaughter is so unremitting it is almost impossible to write about anything particular."

It became impossible for the Iraqi Institute of Peace to operate from its original base in al-Khadamiya. This overwhelmingly Shia neighbourhood of Baghdad was under constant attack from the predominantly Sunni neighbourhood of al-Adhamiya across the River Tigris, and of course it was far too dangerous for the IIP's non-Shia clients to be seen there. In spite of all its difficulties, however, the IIP is still functioning today, with funding from the United States Institute of Peace. I have been trying to remove myself from its leadership, as is only right, but in fact my involvement has only increased. Fadel Alfatlawi has had to leave Iraq because of the huge price on his head, and he has been replaced as the IIP's secretary general by Essam al-Saadi. A former lawyer, like Samir, Essam also works for Iraq's National Security Adviser, Dr Mowaffak al-Rubaie, as his head of media relations. He is a Shia in his late thirties, highly dependable, very well connected on all sides and able to make things happen. Like me, he now lives in the Green Zone and since 2006 we have met every evening to talk things through. He has been present at all the Foundation for Relief and Reconciliation in the Middle East (FRRME) international summits (for which he also handles the media), and he and Samir and I have become known as "the Triangle". I had so many people in my team in Iraq at one stage, but now it often seems as if there are just the three of us.

Samir Raheem al-Soodani, who was originally my driver after the war, is now the Iraq director of the FRRME and the man I most rely on. He translates for me nowadays, as Professor Sadoon al-Zubaydi, Saddam Hussein's interpreter who subsequently worked with me, has gone to live in Jordan. Everyone we work with knows Samir and trusts him, and he, too, is someone who can make things happen. (I divide the world into people who can make things happen and people who can't. I reckon that only 4 per cent of humankind come into the first category, and these are the people I work with.) It is no longer safe for Samir's wife and daughter to stay in Baghdad and so, with the help of the Pentagon, they have won "special parole status" in America. Samir himself has permission to live there when he is not in Iraq, but that is not very often and so he sees them very rarely.

All of us have faced serious death threats. I have had to flee Iraq on several occasions – most recently in July 2007, when pictures of me were posted up around Baghdad with the caption "Wanted dead or alive'. They announced that if I did not leave the country, the hostages I was trying to recover would be killed (so the threat probably didn't come from al-Qa'ida). The British embassy ordered me to go and the next day I flew secretly to Bahrain. Even in England, in rural Hampshire, my wife and children had to move out of our home for a while because they were thought to be at risk. Caroline told me it was the first time she had been afraid because of my job – though I don't think the boys were bothered. After a month in Britain, I returned to Iraq. My colleagues had continued our work for peace without me, but I had St George's Church in Baghdad and the chapel in Saddam's old Republican Palace (now the American embassy) to look after as well. I have to admit that, although I have contemplated the fact that one day I may be killed in Iraq, or abducted, the thought has never once troubled me.

I have been very fortunate in the men who guard me – they have been outstanding. Originally, our security was provided by men of the Controlled Risk Group, at a (hugely discounted) rate of £750 a day. One day in 2006, I was sitting in my trailer in the Green Zone when there was a knock at the door. It was Paul Wood, a former Parachute Regiment officer who was now managing operations in Iraq for Kroll Security International, with whom we had worked closely on several hostage cases. He asked me how much we were paying for our protection and offered to halve the price. When CRG said it would match this, Paul said that Kroll would look after me and Samir for nothing. Since that day, his men have cared for me as if I were one of the family. Kroll was subsequently taken over by the Canadian company GardaWorld, which today takes care of all my needs in Baghdad, including my accommodation, my food, and even my laundry. In May 2007, it was presented with the FRRME's first Prize for Peace in the Middle East in recognition of the phenomenal service it has given us.

In 2006, the Iraqi government was proving to be divided and ineffectual. Continued wrangling over the new constitution was jamming the legislative programme, with disputes in particular over the decentralization of power to new autonomous "regions" and the distribution of oil and gas revenues. Crucial bills were not being passed. The Council of Representatives (that is, the parliament) that was inaugurated in March soon began to lose faith in the Council of Ministers, who seemed unable to deliver on anything that really mattered to the country. Some people might say that these were the inevitable teething troubles of a new democracy, but Iraq could not afford such problems while the escalating violence was shutting down every basic service from electricity to education.

The government of Ibrahim Ja'fari fell at the beginning of May. I used to have regular meetings with Dr Ja'fari and I got on very well with him – he is a nice man, and a good one, though he was a weak prime minister. There was no obvious man to take his place, but eventually the big Shia coalition that had put Dr Ja'fari into power chose Nuri al-Maliki, the leader of the Da'wa Party. At first I didn't think he would have enough authority to survive, but I turned out to be wrong. He is a strong supporter of our work for reconciliation – he knows how difficult it is but realizes that it is the only way forward. I always enjoy my meetings with him.

Meanwhile, al-Qa'ida had become more active and effective in Iraq. In the early years after the war, its mostly foreign fighters had actually played quite a small role in the conflict, but it had the most recognizable terrorist "brand" in the world and had (wrongly) been linked with Saddam in the build-up to the invasion, and so it is not surprising that its presence among the insurgents had a high profile in the Western media. There was great jubilation in the Pentagon when al-Qa'ida's "emir" in Iraq, the one-legged Jordanian Abu Musab al-Zarqawi, was killed in an air strike in June 2006 – but in fact its role in the conflict only grew bigger after that. Most of its fighters in Iraq today are Iraqis, and their impulse seems to be to attack anyone who does not share their extreme Sunni ideology. They see their country as the front line in their war against America, and want to prove to the world that the Americans are defeated – though in fact most of their victims have been their compatriots.

The struggle towards peace and reconciliation continued, but progress was painfully slow. Since the beginning of 2005, our primary objective had been to organize a major summit that we hoped would produce a statement similar to the Alexandria Declaration, agreed and signed by the key leaders of all the faiths represented in Iraq. Samir and I and the young American Peter Maki, who was then my director of operations, sat through endless meetings with politicians and religious leaders, inching our way towards this goal.

Then, one day in June 2006, I was informed by Jerry Jones, my friend and ally in the Pentagon, that the Department of Defense had decided to pay for the whole series of summits we were trying to arrange. This was a very significant breakthrough. The British Foreign Office had undertaken to fund our work for a year after the end of the war, and after the year was up that funding ceased. The American military had never invested in anything like this before, but now we had their support – and they are, without question, the biggest power in Iraq. Some people can only see the Pentagon as the enemy of peace, and cannot understand how we could accept its money and work so closely with its people. The fact is, however, that in Iraq the US Army has become our most important partner in the search for peace. Every day, I see the way its soldiers (sometimes literally) lay down their lives for this country. I see their strength and courage, and their commitment. It is difficult for some people to accept this, but the truth is that the greatest peacemakers in the world today are in the armed forces. Furthermore, in Iraq the US Army detailed its military chaplains to work with me.

The man behind these decisions was Gordon England, who in 2005 had succeeded Paul Wolfowitz as Deputy Secretary of Defense after the latter had moved on to head the World Bank. Mr England is a delightful man, and quite devout. Today, he is very much involved with our work. I always go to see him when I am at the Pentagon and he always listens attentively. Another useful ally there is the retired general Mick Kicklighter, a remarkable man of God who was a regular member of my Anglican congregation in the Palace back in 2004. He has never made any bones about the fact that he regards "this Iraq business" as the Lord's work – and now he is the inspector general of the Department of Defense.

In the autumn of 2006, we began to make concrete plans for the first of the meetings of what was to become known as the Iraq Inter-Religious Congress, or II-RC. At first we intended that this should take place in Britain, and I and my colleagues at the FRRME spent days making the arrangements and discussing the issues with the Foreign Office. The cost of security was a major concern. We had planned to meet in Surrey, in the south of England, but the police told us it would cost in the region of £1 million to ensure our safety. The Foreign Office told me I had three days to find the money, and obviously didn't think it was possible. I did find it, not in three days but one. When I informed the people at the FO, they told me the summit still couldn't take place in Surrey. I think they were always intending to say no: they support what we are doing, but they didn't want to see such a high-risk group of people in Britain.

Frustrated, we started afresh. We wanted to find a venue outside Iraq for many reasons: Baghdad was dangerous and many people were very reluctant to go there – the daily slaughter was just unremitting. It was unpleasant in other ways: even in its best hotel there was often no water in the taps. We looked at the possibility of meeting in Italy (where I had good relations with one of the intelligence services, after helping to secure the release of several Italian hostages in Iraq). We also considered Malta, because a friend of mine worked in its high commission in London, and the island offered some obvious advantages. However, neither government would give us permission, and in the end we decided that Baghdad was the only option.

The negotiations took many, many weeks. Often I would work into the small hours, only to be woken at six by a barrage of rockets. Before the summit itself, we went to Amman in April 2007 for a "pre-conference" with some of the key Sunni leaders who would be attending. My American friends Bill and Connie Wilson, who are our principal "prayer partners", came over from Jerusalem to pray for us in their room, and Colonel Mike Hoyt, the most senior of the American chaplains in Iraq, also accompanied us. For some reason, he spoke eloquently to the delegates about the concept of "the separation of church and state"; but they couldn't really grasp it. To their minds, it was a nonsense: the two are indivisible.

I was constantly being told by Sheikh Dr Abdel Latif Humayem that we were still waiting for the most important delegates to arrive from Syria. Eventually they turned up and I sat down to talk to their leader, an Iraqi in his forties. I know who this man is, but I cannot identify him. He came across as an educated and cultured man and was well dressed, in Western clothes, but he proved to be the nastiest person I have ever met – and I have met some nasty people. It was a very difficult meeting, and at times I felt very angry. I believe Sheikh Dr Abdel Latif hoped that I could engage with this man, but it was soon evident that he had come only to threaten me. He told me at great length how both Britain and America were going to be attacked in retaliation for what they were doing in Iraq. He made a comment I will never forget, though at the time I did not understand what he meant: "Those who cure you will kill you."

That night, I wrote in a "spiritual update" to supporters of my foundation, "I met the Devil today." A few days later, when I happened to see a senior official from the Foreign Office, I told him some of what this man had said, but I did not pass on that one, cryptic sentence: "Those who cure you will kill you." Within a few months, at the end of June, a plot to set off two car bombs in the West End of London was discovered, apparently in the nick of time. A day later, two men tried to explode a car full of propane-gas cylinders at Glasgow International Airport. In all, eight Muslim people were arrested in connection with these crimes. Five of them were doctors and two more were reported to be medical students.

On 3 July, I was sitting in al-Rashid, drinking tea with one of my very few British friends in Iraq, Debbie Haynes, and I told her about my meeting with the Devil and what he had said. I knew she was a journalist, but I didn't really think anything of it. The next day, "Those who cure you will kill you" was the main headline on the front page of the London *Times*. That was the end of my low profile in Iraq. I gave seventy-eight interviews to the media that day – they virtually had to form a queue.

It was at al-Rashid that we had finally held the first meeting of the II-RC the previous month, from 11 to 13 June. There was little electricity and no air conditioning, though the temperature rarely dropped below 45°C, and there was the constant threat of attack by rockets and bombs. At the time, I recorded my thoughts in these words:

> *Two-and-a-half years of non-stop work for two-and-a-half days of meeting. We spent well over $2 million in preparation and spent months sitting with some of the most difficult people imaginable. In the past few weeks, [my team in Britain], Samir and I have literally worked day and night organizing this event. I have worked hard for years, but nothing has ever been like this. In the last day, [we] have been hardly able to talk. I found one of my staff today asleep on the floor. This peacemaking business is not easy...*
>
> *Doing the event in Iraq has been far more complicated than anywhere else. The security is immense – we have helicopters, tanks and ground troops even though it will be in the [Green] Zone. The good thing is that the [US] Army is taking this very, very seriously and risking nothing. I just hope and pray that the delegates will all arrive safely. The whole future of Iraq is at stake.*

In fact, this conference was the largest interfaith gathering of religious leaders ever to take place in Iraq. Some seventy religious and tribal leaders attended, from all across the country, including Basra, Falluja, and Saddam's home town, Tikrit. The Kurds and Christians were represented, too. Dr Mowaffak was present, and several members of parliament, including the Minister for Human Rights, Wijdan Michael Salim, a Chaldean Catholic who is one of the outstanding people in the government. (She and her whole family have become very good friends of mine. The eldest of her three teenage sons, Osama, came to Britain in 2008 with some of the young people from St George's.)

The wording of the accord they signed (in the presence of the ambassadors of America, Britain, Denmark and Italy) was similar to the Baghdad Religious Accord of 2004, though it wasn't consciously modelled on it, but there was one crucial difference: for the first time, Iraq's Sunni as well as Shia religious leaders denounced al-Qa'ida by name. This was also the first broad-based religious accord to recognize the constitution and to call on the Iraqi government to engage at a senior level with religious and tribal leaders. It also declared that the proliferation of unauthorized weapons was an offence. The delegates expressed a desire to continue to meet regularly to look at ways to reduce the violence, and they set up a number of working parties that would address specific issues, such as "religion and culture" (fostering good relations between the different faiths and finding common ground on matters of morality and behaviour) and "reconstruction" (rebuilding everything from mosques to sewers). It had the personal endorsement of the Prime Minister, Nuri al-Maliki, who sent his religious affairs adviser Sayed Dr Fadel al-Shara to sign it on his behalf and promised funding from the government. We understood, too, that Grand Ayatollah Ali al-Sistani – the single most authoritative figure in Iraq – was particularly supportive of the condemnation of the proliferation of weapons.

One thing I was very particular about was that we should bring together the various strands of peacemaking in Iraq, including not only the Baghdad and Dokan Religious Accords and the work of the IIP but also the so-called Mecca Document. This was the product of an independent initiative sponsored by the international Organization of the Islamic Conference, which had been approved by Grand Ayatollah al-Sistani and endorsed by the Grand Imam of al-Azhar, Sheikh Tantawi. It affirmed that "the blood, property, honour and reputation of Muslims', as well as *all* places of worship, are sacrosanct, prohibited abuse and vilification, called for the release of all hostages and the return of all the displaced, both Muslim and non-Muslim, and quoted the words of God in the Qur'an: "Reconciliation is best." Sheikh Abdel Halimjawad Kadhum al-Zuhairi, who chaired the gathering of twenty-nine Sunni and Shia scholars who signed this document live on Iraqi television in 2006 (and who was subsequently appointed chief religious adviser to Prime Minister Nuri al-Maliki), has worked with us since October 2007.

A weakness of our second Baghdad accord was that as all of Iraq's most senior Sunni leaders now live in exile, none of them had been able to attend and so it did not carry any of their signatures. For that reason, in August 2007 we brought a handful of them together in Cairo, along with one of Grand Ayatollah al-Sistani's most senior men, Ayatollah Ammar Abu Ragif, himself a crucial new participant in this process. It is normal in Arabic culture for the most exalted people to send representatives to meetings, but in this case both Sheikh Dr Ahmed al-Kubaisi and Sheikh Dr Abdel Latif came in person. Few of these men had even met each other before, and a great deal of mutual distrust had to be overcome. Moreover, these were all people who bitterly opposed the American presence in Iraq and had previously refused to meet any representative of the Coalition – and yet here they were engaging with my colleague Colonel Hoyt. (They do accept the US Army chaplains as religious leaders in their own right, though it has not been easy to integrate these Americans into the reconciliation process because they are also soldiers, and look like soldiers. When one of them showed up at a meeting in army boots, some of the Iraqis took me aside and said, "Those are the boots that kicked down our doors.")

In the end, after long discussion, these very senior men confirmed their support for the two Baghdad accords of 2004 and 2007 and decided to become, in effect, an implementation committee for everything that had been agreed. They then added their own commitment, "to end terrorist violence and disband militia activity in order to build a civilized country and work within the framework of law", and resolved to seek to involve "the highest-level religious leaders as soon as possible" and "engage with other influential and proactive religious leaders with the highest qualifications in order to work towards issuing a comprehensive *fatwa*". Implicitly, they also urged other senior Sunni leaders to return to Iraq from exile to add their weight to the push for reconciliation (as I believe Sheikh Dr al-Kubaisi and Sheikh Dr Abdel Latif themselves will do one day). It was a simple statement, but one that could have profound consequences.

By this point, the much-heralded "surge" had at last begun to take effect in Baghdad and the so-called Sunni Triangle. "The New Way Forward", as it was more formally known, had actually started at the beginning of the year. The multinational forces in Iraq had been reinforced with about 30,000 American soldiers, most of them deployed in Baghdad. The new strategy had a new focus: to help the Iraqis to take the lead in protecting their own neighbourhoods. The Iraqi army was still predominantly Shia, but a lot of Sunna were now joining it, and with the first-class training its men were receiving from the Coalition it had become a powerful force – far better than the one that had largely melted away before the Coalition in 2003. Dr Mowaffak now made sure that it gave the American troops full support and it began to conduct joint operations with them, including joint patrols led initially by Americans but later on by Iraqis.

General David Petraeus had arrived in Baghdad on 26 January 2007 as commander of the Coalition forces. I would put a lot of the success of the new strategy down to him. He is a wonderful man, quite serious and yet very engaging, and he managed to win the respect of the country's tribal and religious leaders. I had a very good relationship with him. Not least, I found that if I couldn't say something to him in the week I could often say it to him from the pulpit in chapel on Sunday. Whenever my team had an important meeting, I would e-mail him about it and he would always reply – usually, being a soldier, with a one-liner. Another route to him was a subordinate of his called General Moore to whom I used to report everything we did.

At first, the surge had seemed to make no difference to the death toll. On 3 February, a single bomb had slaughtered 135 people in a crowded market in central Baghdad. Over 300 more had been injured. A month later, a string of attacks on Shia pilgrims had left 137 dead and 310 wounded in one day. One effect the surge did have was to displace the violence farther afield, even to the Kurdish-dominated north (which previously had been quite peaceful), as al-Qa'ida concentrated its attentions on parts of the country where there were not so many soldiers. On 27 March, for example, the deadliest single attack in Iraq since the end of the war killed 152 people in Tal Afar, close to the Syrian border. (The bloodletting continued the next day, when Shia gunmen, including off-duty policemen, roamed the town's Sunni neighbourhoods, handcuffing any men they found and shooting them in the head. At least seventy men were killed in these reprisals, and forty more were abducted.) Not that the centre of Iraq was quiet: in April, a hundred people were killed in two separate suicide attacks in the Shia holy city of Karbala and a car bomb in Baghdad killed 140. These, of course, were just the massacres that hit the headlines. In fact, the bloodshed continued every day.

Nonetheless, the American strategy began to show results. A crucial development was that many of Iraq's Sunni insurgents in effect changed sides. General Petraeus was told by his intelligence in al-Anbar that the Sunna there felt that the al-Qa'ida men who had been fighting alongside them were taking control of their province and were now a bigger threat to their communities than either the Coalition or Iraq's Shia-led government. He asked me to enlist the help of Sheikh Dr Abdel Latif, who has a lot of influence with the Sunni sheikhs and tribal leaders, and I spent many hours explaining the general's plans to him. Soon, armed men – whom the Americans called "concerned local citizens" – were reasserting control of their streets, not only in al-Anbar but also in Baghdad and the adjacent provinces of Babil, Diyala, Salahuddin, and Nineva. They became known as "the Sons of Iraq', or "Tribal Awakening". By April 2008, more than 95,000 people were involved, including Shia as well as Sunna. Almost all of them were under contract to the US Army and were being paid $300 a month to maintain law and order.

This strategy has not been uncontroversial, and critics in the West have said that it is buying short-term peace at the cost of encouraging tribalism, "warlordism" and sectarianism. The Prime Minister, Nuri al-Maliki, has warned that these "concerned local citizens" are an armed Sunni opposition in the making. A different way of looking at it is that, as one senior Sunni leader put it to me, by giving people authority and respect as well as money General Petraeus has given them back their country. The fact is that this is the only way to get peace in many parts of Iraq – and it has succeeded. The millions of dollars this has cost first the Pentagon and then, since October 2008, the Iraqi government is much less than the cost of the mayhem that would otherwise have continued unabated. Nonetheless, the peace is still fragile and could easily be lost if it was taken for granted. The Iraqi government has promised to incorporate 20 per cent of the Sons of Iraq into the regular armed forces and to go on paying the rest until they can find civilian jobs, but I would prefer to see them all taken into the army.

At one point, the Pentagon even asked me if we could form our own Christian "Sons of Iraq". I said that this was not appropriate: perhaps in America armed Christians might patrol the streets, but not in the Middle East! Sadly, the plight of the country's Christians became very much worse in 2006, when they began to be targeted in earnest by the Muslim militias. At one point in 2007, an American officer in the al-Dora neighbourhood of Baghdad said that over 500 Christians were being murdered there every month. All the churches there were closed down, and there was a great exodus. Once, there were reckoned to be some 700,000 Christians in the country, though by early 2003 the sanctions and the war had already driven maybe 200,000 abroad. Today, no more than 55,000 remain. Many have fled, to Jordan, Syria or Lebanon or to the West – especially Sweden, where for a while it was very easy to get asylum. Increasingly, it is only the poorest who are still left in Iraq. The same is true for the country's other religious minorities. Most of the 25,000 Mandeans counted in the 1997 national census have now gone, for example – and of the 109 Jews who lived in Iraq in 1997, the last of a community that dates back to the time of the Second Exile in Babylon in the sixth century BC, just eight remain in the country today. As the tiniest of Iraq's minorities, they are very fearful for the future.

Between the Shia and the Sunna, however, the conflict has begun to abate. In the period from June to November 2007, the monthly death toll nationwide fell by 70 per cent. As well as the surge, I believe that our work for reconciliation was beginning to bear fruit. Consider the reaction to the successive attacks on the al-Askari Mosque in Samarra, which is venerated by the Sunna but is especially sacred to the Shia as it contains the tombs of the tenth and eleventh Imams. In February 2006, when its golden dome was destroyed by bombs, a string of reprisals across the country claimed thousands of Sunni lives. In June 2007 – actually during the press conference that followed our first II-RC summit in Baghdad – the mosque was attacked again and two of its minarets were blown up. All of our delegates, Sunna as well as Shia, joined in condemning this. A month later, the mosque's clock tower was also blown up. Remarkably, no one was killed in retaliation. Muqtada al-Sadr responded to the provocation by saying he did not believe that Sunni Arabs could be responsible and called for three days of mourning and peaceful demonstrations. In August, after our Cairo meeting issued its denunciation of al-Qa'ida, the ranks of the Sons of Iraq were noticeably swelled, while on the Shia side Muqtada al-Sadr ordered his Mehdi Army to cease fighting.

Seven months later, he sent his chief spokesman, Sheikh Salah al-Ubaidi, to our next round of discussions in Cairo. In spite of everything, we seemed to be making progress!

CHAPTER 5

Knowing the Right People

Even so, there were still new depths of horror to plumb. On 14 August 2007, suicide bombers, almost certainly from al-Qa'ida, detonated a fuel tanker and three other vehicles packed with explosives in the Yazidi villages of al-Qataniya and al-Adnaniya, in the north-west of the country near Mosul. Many of the houses, which were built of clay and stone, were completely flattened, burying those inside. Someone at the scene said that it looked like the aftermath of a nuclear explosion. Initial estimates of 250 dead soon rose to 500, with as many as 1,500 more injured. The Americans eventually put the death toll at 796.

The victims belonged to the ancient community, mainly Kurdish but defined by their religion, that lives in villages around Lalish and spread out across northern Iraq. It is reckoned that there are just over 200,000 Yazidi in the country, which is maybe half of their total number worldwide. They are often regarded as Devil worshippers, but this is based on a misunderstanding. They revere a being they call Melek Taus, the Peacock Angel, whom they also know as Shaytan – which is the name the

Qur'an gives to the Devil. Yazidi generally get on well with Iraq's Christians, but the more extreme Muslims hate them and have often attacked both them and Christians together. Unfortunately, most Yazidi are very poor and could not afford to leave Iraq even if they wanted to. The threat to them increased considerably in April 2007 after a seventeen-year-old Yazidi woman was stoned to death by her community, reportedly for wanting to convert to Islam so that she could marry a young Muslim. Shortly after, twenty-three mostly elderly Yazidi men were taken off a bus in Mosul, lined up against a wall and shot to death.

So it continued. In October, a suicide bomber on a bicycle massacred thirty police recruits in Baquba, in the eastern province of Diyala, which had seen a big increase in violence since the surge began. (On the same day, close by the same city, twenty headless corpses were discovered but could not be identified.) In December, two suicide bombers targeted Awakening patrols in Diyala and Salahuddin, killing thirty-three people and wounding another seventy-seven. There was a growing number of suicide attacks on the queues of young men throughout the country who – desperate for work and desperate for peace – were trying to join the security forces. The new year saw a horrible new development: on 2 February 2008, two bombs strapped to women with Down's syndrome were set off by remote control, killing ninety-nine people in two pet markets in Baghdad. These were the city's worst attacks in six months and seemed to mark a new level of depravity. Three weeks later, in the ancient city of Iskandariya, a suicide bomber killed sixty-three pilgrims on their way to one of the holiest of Shia festivals.

It was in February 2008 that we held another major conference in Copenhagen, at the invitation of its Lutheran bishop. The Danish government paid for this. There are several reasons why our work has won support from this country. First, I live next door to its embassy in Baghdad; its ambassador until recently, Bo Eric Weber, is a very good friend of mine, and his deputy, Torqild Byg, is the longest-standing member of my Anglican congregation in the chapel at the Palace. A second factor is that after a Welsh woman living in Denmark contacted me about the plight of Iraqi asylum seekers there, her church began to support my foundation and eventually the Danish government allowed her pastor, Niels Eriksen, to come and visit me in Baghdad. There is now a memorial fountain in the garden of St George's that lists the names of all the Danish soldiers who have been killed in Iraq.

The Iraqi Reconciliation Conference brought together the broadest range of delegates yet, including Christians, Yazidi, and Mandeans as well as Sunna and Shia, and Armenians and Assyrians as well as Arabs and Kurds. There were also politicians from the Council of Ministers and the Council of Representatives, including Dr Mowaffak and Mrs Wijdan. As well as issues of human rights (in particular, for women and children), there was frank discussion of the proper role of religion in government. Several people – members of the government and religious leaders – who had previously refused to be reconciled were so.

This gathering took place within a few days of the reprinting by many Danish newspapers of the notorious cartoon of the Prophet Muhammad with a bomb in his turban, after the police apparently foiled a plot to murder the man who drew it. Many of the Muslim delegates threatened to boycott the conference as a result, but in the end we persuaded all but three to come. The Danish government, to its credit, was all the more determined that the event should go ahead. The three days bore fruit in a strong statement signed by everyone who attended which presented their detailed vision for the future of Iraq and how this might be realized.

The following month, on 13–16 March, the third of the Pentagon-sponsored II-RC meetings took place, again in Cairo. This time, eighteen people were present, including Sheikh al-Zuhairi, Muqtada al-Sadr's lieutenant Sheikh al-Ubaidi and representatives of the reclusive Grand Ayatollah al-Sistani as well as some very senior Sunni clerics. The statement they issued announced a total rejection of all violence. It was a major achievement. As well as the formal outcomes of such meetings, however, the informal business that goes on between sessions is just as important. On the last evening, we were all crammed into a small bus on our way to a final meal together when one of the Sunni sheikhs started singing a Sunni religious song and one by one the others joined in. When Ayatollah Abu Ragif asked them to sing a Shia song, there was a moment of tension before they obliged and then everyone, Sunni and Shia, began laughing and singing. It was amazing how different the atmosphere was after the mutual suspicion of the first day. When the same sheikh launched into a song about Fatima, the wife of Imam Ali, who is especially revered by the Shia, Ayatollah Abu Ragif began to cry. He told us afterwards that he loves Fatima so much and it touched him to hear Sunna and Shia singing about her together.

Later that evening, Peter Maki was chatting to a delegate who was representing al-Fadhila, the Shia party led by Ayatollah Muhammad Ya'qubi whose militia has sometimes clashed with the Mehdi Army. This man confessed that he had heard many things about Sheikh Dr Abdel Latif and his links with Saddam and had been prepared to hate him; yet, having talked to him and eaten with him, he now appreciated that the sheikh was a delightful man who, like him, wanted to end his country's torment. He was going to tell Ayatollah Ya'qubi, he said, that they could put the past behind them and work together to build a free Iraq. The same man also mentioned that a close relative of his had been jailed over a month before by the Americans, who had given no explanation except that they needed to question him. It hurt his heart, he told Peter, to see things like this happen that undermined all the good that democracy had brought to Iraq – and yet, he said, he was still willing to engage with the Coalition.

Within days, however – as if to demonstrate the ambiguities of peacemaking in Iraq – there was heavy fighting on the streets of Basra as the Iraqi army made a concerted effort to wrest control of the country's only port from the Mehdi Army and restore law and order. This, too, was highly significant – a massive onslaught on a Shia militia ordered by a Shia-led administration. Finally, after six days, the Mehdi Army requested a ceasefire and withdrew its gunmen from the streets, and things began to quieten down.

Since then, things have progressed quickly. I have been in contact with the key Sunni and Shia leaders almost every day, and we meet with them every two months; but the greatest advance is that every other month they meet each other without us. Meanwhile, other good work has continued at the grass roots, where our allies at the US Institute of Peace and others have had remarkable success. Of the working parties established by the Baghdad Conference in June 2007, all but one are still meeting regularly. Sadly, after we had done a huge amount of preparatory research, we had to disband the one devoted to reconstruction as everyone vainly expected the Coalition to pay for all the work. The most active of the working parties is one that the Iraqi religious leaders themselves insisted upon, which deals with the welfare of women and children.

Finally, in August 2008, I met with the most senior II-RC delegates in Beirut. Of the five we had expected, only Muqtada al-Sadr's representative did not turn up. Although they expressed their distress and frustration that "nothing had happened" in 2006 and 2007, there was now a sense that the time had come to work seriously and resolutely for peace. The great prize of those five days together was the first ever *fatwa* against violence issued jointly by Sunna and Shia:

> *In Islam it is known that our God of mercy has chosen and blessed Adam's sons more than all other created beings (Holy Qur'an, al-Isra 70).*
>
> *It is known that all Muslims are totally prohibited from harming anybody, as stated in the Holy Qur'an, al-Ma'ida 32.*
>
> *The Prophet Muhammad prohibited the spilling of blood by a Muslim against a Muslim. Therefore, all suicide bombings are totally prohibited.*
>
> *Therefore, as Sunni and Shia religious leaders, we declare that all killing must be stopped now. We also declare that the killing of non-Muslims is also totally unacceptable. The process of reconciliation and tolerance is the only way forward and the only solution to the conflict in Iraq. This is also seen in the Holy Qur'an, in al-Hujurat 9. We see it as both our religious and our ethical duty to urge people to hold to shari'a law and to see it as a refuge and the only solution to the conflict. We acknowledge that these are difficult times but we demand that all violence, killing and provocation be stopped. We ask that all involved in violence join with us to support reconciliation and tolerance, in accordance with al-Nisa 65 in the Holy Qur'an.*
>
> *It is the ethical and religious duty of all Iraqis to abandon all violence and live under the rule of law.*
>
> *This is our* fatwa *to all Iraqi people and all Muslims. From*

our God we have been told, and have delivered this message, may our God be our witness!

After the war, I had been concerned to forge relationships with as many of Iraq's religious leaders as I could. However, although it is essential in Arabic culture to maintain good relations, once formed, in order to prevent friends from actually becoming enemies, our emphasis today is on *reducing* the number we are dealing with, so that we can concentrate on the absolutely key people. Unlike the Sunna, the Shia have a religious hierarchy, not dissimilar to the Roman Catholics. There are five *Maraje* (who are the supreme legal authorities in Shia Islam) living in Iraq today. The most senior of these is Grand Ayatollah Ali al-Sistani, who has enjoyed that pre-eminence since 1999, when his predecessor, Muqtada al-Sadr's father, was assassinated by Saddam's agents. He lives in the holy city of Najaf, along with the ayatollahs closest to him, and he declines to meet anyone who is not an Iraqi. However, I am told by Dr Mowaffak and Ayatollah al-Sadr that he strongly approves of our work – and since 2007 one of his key people, Ayatollah Abu Ragif, has been attending our meetings.

Grand Ayatollah Muhammad Taqi al-Modarresi is the leading authority in Karbala, the second Iraqi city that the Shia consider holy. I have met with him, as I have with Grand Ayatollah Muhammad Sayed al-Hakim, who commands the powerful militia of the Supreme Council for the Islamic Revolution in Iraq, better known as Sciri. I have never met Iraq's other two grand ayatollahs, Bashir Hussein al-Najafi and Muhammad Ishaq al-Fayyad, but Ayatollah Abu Ragif is close to them.

In Baghdad, by far the most important Shia is Ayatollah Hussein al-Sadr, who presides over the third-holiest Shia shrine in Iraq, the al-Khadamiya Mosque, and exerts influence through his own TV channel. He has been committed to peace from the beginning, and remains my closest spiritual ally in Iraq. His nephew Muqtada al-Sadr is not a senior cleric, but is important because he controls the Mehdi Army, the largest militia in Iraq. He doesn't attend our meetings (though he has rung me more than once), but he sends his chief spokesman in his place.

Among the Sunna, there are three sheikhs who are supremely important: Dr Ahmed al-Kubaisi, Dr Abdel Latif Humayem, and Dr Harith al-Dari. Of these, only the last, who is the head of the Association of Muslim Scholars, has not honoured his commitment to work with us for peace. He now lives in Syria and Jordan, and we no longer have anything to do with him.

Sheikh Dr al-Kubaisi has been to Iraq only once since the war. He lives in great luxury in several houses in Dubai, where he fled after falling out with Saddam many years ago. At the age of over seventy, he has just become the father of twins! He exerts huge influence in Iraq through his almost daily television programmes. I have a really warm relationship with him, and believe that he is committed to what we are trying to achieve. His principal lieutenant in Iraq was Sheikh Dr Abdel Qadir al-Ani, who worked with us in the early days after the war but then fled to Jordan in 2004 after his house was bombed and he was accused of being a traitor and collaborator. He comes to most of our meetings in Amman.

Sheikh Dr Abdel Latif, too, has been back to Iraq only once since the fall of Saddam, in 2004 (when he was greeted with remarkable warmth by Ayatollah al-Sadr). The reason he gives is that the National De-Ba'thification Committee (chaired by Ahmed Chalabi, who is not exactly beyond reproach himself) then seized all his assets, amounting to over $70 million, and he can no longer afford security for himself. Today he lives in Amman, in a fairly modest apartment, while I work hard with the Americans to restore his fortune to him. He has played a crucial role in reducing Sunni violence. His genuine commitment to the cause of peace and reconciliation, which is rooted in his ten-year relationship with me, has strengthened since we introduced him to Ayatollah Abu Ragif in Cairo. They have become not only allies but friends, which is a perfect example of what the FRRME has been trying to achieve. He will never enjoy the amount of influence and prestige he had as Saddam's personal imam, because Iraq is a democracy now and the Sunna are a minority; but we have been able to give him something back of what he lost in 2003.

The Foundation for Relief and Reconciliation in the Middle East, which I launched with the former Archbishop of Canterbury George Carey in June 2005, just before I quit my job at Coventry Cathedral, is now the vehicle for everything I do. Lord Carey, its original chair, continues to work very closely with us as its patron. Our trustees are now chaired by David Harland, the pastor of a church in Brighton that strongly supports us, and we also have an outstanding board of advisers who meet with me regularly in central London. This group is made up of Christians, Jews and Muslims and has a mix of businesspeople, religious leaders, peacemakers and diplomats, including several former British ambassadors to the Middle East. Its chair is Lord Hylton, a Roman Catholic peer who has a strong interest in that part of the world. It is with this group that I discuss the practicalities of our work, and their advice is invaluable.

In America we have a similar board of advisers who likewise meet regularly, chaired by Robert "Bud" McFarlane, who was Ronald Reagan's National Security Advisor from 1983 to 1985. Many of its members are people we have worked with in Iraq, and Bud himself has attended many of our gatherings of Iraq's religious leaders, including the key ones in Cairo and Beirut. Whether we have met in Iraq itself or in Lebanon, Egypt or Jordan, he has been there to give us insight and direction. He is a man of wisdom, who survived the disgrace that followed the Iran-Contra scandal to become a very committed Christian.

Bud is a friend of John McCain, having served with him in Vietnam, and as a result I often receive messages of support and encouragement from the senator, who even promised me that if he became President he would meet all of the key Iraqi leaders I am working with. (When I mentioned this to them, they each started telling me in private that they were the most important and should meet the President on their own!) There is no question that the outcome of the American election will have more impact on the streets of Baghdad than it will on those of Washington or New York. I have been deeply impressed by Barack Obama as a person, but I was most struck by Senator McCain's words, "I'm a great believer in reconciliation and redemption." I can't deny that for the sake of Iraq I hoped and prayed that he would win.

In 2008, the FRRME awarded its Prize for Peace in the Middle East to Dr Mowaffak, in recognition of the crucial part he had played in our work for the past five years, not only as chair of the IIP but also as my principal adviser and one of my closest friends. The presentation was made twice: in Baghdad by Lord Hylton and in London at the House of Lords by Lord Carey.

We have spent so much time and effort working for the

healing of a whole nation, and yet so often our highest priority from one day to the next has been to try to save a few individual lives. To date, I and my team have been involved in negotiations for a total of 142 victims of kidnapping. Ninety-eight of these were taken for money, and we managed to get thirty of them released. The other forty-four were abducted for political reasons, and sadly we have so far got only nine of them back.

In the second category are five men who have preoccupied me since 29 May 2007, all of them Britons. Four of my bodyguards from GardaWorld were protecting an IT consultant at the Ministry of Finance in Baghdad when they were all kidnapped by dozens of men, some in uniform, who arrived in a large fleet of police cars. Ever since that day, it has been the highest priority in my work to try to locate them and secure their release. My trailer is inside the GardaWorld compound, and these men lived opposite me. Not only were they my protectors, they are my friends. One of them, who had been a medic in the army, was meant to have started at medical school in south London in September 2007. As this book goes to press, in February 2009, they have still not been found or freed. I have had meeting after meeting, with so many different people. Literally every day I work on their case, and it has seriously affected our other work, not least in Israel/Palestine. I can never make an absolute commitment to be anywhere or do anything, because I have to drop everything if something comes up in connection with these hostages. Everything else has to be provisional.

In a spiritual update in May 2008, I wrote this:

The past year has been very difficult and until now I have not been able to talk about it. At times I have not even been able to communicate with people. This has been because of the search for the five British hostages. The 29th of May will mark the first anniversary [of their kidnap]. All year we have been working on this case non-stop. It has been very difficult – it took us six months even to get on the right lines. You can never say for certain that you are dealing with the right people, but it now looks as if we are.

In the last year, I have spent a huge amount of my own money and the Foundation's money on [this matter]. To date, we have spent nearly $700,000 ... to meet with the right people, and even to bring people in from Iran. Paying for security [for them] has been immensely expensive. We have not been able to ask for people to support these initiatives – it has all been carried out in secret with just a few people praying for us. On Sunday I had a secret meeting at the church with people from Iran. It cost $50,000 just to have this meeting. It was difficult, but [at least now] we had clear demands, one of which was to go public [and talk to the media]. Despite there being no ransom demand, both the [Foreign Office and GardaWorld] had wanted to keep everything quiet. ...

Yesterday was one of the most difficult days of my life. It all looked so awful, as if the whole venture would be lost. I felt very angry and wanted to tell [GardaWorld] I wanted to give up and their attitude was totally wrong. I sat down to send the e-mail and God told me not to send it. I had an e-mail from a friend in the USA telling me to love, love and love. I agreed with this as regards the really bad guys, but did this apply to governments and companies as well? God said yes, it did. I did not send the e-mail and knew that it was now up to God.

Such a hard day followed. I struggled, I prayed continually. I was not focused. In the afternoon, I met with people from the US chapel and St George's, including many of the children. This really lifted my spirits. Samir told me we could not give up. I agreed, not because I felt like continuing but because I knew that was what our Lord was saying. I returned to base yesterday evening to hear that everything had changed. Both the British Government and the *company had agreed that we should go ahead with our plan. So, for the first time, I will soon – not yet – be able to talk about this case. For the first time since the kidnapping I will be able to talk to the media.*

We are told that following an active [media] campaign there will be a release. The kidnappers have said that 11 times they have been approached by the Iraqi government but have refused to engage with them. They said they decided to deal with me because they knew of my involvement in the Bethlehem siege resolution and because I was a religious leader. Since then, most of our meetings have happened in secret at the church. The security has been immense, but secret. Soldiers have literally hidden and watched from rooftops and inside the church. Our church people have always prayed fervently in these meetings. Our staff have cared for and looked after our visitors, feeding them well.

We now need your prayer fervently in the next month. I will return to the UK next week to start working on this campaign. In a short while, I will be able to talk to the media about this issue. First, though, we need to make a video that will be widely distributed. So, we enter another really important period. I ask your prayer for Al, Alan, Jason, Jason and Peter, the five [hostages]. Please pray that we will get them back soon. We are told that if the kidnappers are happy with what we do they will soon be returned.

In many ways, this case is typical of much of what we are doing here. Nothing is quickly achieved and nothing is certain. We will not even know for sure that we are dealing with the right people until these hostages are actually returned to us. The search for them has already cost us so much in both time and money. But I will not give up. Every Thursday the people of St George's meet to pray for their release, and it will happen. I cannot go into the details of what we are doing to secure it, but one day I will be able to tell the whole tale.

Their story is a tiny sample of the ordeal that Iraq has suffered since 2003. Today, it seems that more and more people in the West condemn the invasion of Iraq. The cost in human lives has greatly exceeded what almost anyone predicted, and the cost in billions of dollars vastly so. So many people say to me: "Look at the situation now! How can you say the war was not a terrible mistake?" I can say it easily, because I saw this country before the war. I witnessed the oppression, felt the intense, pervasive sense of fear. I heard people whispering that they needed to be released from tyranny. I will never forget the horror in my Mukhabarat minder's face when I told him I would not have dinner with Saddam's sons. If I didn't go, he said, he and his family would all be killed. It was then I understood just how evil that regime was.

I am not saying that everything in Iraq is rosy now, because it is not. So many times I have sat on my bed at night and cried over the death of an American or Iraqi friend. At times, I have thought that the suffering was just too much to bear. Then I remember that we are engaged in the rebuilding of a nation. Yes, there is still fear, but there is also hope. We know that one day this will again be the great country that it used to be. Unless you have been here, you cannot imagine the pain Iraq has gone through – but unless you have been here you also cannot have any idea how much good has already been achieved. Despite all the violence, the work of building or restoring hospitals, power stations, schools, and roads has gone on. Most civilian contractors have long ago fled Iraq, despite the huge sums of money they were paid; today, the construction work is being done by the US Army – often by reservists, men and women with other jobs and other lives who are making great sacrifices to serve both their country and the Iraqi people.

As I write this in October 2008, it has been announced that last month 359 civilians were killed in Iraq, compared with 884 in September 2007. This is a measure of how much the situation here has improved – and of how terrible it still is. This is still the most dangerous country in the world. Baghdad is still the most dangerous city in the world. Even now, some of the children from St George's have just rung me to say that this morning two large bombs went off near their school and they were showered with glass as all the windows in the building shattered. Some people are dead. It is another normal day. Nonetheless, the violence *is* diminishing. I know this not just because the statistics say so but because my congregation tells me so. In the Green Zone, where I live, we used to be bombarded with rockets every day; now, such attacks are rare. Things have changed enormously for the better, though this has yet to be recognized by the international media. It is still not possible for ordinary people to walk down the streets of Baghdad or Mosul in safety, there are still murders and abductions every day, and yet the fact is that order is slowly but surely being restored – and we hope and pray that peace and reconciliation will follow.

CHAPTER 6

Giving Peace a Chance

Almost every day I am contacted by people who want to talk to me about peacemaking. Often they have good ideas – they want to develop inter-community relations, perhaps to host some sports activity that would bring together young people of different religions, races, or tribes. Initiatives like these are important, but I have to confess I have very little experience in this area. In Iraq, to be honest, I have learned that the established strategies for resolving conflict – working through political issues, restoring civil society, supporting the moderates, involving women – are mostly ineffectual. What is more productive, I have found, is to gain an understanding specifically of the people who are responsible for the violence and of their culture, religion, traditions, and everything that shapes their expectations. These are the influences that propel people into conflict; these are the factors that complicate its resolution.

In the early days after the liberation of Iraq, so much of what we did was aimed at finding political solutions that we thought would engineer change and generate hope. It would have been wonderful if those initiatives had worked, but most of them did not. Of the six working parties set up by the Iraqi

Centre for Dialogue, Reconciliation and Peace in early 2004, for example, only the one concerned with women, religion, and democracy ever bore much fruit. Some of the key women's leaders we identified were subsequently elected to Iraq's new parliament and did a very important job – though now they tell us that their male colleagues only laugh at them. Mrs Samia Aziz Mohamed, the Faili Kurd who led this effort for us and became an MP herself, lost three of her relatives and her house in 2006 in an attack by Shia gunmen.

So much of my work now is about helping people simply to stay alive, and to keep their remaining loved ones alive, amidst the constant violence. There is no knowing how many people have been killed, or even how many have been abducted, since the fall of Baghdad in 2003. Those who are taken are very rarely returned. The humanitarian situation, too, is dire. People often ask me why my foundation is involved in relief work. The answer is simple: because no one else is. Those foreign aid workers who were here in the heart of Iraq have fled. Many have gone to the north of the country, to the beauty and comparative peace of Kurdistan. They tell their supporters they are working in Iraq and of course it is true – but they are in a different world from the one we are operating in.

Many of these people work for Christian agencies. They were not wrong to leave central Iraq – they had to. It would have been far too dangerous for them to remain here. If they had stayed, they would have achieved little and most probably would have been seen as missionaries trying to convert Muslims. They themselves would then have been at serious risk of being kidnapped or murdered, while any Iraqi Christians associated with them would have been reckoned as supporters of the "Crusader" ideology of the West. This is the perspective of militant Muslims who do not realize that Christianity took root here long before Islam, and long before it took root in the West. Such thinking is dangerously prevalent here.

The flight of the major relief organizations from the heart of this country has increased the burden on the FRRME massively. Fighting for peace in the Middle East is always hard, but at times in Iraq it is soul-destroying. So, what is the role of a peacemaker in this country, amid the trauma and chaos that have become so normal here? You soon discard the idea that success may come quickly: any strategy has to be long-term. You are also soon disabused of the idea that imposing Western-style democracy will bring peace. Whenever a democratic system has been introduced to the Middle East in the recent past, the outcome has generally been bad. Democracy has given Iran a malignant president and Gaza a terrorist government, and Iraq, too, has suffered enormously because it took so long for people to agree on who should run it. In fact, the most stable governments in the region are those of Morocco and Jordan, which are essentially benevolent hereditary dictatorships.

Attempts by the West to foster peace in the Middle East by encouraging democracy show that our politicians have not considered the core values of these societies, and in particular their religious identity, their culture of honour and shame, the influence of the family and the pervasive role of tradition. Many of our Western ideals simply do not work in this part of the world. It sounds very fine, for example, to try to bring about change from the bottom up, and in the West it may work; but here it does not. Here, the only way you can really effect change is to work from the top down. In particular, it is the religious leaders who determine which way a society will go – and in order to influence them we have to make friends with them. This, I believe, has been our most crucial mistake in the West: we have failed to understand that at the heart of Middle Eastern society is the idea of relationship, which means that establishing and nurturing relationships have to be absolutely central to our work.

What is important is not only how strong our relationships are but who they are with. We can make progress in peacemaking only when we are engaging with the key people on both – or all – sides of the conflict. In Israel/Palestine, that is comparatively easy; but in Iraq it is much more complex. The parties to the violence include the Sunna, the Shia, the Kurds, the Americans and their partners in the Coalition, and the Iraqi government and its security forces. Moreover, there is fighting not only between communities but also within them, as different factions struggle for control. Everyone needs to be involved in the quest for peace. Peacemaking of the old woolly-liberal kind no longer works, if it ever did. We cannot succeed if we do not engage with the military. By the same token, we have to engage too with the people who choose to kidnap women and children and blow up buses. We cannot confine ourselves to sitting down and drinking tea with nice people.

Not everyone is approachable, of course – some groups, such as al-Qa'ida, are impossible to engage with at any level. How great it would be to meet with them and talk sense, to restore to them what they feel they have lost and seek peace and reconciliation! But that is simply not possible, because it is of no interest to them. They are set only on killing and maiming in the name of God. I have, however, got very close to the most senior people in the Mehdi Army and other such radical groups, and I continue to be so. (This can be quite disconcerting. One day, I was sitting in my study in leafy Hampshire when I had a phone call from Muqtada al-Sadr. He had heard it reported that the Archbishop of Canterbury, Dr Rowan Williams, had said that *shari'a* law should be introduced to England and he wanted me to tell Lambeth Palace how much he approved.) If anyone who is responsible for violence is willing to deal with us, we have to engage with them if we are to have any hope of bringing peace to Iraq. It is often difficult to get these people to meet representatives of the Coalition, because Western governments do not want to be seen to be talking to "the bad guys" – though in private they are glad we are doing it, and the Pentagon especially is now happy to finance this aspect of our work.

I am involved with both religious and political leaders and I find they often fail to understand each other. Western politicians do not appreciate that religious extremists need to be addressed in religious language. On the other hand, most religious leaders have little insight into the nature of Western politics and are unaware that most of our politicians find violence in the name of God incomprehensible. Often, a further obstacle to mutual understanding is the belief shared by both kinds of leader that the only way to deal with the other kind is by force. Both of them tend to assume that if you hurt someone enough they will submit to your will. The problem with this assumption is that usually it results only in an escalation of violence.

There is no simple formula, no secret, to getting these people to engage with us or with each other, or to change their tactics; and there is little rhyme or reason in how we have achieved it. It can take months merely to get to know some people – and yet often it is when we get to know them, and even make friends with them, that solutions begin to emerge. Fortunately, Christianity encourages us in this approach, because Jesus taught us to love our enemies and forgive them. (Most of those I deal with in the Middle East, however, are Jews or Muslims, and this concept of loving and forgiving your enemies is foreign to their religion. It can be difficult to explain it to them.)

As a third party, I and my colleagues play a vital role not only by mediating negotiations but also by facilitating the forming of relationships across the divides. Often, our starting-point is enabling each side to hear the other's story. As the American poet Longfellow once wrote: "If we could read the secret history of our enemies, we should find in each man's life sorrow and suffering enough to disarm all hostility." Or, as someone has said, "Who is my enemy? It is the person whose story I have not heard." Merely to get to this point of listening to each other can take many months or even years, but once we have reached it we find that people are often astonished to learn of the pain the other side is experiencing in the conflict.

Such encounters may be the beginning of a road that leads to reconciliation, but we need to find a way to keep people moving along it. This may involve arranging regular conferences, seminars or private meetings between religious and political leaders, or it may mean something more informal, such as a meal together. All of this sounds easier than it actually is. In fact, progress can be excruciatingly slow. Once I thought we could achieve things quickly, but it did not take long to discover that in Iraq you have to operate by Middle Eastern, not Western, time. Something that in Britain or America you might hope to accomplish in a day can take over a year here.

In the meantime, our task is often just to get to know people's concerns and to hear them tell their stories in the way they want to tell them. This in itself can be very difficult: time and time again I encounter views I know to be seriously flawed or grossly inaccurate. Everything requires tact and patience. The fact is, however, that while summits can produce stirring declarations (and I have been involved in many of them), on their own they will achieve nothing. It is the individuals that come to such gatherings who can make the difference – as long as we invest enough time and money in working with them. And they, too, need to spend time meeting with others, on their own side and the other side, who also have the influence to make a difference. In August 2007, I met in Cairo with a number of Iraq's most distinguished religious leaders. When Abu Ragif, a Shia ayatollah, and Dr Abdel Latif, a Sunni sheikh, said they wanted to meet at least once a month, I thought they were being far too ambitious – they didn't even live in the same country. And yet that is what has happened. One of Iraq's most senior Shia leaders has been sitting down regularly with one of its most senior Sunni leaders. This is how change is brought about. Declarations are all very well, I have learned, but they must be followed by action – and it is relationships that make this possible.

Once we have established relationships – and set up the congresses or institutes or whatever that will sustain them – we then have to dedicate ourselves to developing them. Every day, we have to address the various issues they throw up, and this involves meeting with all the different parties involved – diplomats, politicians, soldiers, religious leaders, and terrorists. Every meeting is different in character.

All of the diplomats I talk to in Iraq work for one or another member of the Coalition. Generally, my engagement on this front is at a very high level, as I usually deal with the ambassador of a country or his deputy. My conversations with these people are always wide-ranging. Some governments are involved in funding specific aspects of our work with religious leaders and so their embassies need to know how these projects are developing, to be assured that their aims are being achieved. Often, I am asked to arrange meetings for them with various sectarian leaders, and sometimes I am able to and sometimes not.

Often my discussions with diplomats focus on ways to reduce

political sectarianism and encourage the building of coalitions across the tribal and religious divides. (In Iraq's first democratic election, for a transitional assembly in January 2005, over 120 different groups and parties put up candidates, which was impractical as well as daunting for the voters.) I always leave these meetings with a long list of things to do. My unique ability to relate to Iraq's religious leaders means that when I meet with diplomats from Coalition countries I can inform them of the views I have encountered "on the ground". One question that has been central to our deliberations is: How can religion advise, rather than supervise, politics? Often I find that diplomats have only a very limited understanding of the nature of religion in Iraq, and so these meetings can be very educational.

With some diplomats, I am frequently involved in complex hostage negotiations. In these cases, the character of our meetings is totally different. They ask me for details about our dealings with the people we think may be the kidnappers, and sometimes I can give them that information and sometimes I can't. I cannot betray people's trust, even when they are generally perceived as "really bad" people. It is crucial in such negotiations that everyone recognizes that I and my team are not working for any government. (It is no secret that a large part of my foundation's funding comes from the Pentagon, but the Americans have never once told us what to do and I always make this clear to the people we are dealing with – and they accept this.) We have to approach these matters as religious, not secular, leaders. It is this that wins us respect in Iraq and enables us – not always, but sometimes – to accomplish what we are trying to do.

My relations with Iraqi politicians are not always easy, but they are always very civil. Some of them, such as the National Security Adviser, Dr Mowaffak, I have become very close to. All of Iraq's prime ministers since the war have also become my friends. When I meet with these people, we talk through every aspect of their work and ours, from trying to combat religious sectarianism to caring for my congregation at St George's. I also have to engage with politicians from the various countries in the Coalition, and especially our major partners, America, Britain, and Denmark.

My dealings with members of the armed forces, both foreign and (to a much smaller extent) Iraqi, are always precise and to the point, focusing strictly on what needs to be accomplished and how it can be done. The key issue is how the violence can be reduced, for the fact is that the principal peacemakers in Iraq today are the military. Indeed, I often remind them of this fact. Once again, I deal chiefly with the senior officers and have little to do with the lower ranks unless I see them at chapel. I have especially close relations with the American military, both on the ground in Iraq and at the Department of Defense in Washington.

My encounters with religious leaders are always intense. It's essential that I maintain a good relationship with them in whatever country or situation we find ourselves. All of the leaders I work with carry great authority in both the political and the religious sphere, and it is often difficult to get across to them the fact that in the West religious leaders do not have the same influence. Many of these men now live outside Iraq, and so I and my colleagues are constantly flying to other parts of the Middle East. Our endless phone calls are not enough: we have to visit them as often and as regularly as we can – and take them presents, as their culture requires. We spend hours in deep discussions with them about matters relating to Iraq, and usually they have complaints about the multinational forces, the government and other religious groups and leaders.

Engaging with these people can be very expensive as well as time-consuming, but it is essential because even those who live in exile still wield great influence through their broadcasts on television and through the major organizations they are involved in running in Iraq.

The most important people I deal with, however, are the terrorists. If our concern is to stem the violence, we have to work with those who perpetrate it. As I have said already, this is not always easy, or even possible, and there are groups such as al-Qa'ida that refuse to engage with the Coalition except in battle. In these cases, armed force is the only remaining option. Many people object to the idea that military action has an important role in peacemaking, but I believe it is true more strongly now than ever. In other cases, however, you realize that there are non-aggressive ways to pacify people. For example, many Iraqis have resorted to violence because they perceive that something precious has been taken from them. They may have lost territory, money, prestige or political influence, but in the end it all boils down to a loss of power. The solution is some sort of concession. To win them over to the cause of peace, we have to persuade the Coalition and the Iraqi government to give them something back. I can't reveal what this has meant in practice – regrettably, for security reasons, much of what we do cannot be disclosed. All I can say is that mediating the negotiations that this entails constitutes a major part of my work and it is often very complex and time-consuming.

It is essential in all this that people come to trust me and my colleagues. This does not happen automatically. A crucial factor is that first and foremost I am regarded as a religious leader. That is the only reason I can do this job. If I were not a priest, I could not do it. I am frequently told by members of the Iraqi government that my two most important qualifications for my work are that I am a cleric and that I have been in Iraq for a long time, now over a decade. It makes all the difference that I am ordained because here there is very little distinction between religion and politics. In the West we may talk about the separation of church and state and it may have big advantages, but the reality in Iraq – as, indeed, in much of the non-Western world – is very different. Recently, when one of my team asked some of Grand Ayatollah al-Sistani's people what they thought of Iraq's new government, they told him matter-of-factly, "*We* are the government." Here in Iraq, religion and politics are inextricably entwined. I was in a discussion group with Madeleine Albright at the launch of the Clinton Global Initiative in 2005 and she admitted that her biggest mistake in office, as America's Secretary of State from 1997 to 2001, was not to take seriously the role of religion in diplomatic affairs. As she points out in her brilliant book *The Mighty and the Almighty*, it is futile to try to "keep religion out of politics'. It is bound up in so much of the conflict in our world and we cannot be serious about peacemaking unless we are serious about engaging with it.

The mutual incomprehension between the Islamic world and the West is certainly one of the biggest problems facing humankind today. Many Muslims do not understand the fundamentals of Western society. They see it in simple terms, as recklessly secular, with no God-given ideals. Unfortunately, this perception is confirmed by much of our television, whose witness they see and believe. You only have to watch a little Arabic TV to see the difference. (Curiously, the divorce between religion and politics in the West goes even deeper in those countries where it is unofficial, such as Britain, than it does in America, where it is established by the constitution.)

The West, in return, has many false perceptions of Islam,

which it associates increasingly with radicalism and terrorism. We forget that for hundreds of years Christians, too, waged war in the name of God. Violence in God's name is always wrong, whoever it is committed by, but we need to grasp that only a small percentage of the Muslim community is guilty of this evil. (Indeed, it is not only Muslims who suffer from our prejudice in the Middle East – Christians from the region are viewed with the same suspicion. If you are a Palestinian or an Iraqi, you are regarded as a security threat whatever your religion. Western unfamiliarity with Arabic names does not help. Two of my closest Christian friends from Iraq are called Osama and Jihad. These are everyday names where they come from, but in the West they set alarm bells ringing.) The remarks of Iran's president, Mahmoud Ahmadinejad, about Israel have further reinforced the idea that Islam, and especially Shia Islam, is essentially aggressive. Nothing could be further from the truth. The majority of Muslims in Iraq are Shia and I have found most of them to be peace-loving people.

This is not to deny the worldwide threat of al-Qa'ida. Today the danger it poses is real. Kenya, Tanzania, America, Indonesia, Spain, Britain, Algeria, and Pakistan, if no others, have all suffered the consequences of its fundamentalist zeal. The result is that not only Islam but religion in general has gained a very bad name. So often when people in the West learn that I am a priest they start complaining about religion. They tell me that it is a major cause of most of the wars in the world today. I totally agree with them. They find this shocking, but I tell them that religion is like a hammer and chisel: it can be used either to create something beautiful or to cause total havoc. Too often it does the latter – as I point out when Christians tell me, as they often do, that what the world needs now is more religion. Sadly, when religion goes wrong, it really does go wrong. My job, however, is to try to make it go right. As I frequently tell people: If religion is part of the problem, it must be part of the solution.

I often watch Christian television when I am in Iraq. Most of it is American, and most of it shows a profound lack of understanding of what is happening in the wider world. Generally, it seems to be concerned only to make individuals feel good about themselves and to tell them how they can prosper financially. I find this hard to take when my people at St George's have nothing. There is no financial prosperity in store for them, and yet they are so sincere in their love for the Lord. On the other hand, I find great encouragement in channels such as the British-based GOD TV that have helped the FRRME so generously to help those who have nothing. I often say to Christians that we not only must pray for peace, we also must pay for peace. Too often we expect results to come not only quickly but cheaply. This is a point I am constantly making to governments and charitable trusts as well.

Demonizing Islam is not the only mistake we have made in the West, however. We have misunderstood the very nature of this faith. When we talk of the need to "strengthen the moderate Muslims" and deal only with them, who do we have in mind? Those Muslims who share our Western ideals. As a Christian and a priest, I would take great offence if I was called a "moderate" believer. I am not. I am serious about my faith and my tradition. When I say the creed on Sundays, I mean it. And I share the concern of my Muslim brothers and sisters over the growing secularism and apostasy of Western society. True Islam, like true Christianity, is anything but moderate. Unfortunately, when we describe as "moderates" those true Muslims who shun violence and abhor terrorism and are tolerant of "the other", whether Christian or Jew, we only strengthen the position of those who do not and are not, and we encourage the view that it is they who are being true to their faith. I spend most of my time in the Middle East, and most of my colleagues are Muslims. Some of the people I trust most are Muslims – including those who translate for me now at church services. Not one of them is a moderate. They are ardently opposed to all forms of violence, but they are also extremely serious about their faith and their commitment to serving God. I have to say that I have more in common with them than I do with many of my so-called Christian colleagues.

If we genuinely want to resolve the very real problems between the West and the Islamic world, we need to begin by using the right language. In the first place, we have to abandon this talk of "moderation". We need truly to respect Islam, which means having regard for those Muslims who are serious about their faith. In my experience, most Muslims are tolerant and ready to work with others, but they want other people to respect them, and even to be willing to learn from them. Indeed, it may well be that the West – and even the church – has a lot to learn from Islam. Perhaps we should begin by looking at ourselves and asking how we can become more serious about our beliefs. We should also disabuse ourselves of the idea that the best people to engage with Muslims are the liberal Christians. We need people in this field who are orthodox in their faith and committed. That is what Muslims expect all Christians to be.

Front-line peacemaking can be immensely stressful. This is not the kind of work where you can ask people to wait until another day. Often, your response has to be immediate, when a mosque or a church is blown up, a hostage is taken or a member of your staff is killed. On several occasions I have sat with my colleagues in Baghdad and cried at the news of a disaster or death we had tried to prevent. It has been an incredibly painful experience. However, there have also been times of immense joy. This is the nature of our work, put very simply. It is complex and intense and, for the present, much of it cannot be revealed, though one day I may be able to tell the full story. Searching for peace in the midst of violence is a risky business. It is so dangerous sometimes that very few people can do it. Nothing is certain about it – except that it has to be done. People must realize that it takes a very long time and we must not give up. Here in Iraq the work is often very solitary, very lonely, and widely misunderstood. There are times when I wish I had a different calling. Then, suddenly, comes a small sign of progress: a Sunni and a Shia cleric share a meal together or a hostage is freed and, in a moment, hope is renewed.

This hope is often far more theological than political. Often Iraqi politics offers very little reason for optimism, but then unexpectedly the hope of the resurrection breaks through. I think of days when all has seemed utterly bleak and I have gone in my mind to the empty tomb of Christ and just stood there. That empty tomb has been my inspiration. So, we take heart. The Spirit and the glory of God are here and, with the angels, are filling the atmosphere with the presence of the Lord. He is working in our world and I believe that the Middle East is at the centre of his purposes. The more I have worked in this region, the more I have come to see that it is God who is in control. I know that of myself I can do nothing, but with God I can do everything. I have come to realize that what is happening in the physical realm is often just a manifestation of what is happening in the spiritual realm.

If you had asked me a few years ago what peacemaking boils down to, I would have given you a long and convoluted answer. Nowadays, I would simply say one word: love. It is love that leads us to forgiveness, which is the only thing that can prevent the pain of the past from dictating the future. Jesus taught us to love our enemies, but generally we do not even like them very much. So much of my time is spent with unpleasant people, and so before I approach them I simply pray: "Lord, help me to love them!" If there is one passage in the Bible that is a prescription for my work, I would suggest it is Romans 12:9–21:

> *Love must be sincere. Hate what is evil; cling to what is good. Be devoted to one another in brotherly love. Honour one another above yourselves. Never be lacking in zeal, but keep your spiritual fervour, serving the Lord. Be joyful in hope, patient in affliction, faithful in prayer. Share with God's people who are in need. Practise hospitality.*
>
> *Bless those who persecute you; bless and do not curse. Rejoice with those who rejoice; mourn with those who mourn. Live in harmony with one another. Do not be proud, but be willing to associate with people of low position. Do not be conceited.*
>
> *Do not repay anyone evil for evil. Be careful to do what is right in the eyes of everybody. If it is possible, as far as it depends on you, live at peace with everyone. Do not take revenge, my friends, but leave room for God's wrath, for it is written: "It is mine to avenge; I will repay," says the Lord. On the contrary:*
> *"If your enemy is hungry, feed him;*
> *if he is thirsty, give him something to drink.*
> *In doing this, you will heap burning coals*
> *on his head."*
> *Do not be overcome by evil, but overcome evil with good.*

There are times when it is very difficult to love, when you feel you have given so much and got nothing in return. Especially this is so in long-running hostage negotiations. Sometimes I feel angry as I make my way to a meeting, but I know that, if there is to be any prospect of progress, that anger must give way to love. In all my dealings with terrorists, it has been clear that they want something; but often I have had nothing to give them but love. This is in itself a form of sharing Jesus. So, we love, love and love, and pray, pray and pray, and hope, hope and hope, that change will be brought about through the glory of God.

CHAPTER 7

The Most Wonderful Church in the World

It was on my earliest trip to Iraq, in 1998, that I first set eyes on the Anglican church of St George of Mesopotamia. The Art Deco brick building, which dates from 1936, was then rather derelict, filthy, and infested with pigeons – though the stained-glass windows, adorned with various British regimental crests, were all in good repair. No one had worshipped in it for fourteen years. A new caretaker had lately been appointed, a former soldier called Hanna who had spent seventeen years as a prisoner of war in Iran, but he had never been given any instructions. In fact, though he was being paid $50 a month – more than ten times what most Iraqis were earning – he seemed to regard his job as part-time and spent most of his day selling cigarettes. I showed him what he had to do, and he immediately set to work. Within a matter of days he had transformed the church – from a dirty shell to a clean one. It didn't look very Anglican. Hanna is a Chaldean Catholic, and he had filled the building with plastic flowers, pictures of Mary and the smell of burning incense.

I said evening prayer in St George's most days during that

first visit to Baghdad. The only other people in attendance were Hanna and the various members of the Mukhabarat who had been detailed to watch me. The church was a sad, sad place in those days. On my second visit to the country, I was accompanied by Colin Bennetts (then my bishop at Coventry), Peter Price (now Bishop of Bath and Wells, but then of Kingston) and Clive Handford, then Bishop of Cyprus and the Gulf, who had briefly been rector of St George's himself in 1967 and loved the place. I vividly remember the service in the church that Sunday, when the congregation consisted entirely of bishops, spies, and the caretaker.

The years went by. Tariq Aziz, the Deputy Prime Minister under Saddam, gave me permission to take services there whenever I was in Baghdad, but every time I visited the church I wondered whether it would ever really function again. Apart from the Mukhabarat, my congregation was now made up mainly of United Nations staff. Hanna continued to look after the place. He got married to Rema, and they had a little girl named Mariam (Arabic for "Mary"). Three years later, they had twin boys and called them Martin and George (after the church). After another two years, they had another boy and named him Andrew Clive after me and the bishop.

For five years, the church remained in disrepair. None of its outbuildings had doors or windows. Inside, they looked fit for nothing except to be pulled down. Really, there was no point in doing anything to them because they were so little used. As war loomed in 2003, I became increasingly anxious about Hanna and his family, who lived in the church hall. There were major government buildings around St George's – the Ministry of Information was its neighbour on one side and the National Theatre on the other – and I was very worried. I phoned Hanna and told him to take his family somewhere safer before the bombing started. He assured me that he would, but said that he himself had to stay behind at the church to look after it. Eventually I agreed to this, but I worried about him every day until the war was over.

When I returned to Iraq in May 2003, I was amazed to find that St George's was unscathed though the buildings on either side had been totally destroyed. Hanna, too, was in one piece, but in the chaos after the fall of Baghdad looters had broken into the church and tied him up while they stole everything except the marble font, the safe (which they had blown open) and, inexplicably left behind in it, a single cross of solid silver given in memory of a British soldier who had been killed in the First World War.

I will never forget the first service we held there after the liberation of Iraq. The congregation of about fifty consisted mostly of military personnel and diplomatic staff, though the Patriarch of the Ancient Church of the East (Old Calendar) turned up as well. The building was ringed with tanks and armoured personnel carriers, and helicopters clattered overhead like noisy angels. The security was so tight because there was reliable intelligence that someone was planning to blow the church up. I only learned this the next day, but apparently the Coalition people knew but came anyway. Canon Justin Welby, who was then co-director with me of Coventry's International Centre for Reconciliation, presided, and I preached from Haggai 2:9: "'The glory of this present house will be greater than the glory of the former house," says the LORD Almighty. "And in this place I will grant peace," declares the LORD Almighty.'" The same verse, carved in stone, is set into one of the ruined walls of Coventry's old cathedral. I saw it almost every day when I was there and it expressed my hope for St George's. At that stage, I imagined that the "greater glory of this house" would consist in the political changes for the better that we all expected to see. In fact, what followed was quite different.

Within weeks, the congregation became increasingly Iraqi. Soon the services had to be conducted in Arabic and my sermons were being translated by my assistant (and, by now, very close friend) Georges Sada. It wasn't long before almost 200 Iraqis were attending the church – though, as Baghdad outside the Green Zone descended deeper into darkness, all the Westerners stopped coming except one, the daughter of the British ambassador to Kuwait. Soon I appointed our first lay pastor, a fine man called Maher who as a convert from the Mandean faith had established his own evangelistic ministry. Whenever I was away, he did a wonderful job looking after the church and its congregation, while the services on Sundays were taken by my friend and colleague Colonel Frank Wismer, an Episcopalian who was chaplain to the Coalition Provisional Authority. By Christmas, we were regularly getting 300 people, including over a hundred children. With funding from the British government and the diocese of Cyprus and the Gulf, the doors and windows had been repaired, the brickwork cleaned inside and out and a carpet laid.

Even as St George's was coming to life, however, things were becoming more and more difficult for me. Merely getting there was hard work. I lived only two miles away but the roads were so congested that the journey through the heart of Baghdad could take as much as five hours each way. The traffic was terrible in the early days just after the war because so many people had celebrated their freedom by buying a new car. By the summer of 2004, however, it was hard to get petrol, and drivers would queue for two days or more just to fill up their tanks. After a while, I moved to a house by the Tigris, on the other side of town. My new home was twice as far from the church, but because we no longer had to drive through the city centre it never took more than an hour to get there.

The congregation at St George's continued to grow steadily, and in the space of a few months the outbuildings which I had thought were beyond hope were beautifully restored. In April 2005, however, we had very bad news. Maher and his wife and their fourteen-year-old son had gone to a Christian conference in Jordan, accompanied by his assistant. On their way home, they rang me on a satellite phone as they crossed the border back into Iraq – and that was the last we ever heard of them. Neither they nor their driver, nor three others in their party, were ever seen again. It seems likely that they were abducted and killed – many people were being kidnapped at the time – but we never received a ransom demand. I appointed a temporary replacement for Maher while we waited in vain for news of him. We also had to take care of his surviving child, a teenage girl.

In all, eleven of my staff were killed or disappeared that year. Eventually, the British ambassador decided that it was too dangerous for me to live outside the Green Zone and so I moved inside its fortifications, from my lovely, nine-bedroomed, riverside house to a new address: 27 Foss Way, Ocean Cliffs, Baghdad. There were no cliffs, however, and certainly no view. My new home was a small plastic trailer in an underground car park. It was not en-suite, so I had to use the public "rest rooms". (Bizarrely, these were all named after Oxford and Cambridge colleges. Of course, I went first to the room named after my old college, Clare, but I found it was for women only. The one next door was named after All Souls College, Oxford, but someone had crossed that out and written "Trent Polytechnic" instead – a much less august establishment, but rather more appropriate.)

In the end, I was told it was too dangerous for me even to go to St George's. Indeed, it was dangerous for the congregation to go there, and so from then on they came into the shelter of the Green Zone every week. We held our services in either the prime minister's office or that of my friend and colleague Dr Mowaffak, and there we would worship for hours at a time in freedom and safety. The children came in their hordes along with their mothers and the few fathers who were still alive. I am sure we were the only church in the world that met in the office of a Shia Muslim, and I often described this as interfaith relations at the cutting edge. Most of the security men who guarded these premises were South Americans, and being good Catholics they loved to join us for Communion – and we loved to have them with us. Sometimes I was able to get one of the American military chaplains to come and preach, and I often conducted baptisms with a red plastic washing-up bowl.

One disappointment we had was when the father of Philip Rizk, then the FRRME's man in Gaza, sent us a load of illustrated children's Bibles and the truck that was bringing them was stolen en route to Iraq. We had plenty of Bibles for adults, but none for the children. A few months later, we were holding a service in Dr Mowaffak's office when a man called Ali came in. "*Abuna* ['Father']," he said to me, "you never told me all the children come here." Of course I hadn't: Ali is a senior member of the Mehdi Army. However, he left the room and five minutes later returned with dozens of children's Bibles. I looked inside them and saw they were the very ones that had been stolen. They might not have reached us by the route we intended, but by God's grace they had got to us nonetheless. The children were delighted.

One of them, a six-year-old girl called Vivian, was ill – we were told she had bladder cancer, probably caused by uranium dust. On one occasion when I prayed for her,

her father told me that the radiotherapy machine at the hospital was no longer working. I remember very clearly laying hands on her and asking God not that she would be healed but that we would find the right doctor to treat her. That night, I prayed for her for three hours or so. The next day, I was preaching at an evangelical service in the Palace. When it was over, I stood at the door of the chapel saying "Goodbye, General. Goodbye, Colonel" when suddenly I saw an officer I had not met before. I got talking to him and it turned out that Major Gibbons was born just a few miles from where I live in Hampshire. I asked what he was doing in Baghdad, and he told me he was working at "the Cash" (the combat support hospital).

I asked him what he did there and he said: "Oh, I'm just a urologist." I could have kissed him. "Just a urologist!" I said. "You are the one man in the world I needed to meet right now." I told him all about Vivian and he asked me to bring her to the hospital the next day. It proved to be very difficult to get her in, but with the help of the command surgeon, who was a member of my Anglican congregation in the Palace, we succeeded. It was clear that Vivian's situation was serious: the cancer was developing and her bladder had to be removed. There was no one who could do the operation in Iraq. Major Gibbons investigated the possibility of getting it done in America, but none of the little girl's family spoke any English and that was a problem. Finally, he found a surgeon in Jordan who had trained in America and had specialized in Vivian's form of cancer. This man agreed to treat her at the King Hussein Cancer Hospital in Amman.

I had a week to find about £30,000 to pay for all this involved, which I managed to do – not least with the help of the Anglican congregation in the Palace. We took Vivian and her father to Jordan, where I discussed her extensive treatment and her prospects with the surgeon while she underwent the preliminary chemotherapy. Eventually, it was time for the operation and Vivian had her entire bladder removed. She endured the pain so well! Afterwards, her mother and her brothers were able to join her and we moved the whole family into a house. The day she came out of hospital was a day of great celebration.

I told her I would get her anything she wanted, and it turned out there were two things: a doll from England and a mobile. When we gave them to her, she was so happy! She made very good progress. Fortunately, my former colleague Fadel Alfatlawi, who used to run the IIP, was now in Jordan and he took responsibility for Vivian's family and did a great job. She continued to get better, and it was a joy to see her playing and dancing again. One day, Fadel told her that when she grew up he would marry her. She informed him that that was impossible, as she was going to marry Father Andrew.

Every day, whether I was in Iraq or Britain, I would phone to find out how Vivian was. The news was always good until one day I was told she couldn't see out of her left eye. It was a dreadful blow. I spoke to her doctor and it was apparent that she had a secondary tumour on her optic nerve and there was now nothing more that could be done. When Vivian came home from hospital, she was dying. I had hoped so much and prayed so much for this child, whom I loved like one of my own. All around the world, people were praying for her – Christians, Muslims, and Jews – yet as I was leaving for Britain at the beginning of April 2007 I kissed her goodbye and knew I would not see her alive again. I said the prayer that the old priest Simeon had said when he saw the infant Jesus: "Lettest now thy servant depart in peace, for my eyes have seen the glory of my salvation." I flew back home with a very heavy heart. I thought about Major Gibbons, how we had met, how God had surely been involved. I didn't know why Vivian should now be dying but I knew she was in the care of Jesus. She told her parents that angels kept coming to see her, and I knew it would not be long before she went to live with them.

One night, Fadel phoned me to say that Vivian was in a coma in hospital, where he and her father were with her. The next day, I was due to fly to America to speak at a healing conference led by the televangelist Benny Hinn, but as I was packing my bags early that morning Fadel rang me to say that Vivian had died. I cried as I cannot remember ever crying before. I told my staff I would not be going to America after all, but back to Jordan to take her funeral the next day. It was to be the hardest funeral I had ever taken, but it was also a day of celebration for a beautiful little girl. I told the congregation that she was so wonderful that Jesus needed her. Vivian, my Vivian, was in heaven. I went back to Baghdad and told her relations and friends and all the people of St George's about the service. All of us had tears in our eyes as we celebrated her life together. Her immediate family remained in Jordan until September 2008, when they were granted permission to emigrate to France. I am sure I will see them again, and I will not stop loving them all.

By the start of 2007, the congregation numbered well over a thousand and there was nowhere in the Green Zone large enough to fit everyone in. The violence was starting to abate a little, and I began once more to hold services in the church – though I had to be escorted there by five heavily armed bodyguards from GardaWorld. I hadn't seen St George's for over a year. We furnished each of our people with a photocard so that we could regularly give them food and money. Their needs are immense, and if we do not give, they do not have.

The cost of this provision is colossal and is met primarily by British churches. We also provide food for people who live in the neighbourhood – most of whom are Muslims – as well as for several institutions in Baghdad that help the sick, the elderly, and the disabled. Not least is our commitment to the Mother Teresa Home for children born with serious disabilities, which is a particular concern of our Mothers' Union.

I'm often asked about the Mothers' Union in Baghdad, what it does and why it was set up. Worldwide, the MU is the largest missionary organization in the Anglican Church. As none of my congregation was originally Anglican, I decided that it was important to enhance our Anglican identity in some way. This our Mothers' Union has truly achieved. We launched it on Easter Day 2006 and we now have by far the largest branch in the Middle East. Led by Nawal, the wife of our lay pastor Faiz, the MU is now the biggest group in the church, with over a thousand members. They wear their badges proudly and are at the forefront of our relief work, providing food and making clothes and curtains and other essentials for people's homes. Their room in the church is equipped with several sewing machines and they also have their own kitchen. They meet several times a week to pray and study together, and they work so hard for the whole community.

By the beginning of 2007 we had two lay pastors, Faiz and Majid, both wonderful men of God. One day, I was at home in sleepy Hampshire, walking down my road, when I got a phone call from my young friend David, who lives and works at the church. "They've kidnapped Majid!" he shouted. I took a big breath and said I would phone Samir in Iraq. It was obvious from the information we had gathered that Majid's abductors were seeking financial gain rather than political advantage, which was actually very good news. I told my staff to find out how much they wanted. The answer was $60,000. The church didn't have that much – but that very morning we received a large gift of £20,000 from GOD TV and so we were able to make an offer of $40,000, which was accepted. Majid was returned amid great rejoicing. He told us that throughout his ordeal he had kept praying out loud and quoting scripture, and when his kidnappers had asked him why, he had told them. Their ringleader said that usually they killed their victims but for some unknown reason they couldn't kill him. However, they assured him that they would if he or his family returned to his house, even to collect their clothes, and so he and his wife and children had to move into St George's. It soon became obvious that it was not safe for them even to remain in Iraq and so very sadly we said farewell to them and sent them to Syria.

St George's stands in Haifa Street, which is now one of the most dangerous in Baghdad. In the first few days of 2007, there was a big gun battle there between a number of different groups, including the Mehdi Army and al-Qa'ida. Many people were killed, and when I next came down the street on my way to church I saw fifty or sixty bodies hanging from the trees and lamp posts. Every week, I ask my congregation what they want to tell me and people say, "I went to the market and someone next to me was shot dead" or "A car bomb went off and I just managed to escape." All but a handful of the men have been killed, and a lot of the women dress in black because they are mourning the loss of a loved one. In July 2007, I told the US Commission on International Religious Freedom that "in the past month thirty-six of my own congregation have been kidnapped. To date, only one has been returned." In the first five months of 2008, another eighty-nine were taken or killed. Usually, we are never told why.

In May 2007, after four of its security men were kidnapped,

GardaWorld announced that its employees would no longer venture outside the Green Zone. Thankfully, Dr Mowaffak again proved his friendship and nowadays I am escorted to and from St George's by at least twenty-five men of the Iraqi special forces from his own personal detail. My GardaWorld bodyguards drive me from my trailer to Dr Mowaffak's compound nearby and there, encased in body armour, I take my seat in an armour-plated car with blackened windows. Surrounded by military vehicles, we proceed slowly, stopping at countless checkpoints. When we finally leave the Green Zone, we are met by a convoy of police cars and more military vehicles and now we drive at speed, with sirens blaring and guns pointed out of the windows. If we encounter a traffic jam, the other drivers are ordered through loudspeakers to clear the road. If that doesn't do the trick, our whole convoy simply moves to the wrong side of the road – still at speed. At every crossroads, the police have stopped all the traffic. When we arrive at St George's, the street is closed off. Soldiers run to surround the building while others check inside to make sure it is safe. Only then am I finally allowed to get out of the car, to be met by scores of our children. I never dreamed I would ever go to church like this – but then again I never thought my parish would be in Baghdad.

Despite these pressures, St George's in 2007 was very full and very alive. The congregation still sat on the white plastic garden chairs we had bought after the war, but the worship was out of this world. Every week I fell more deeply in love with this church and all its people. Faiz and Nawal were inspiring. By the end of that year the congregation had grown so large we couldn't fit everyone in at one sitting, so we began to hold two services, one on Saturdays (following the custom of Christians in the Middle East) and one on Sundays (which is a weekday in Iraq – but as most of our people do not have jobs, this is no problem). Once again, GOD TV came to our rescue and paid for pews for the whole church. These are quite splendid, but already they are not enough for the numbers who come and so the garden chairs are back as well – and still people have to sit on the floor or stand, while we worship as I have never worshipped before.

People often ask me what the services are like at this special church, but they are hard to describe. In Britain, a vicar would usually impose his or her own style on their church, but in Baghdad my people impose their style on me and it is simply wonderful. It is a mix of Orthodox, Catholic, and charismatic (which I suppose is essentially rather Anglican). We have pictures of the saints that the people kiss as they come in, and they dip their hands in the font and cross themselves. Everyone stands to pray, with their hands held out in front of them, and there is much bowing. We conduct our services largely in Arabic, with the most important prayers in Aramaic, the language of Jesus. I know enough of both to say the liturgy, though I have to preach in English and pause while my words are translated.

I make my sermons very culturally relevant – I always talk about what has happened locally and recently. I talk about the saints, and especially those these people really revere: Mariam, Jona, "doubting" Toma and the church's patron saint, Gorgis. The people are very serious about their own, individual relationships to God, but they have told me lately that they have learned so much from us and how we explain the Bible to them, almost as though that was never done before. We have just started doing the Alpha course at St George's, which is a basic introduction to Christianity – I've been doing it at the

Palace with Coalition personnel since March 2004 – and over 800 of my people have signed up for it.

I also talk a lot about Iraq in the Bible, where it is referred to as "the land of Shinar" or as "Mesopotamia" (which means "between the rivers", Tigris and Euphrates), or by the name of one of its greatest cities, Babylon. I tell them that the Garden of Eden was here, and the tower of Babel; that Noah built the Ark here; that Abraham came from Ur and Isaac's wife Rebekah from Nahor (where Jacob met his wives-to-be Leah and Rachel), which are both in present-day Iraq; that Jonah went as an evangelist to Nineveh, on the edge of modern-day Mosul, and so did Thomas on his way to India; that Daniel survived the lions' den here and Shadrach, Meshach, and Abednego met the Son of God in the fiery furnace here; that Esther was queen here; that Amos and Ezekiel prophesied here, Belshazzar saw the writing on the wall here, the Magi came from here and Peter preached here. In fact, Israel/Palestine is the only land that is mentioned more frequently in the Bible.

We have a full robed choir and there is a great deal of energetic and enthusiastic singing, accompanied by an electric piano (the church organ was stolen long ago). There is no set length for our services, though people have to get home before it is dark and sometimes the soldiers have to hurry me away for security reasons. Many of the songs we use are songs well known in Western churches translated into Arabic; but too often the sentiments these express are irrelevant to the situation here in Baghdad and so I have written some new ones. One of these appears at the end of this book.

Of all our services, I especially love the children's first communions. They all wear lovely white robes made for them by the Mothers' Union and process into the church singing. At a recent first communion, two of the children – one aged ten, the other eight – were in tears as they walked up the aisle. I took them aside and asked them why they were crying. They told me: "This is the most important day of our lives and as we were walking in, Jesus was with us."

At the beginning of our services, I declare: *Allah hu ma'na* ("God is here'). The congregation reply: *Wa Ruh al-Qudus ma'na aithan* ("And his Holy Spirit is here"). This is how most Anglican services around the world begin; but when you have lost everything, as these people have, you realize that Jesus is all you have left. Recently, I spent two days speaking at a small conference for Episcopalian US Army chaplains in Iraq and I introduced them to some of their fellow Christians from St George's. The man who organized the conference, Colonel Dale Marta, sent this report to his bishop:

> *The meeting with Canon White and members of his congregation … was a profound spiritual experience for me. I will never be quite the same. In the loud rushing wind of media and politics that swirls around Iraq, I heard the small still voice through the humble and precious people of St George's and her spiritual leader. I no longer can hide in the safety of the cave but feel driven to stay engaged with Iraq and her people through St George's.*

At that meeting, one of the chaplains asked what was so special about our church. Everybody replied with the same answer: love. We not only talk about love, we practise it. We love our Lord and Master, we love each other – and I love my people and they love me. I never thought I would love my congregation as I do. I never thought I would be loved by my congregation as I am. We are surrounded by violence and the tools of violence, but when we come to church we come to worship and to love. There is a lot of laughter – sometimes at my expense! – as well as tears.

The fact is that we have the biggest Christian congregation in Iraq. Currently, it is growing at a rate of a hundred a month and it now numbers 1,800, including 500 children. Apart from me there are no real Anglicans in St George's, and yet everyone is so committed to it. They used to go to the Chaldean churches, or the Assyrian, Armenian, or Latin Catholic churches. In fact, the other priests are really cross with me because my congregation is huge and now they have nobody. I feel bad about this, but I didn't exactly go sheep-stealing – these people came to St George's because either they lived near the church or they had heard good things about it. At first, I said I hoped that once the violence had stopped, people would go back to their own churches; but if anyone mentions this nowadays, everyone insists that this is their church and they will never leave it. (It's not an easy issue. Many of Iraq's old churches are threatened by new arrivals. A host of foreign missionaries showed up after the war in 2003, and today there are 12 new evangelical churches in Baghdad. This is a serious disturbance of the status quo. People want freedom of religion – but not too much!)

In June 2008, the new bishop of Cyprus and the Gulf, Michael Lewis, visited Iraq. Everyone was so excited to see him, and he was greeted like a patriarch. One of his duties was to open our new medical and dental clinic. The kidnappers in Iraq had targeted professionals in particular, and by now over 80 per cent of Baghdad's doctors had either been killed or fled the country. As a result, it had become very difficult for people to get treatment. So, we set up a free clinic with funding from the US Army, with three doctors and three dentists – one of them Jewish – all from the neighbourhood. Now, people come to church for the good of their bodies as well as their spirits. Most of our patients are not even Christians, let alone members of our congregation, but it is to the church they come for help and there is no discrimination. Thus St George's not only provides opportunity to worship the Almighty, it also meets people's physical needs. One week we give everyone food, the next we give them money. Sceptics may say that this is why our congregation is so large, and I have wondered that as well – but the people themselves insist: Even if you gave us nothing we would still come for the love.

I can't pretend that there are never any problems within the church, but they are always very minor. Among the teenagers there is a lot of jealousy over whom I love the most. If I rang one person and not another, word would soon go round that *Abuna* had favoured so-and-so. Even as I write this, I have just had a phone call from one of our young people telling me that someone else wants to call me daddy and I mustn't let her. I explained that we must love everybody and after a while I think they got the message.

In the summer of 2008, six of the young people from St George's were able to come to Britain with me. Three of them stayed at my house in Hampshire, and three at the home of some local friends, Robert and Tanya, who have a swimming pool, a tennis court, a lake and a large collection of vintage cars. They had a wonderful time. They travelled around the country – in Oxfordshire they were given lunch by Nina Prentice, the wife of the current British ambassador to Iraq. They even spent two days at the House of Lords with the chair of the FRRME, Lord Hylton, our patron, Lord Carey, and the former Leader of the Lords, Baroness Amos, whose father taught me (and inspired me) when I was at school. When they returned with me to Baghdad, one of these young people said to me: "You took us to heaven. Now we are back in hell." I told him that one day Iraq will be heaven again. After all, the Garden of Eden was in Mesopotamia. Paradise it once was, and paradise I believe it will be again one day.

At the beginning of 2008, some of my supporters complained that the updates I was sending out devoted too much space to St George's. It was true – but that was because at the time the church was my only source of hope and encouragement. To me, it is simply the most wonderful church in the world. I love all my people, and though Baghdad is the most dangerous place on earth I have no desire ever to leave. My mind goes back to my first sermon here after the war, on Haggai 2:9: "The glory of this present house will be greater than the glory of the former house … and in this place I will grant peace." I never dreamed how that promise would be fulfilled in this church, but as I reflect on that verse it strikes me that today St George's is filled with the glory of the Lord and, even though there is violence all around, it is a place of the profoundest peace.

CHAPTER 8

The Kingdom, the Power, and the Glory

I t may sound wonderful practising one's ministry in the corridors of power, but I spend most of my time in much more dangerous places. I have been beaten, held at gunpoint, left for hours in rat-infested rooms and much more besides. On one occasion, I was even locked in a room whose floor was littered with human fingers and toes. I didn't know whether I was next to be maimed. I was fortunate I was not. In addition to all this, my health is not good – I constantly feel enervated, my balance gets progressively worse and at times my speech is slurred and my sight is very poor. Many people would like to see me put out to grass. Almost every day, people ask me how I manage to keep going.

I remember not so long ago contemplating my job while I was sitting waiting for a military helicopter in the Green Zone. When you fly in one of these machines, there is no safety briefing. The doors are left wide open and soldiers lean out with their guns trained on the ground. Usually you are shot at, which takes a little getting used to. I thought of the days when I used to cycle round my old parish in London – now even the ride along the busy South Circular Road seemed utterly serene. I recalled my time at theological college and what I learned there. They didn't teach me to write a *fatwa* for Islamic clerics or to negotiate for the release of hostages, but they did teach me theology and they gave me the tools to understand the scriptures. I took out my Bible and it suddenly struck me that even this looked different. It wasn't bound in beautiful black leather, its pages were not edged with gold. Instead, it was khaki-coloured and its cover said "3rd Squadron of the 7th Cavalry Regiment'. It was an American military Bible. Nonetheless, it contained the same words that keep me going each day. I opened it to Psalm 62 and read verse 2: "He only is my rock and my salvation, my stronghold; I shall not be greatly shaken" (NASB). Yes, I am surrounded by trouble, but my God, the God of Abraham, Isaac and Jacob, does not change, for he is my rock. He sustains me even when everything seems to be going against me.

This is the most vital aspect of my work: that everything I do is underpinned by my faith. Much of the church today has rejected the word "religion" and I agree with a lot of what has been said on this subject, but I also believe strongly that there is a crucial meaning in the Latin root of that word: *ligare*, to bind. I am bound to my God as he is revealed in Jesus Christ, who is my Master, my Leader, and my Messiah. I rely on him completely in my work. I could not attempt to do it without him. It is fine to have debates and sermons on the danger of "the spirit of religion", but here in the midst of conflict that is not our concern. Our priority is doing the work of the Kingdom of God, enabling his rule to come to earth. The more you are surrounded by violence and bloodshed, the more you have to rely on the love of God and the direction of his Holy Spirit. The more you recognize your own inadequacy, the more you realize that nothing can be achieved unless you trust and hope simply in God.

The following is an account I wrote for my supporters of a recent Sunday in Baghdad. It shows the true nature of my work in Iraq. It also shows the true nature of God, our rock and salvation.

Do you ever have days when you know that God's glory is going to come? Well, today was one of those days. I started on Saturday night with my security team. "Tomorrow is a God day, not a political day." "Yes, sir" was the reply.

Early in the morning we made our way to the Prime Minister's offices. Not for politics but for God. It has been decided that it is far too dangerous for me to go to St George's, so we had the service in the Prime Minister's lecture theatre at his invitation. It took the congregation over two hours to enter because of security.
...

I chose as my text just three words from one of the letters of John: "God is love." We had a wonderful service: great singing, OK preaching and tears ... What was clear was that it is only the love of Jesus that sustains these wonderful people at such a difficult time. ...

We then had Holy Communion and as we broke bread God's glory came. I cannot explain why or what happened, but our Lord was there in power. We then baptized a young child, just 17 days old, called Alexandria. Once again there was great joy, joy that God loved this little girl and us.

From the Prime Minister's office we went at full speed to the Palace for the service there. As we arrived, mortar [bombs] came over. The soldiers made us dive for cover and for a short while nobody was allowed into the Palace. I was actually quite grateful for this, because I was late...

Here I am doing a series on people in the Bible who dwelt in Iraq. Today it was the turn of Ezekiel. I spoke of the glory that he saw, I spoke of God's glory that I have seen here, glory like no other place. I told people to expect to see God's glory here. I read them part of a recent e-mail from Brett, Alyssa, and Emily from All Nations Church in Charlotte, North Carolina. People saw that if these young people can experience the glory of God, surely they could as well.

As I celebrated Holy Communion, God's glory came again. As I looked down from the altar I could see military officers, with their guns beside them, in tears. Tough men with big tears. After the service, person after person came and said they had seen God's glory in the service. They stayed by me, and we had lunch together and talked more of the glory of God. …

In the evening [session of our Alpha course,] we dealt with the subject of how we can be sure of our faith. I spoke from 2 Corinthians 5. Once again I read out the email from the girls of All Nations Church as a perfect example of being able to experience God's love. Once again this was a truly glorious session when the Lord was very present. Literally everybody said it was amazing …

So, this was a Sunday in Baghdad, a day when God's glory again broke forth. I know more now than ever that all things are in the hands of God and he decides. He is indeed our rock and salvation. As I left my security team tonight, they said, "Today was very different. Something happened to us!"

When we meet with God, we see not only his glory, we see that he is unmoving, unchanging, and all-sustaining. Without him there is no hope and no future. … This is my God, this is my rock, which enables me to continue the work of the Almighty come what may. All may change but my God is the same yesterday, today and forever. I say again: he is my rock, my strength, my salvation, and my fortress in times of trouble.

People ask me why I spend so much time in places such as Gaza and Baghdad. The truth is, because that is where I am sent. And so I am never afraid. Some people say that it is the very fact that I have no fear that puts my life in particular danger; but the reason I am not afraid is because I have an uncomplicated, almost childlike faith in God. Every night, I begin my prayers in the same way that I did as a boy. Maybe this is why I love and care for children so much. It is in their faces that we can see the face of Jesus in a simple, wholesome way. The more I have done this type of work, and the more I have struggled with the reality of death and destruction, the more I have had to put my trust simply in my Lord and my God. My faith has grown, and I no longer experience my spiritual highs only when I am in a wonderful church service. Now it is a matter of seeing the glory of God wherever I find myself. All that is needed is awareness. Each day I ask God to come with me on my difficult journey and each day I see his glory at work. It is that that sustains me, along with the friendship and support of my colleagues.

Many people are astonished when I say that the people I am closest to in my work are not Christians at all. One is a Jew and the other a Muslim: Rabbi Michael Melchior and Dr Mowaffak al-Rubaie. Both are fine politicians, and both are men of great faith. I consider them to be nothing less than a gift from God. When I say this in public meetings, people are often not just amazed but indignant. They ask: How can my most vital allies be followers of other faiths? I have to insist that the God I serve is not a Christian either. He is the God of Abraham, Isaac, and Jacob. Others who have met Rabbi Melchior and Dr Mowaffak have told me that they, too, have seen God in them. My audiences are often surprised, but then my God is the God of surprises.

However, though I work predominantly with people of other

faiths, it does not mean that my own faith has in any way been diluted. In fact, it is stronger now than ever. I give thanks to God that I have never doubted him. He is indeed for me "the same yesterday, today, and forever". However dreadful the tragedy, my Lord is there. Amidst the greatest havoc I have witnessed in post-war Iraq or in Gaza, or in Bethlehem during the siege, I have still seen his glory – the same glory I saw in the worship at St Mark's, Kennington and at All Nations Church in Charlotte, and in the life and ministry of Sister Ruth Heflin. I have seen the heavens opened and glimpsed something of the majesty, might, and love of God.

When life is full of despair, it is only the glory of God that truly sustains. There have been times when everything has gone wrong, when friends and colleagues have been killed and there has seemed to be no hope. It is at times like this that I ask God to show me his glory. He always does so, though sometimes I do not see it immediately. It has been manifested as a mighty cloud over Baghdad, and on one memorable occasion I have sensed it in the singing of a hymn one Easter morning when the birds were singing and the bombs were going off. God is here, and his Spirit is with us! When one is in the glory of God, miraculous things can happen and one is no longer restricted by the life of humanity. So, as I circulate among the powerful people in the Pentagon, Congress, and Parliament, I ask to see God's glory and in all these places I have seen it. It is when the power and the glory come together that we witness change. That is why I say that my work is about the power and the glory – the power of those who run this world and the glory of the God who runs the universe. For too long people have tried to keep them separate, but God is at work in time and space and they have to be brought together.

When I am sitting in my little trailer in Baghdad, or being bundled from one meeting to another, it is not easy to stay abreast of what is happening in the wider world. Often, people ask me for my opinion on the way the world is going – on globalization, climate change, the growing dominance of China. The truth is that I have nothing to say about these issues. I do not have time even to think about them. To me, they seem to be things that preoccupy people who live in peace and comfort. The questions that plague me are much more immediate. When will the next rocket come? Am I well enough to get to the bunker outside if the barrage starts up again? Have we got enough money for the ransom if I am abducted? Have we got enough money to feed the people of St George's this month? The challenge for us is simple: to survive today. Though I can honestly say I have never been anxious for myself, I do worry about my congregation. I worry, too, about friends like Dr Mowaffak.

Amidst these concerns, I stop and turn to God. I am drawn back to the words that end Isaiah 19:

> *In that day there will be a highway from Egypt to Assyria. The Assyrians will go to Egypt and the Egyptians to Assyria. The Egyptians and Assyrians will worship together. In that day Israel will be the third, along with Egypt and Assyria, a blessing on the earth. The Lord Almighty will bless them, saying, "Blessed be Egypt my people, Assyria my handiwork, and Israel my inheritance."*

Egypt, Assyria – that is, Iraq – and Israel are all places where I work, and I have a profound sense that in the midst of all this conflict the Lord is here and his Spirit is with us. All my hope for this broken world rests in God. And it is a huge hope, a hope I find in scripture and also in hymns. There are four hymns in particular that have had profound meaning for me in the Middle East. Every day I listen to them and every day I reflect on their words. Each one has its own story.

BECAUSE HE LIVES

GLORIA AND WILLIAM GAITHER, 1971

It was Maundy Thursday, 2005. I had to speak at an Easter sunrise service beside Saddam's old swimming pool in Baghdad and I was struggling to find a suitable text. Before I went to sleep, I prayed that God would speak to me and direct me what to say – and in the middle of the night I woke up with a song going through my head. I hadn't sung it since I was a child at Sunday school.

These are the words:

God sent his Son – they called him Jesus,
He came to love, heal and forgive;
He lived and died to buy my pardon,
An empty grave is there to prove my Saviour lives.

> *Because he lives, I can face tomorrow,*
> *Because he lives, all fear is gone;*
> *Because I know he holds the future*
> *And life is worth the living just because he lives.*

How sweet to hold a newborn baby
And feel the pride and joy he gives;
But greater still the calm assurance:
This child can face uncertain days because
> *he lives.*

And then one day I'll cross the river,
I'll fight life's final war with pain;
And then, as death gives way to vict'ry,
I'll see the lights of glory and I'll know he reigns.

There was no doubt that this was to be my message. It was a difficult time and things looked very black. Everyone was wondering what we were doing in Iraq at all. We sang this hymn and the final verse spoke deeply to so many of us that day and gave us hope. It also confronted me and others, with an apocalyptic question: Could this indeed be it, the end of the world, life's absolutely "final war with pain"? And if so, would we see indeed death "giving way to victory"?

A few weeks later, I was visiting Wheaton College, near Chicago, when my mobile phone rang. It was a woman I didn't know. She told me her name was Gloria and she had written that hymn. It was a truly wonderful encounter. It wasn't long before I went to see her and her husband, Bill Gaither. I heard the story that inspired her words, about their newborn son and the pain that Gloria was suffering at the time. Her sentiments had uplifted us 34 years later at Easter in Baghdad.

GOD WILL TAKE CARE OF YOU

CIVILLA D. MARTIN, 1904

The second hymn did not impact me until late in 2007. We didn't have a pianist at the time for the Anglican services in the Palace, so one of the soldiers in the congregation played her flute and she also chose the hymns. When we came to the end of the service, the hymn she had selected brought tears to my eyes. Once again, I hadn't sung it since I was a boy. It was, again, a bad time. Rockets were pounding into the Green Zone, and though the surge was well under way, things did not seem to be going well at the time. Our only assurance was that, despite everything, God would take care of us.

Be not dismayed whate'er betide,
God will take care of you;
Beneath his wings of love abide,
God will take care of you.

   God will take care of you,
   Through every day, o'er all the way;
   He will take care of you,
   God will take care of you.

We came to the second verse:

Through days of toil when heart doth fail,
God will take care of you;
When dangers fierce your path assail,
God will take care of you.

Without question, these words applied to all of us. Every week at St George's, I tell my people that I cannot assure any of them that they – or I – will not be killed; but what I can guarantee them is that we shall all meet again in heaven, and when we see Jesus we shall be like him.

All you may need he will provide,
God will take care of you;
Nothing you ask will be denied,
God will take care of you.

No matter what may be the test,
God will take care of you;
Lean, weary one, upon his breast,
God will take care of you.

NEVER ALONE

LUDIE D. PICKETT, 1897

In May 2008, the Green Zone was coming under rocket attack at least forty times a day. It was rather funny, because every time a rocket landed I would be phoned by members of St George's wanting to know that I was all right. One evening, I was preaching at the evangelical service in the Palace when the sirens started to blare. We were singing a hymn at the time that I had never heard before. Everyone apart from Samir and I got down on the floor. Even the pianist was on the floor, but he managed to keep on playing and so we kept on singing:

I've seen the lightning flashing,
I've heard the thunder roll.
I've felt sin's breakers dashing,
Which almost conquered my soul.
I've heard the voice of my Saviour,
Bidding me still to fight on.
He promised never to leave me,
Never to leave me alone!

No, never alone, no never alone,
He promised never to leave me,
He'll claim me for his own;

No, never alone, no never alone.
He promised never to leave me,
Never to leave me alone.

The world's fierce winds are blowing,
Temptation sharp and keen.
I have a peace in knowing
My Saviour stands between –
He stands to shield me from danger
When my friends are all gone.
He promised never to leave me,
Never to leave me alone!

When in affliction's valley
I tread the road of care,
My Saviour helps me carry
The cross so heavy to bear;
Though all around me is darkness,
Earthly joys all flown;
My Saviour whispers his promise,
Never to leave me alone!

He died on Calvary's mountain,
For me they pierced his side.
For me he opened that fountain,
The crimson, cleansing tide.
For me he waiteth in glory,
Seated upon his throne.
He promised never to leave me,
Never to leave me alone!

"Fierce winds" were certainly blowing in Baghdad, and the

danger was very real; but we trusted in a God who would never leave us, who always stood to shield us. Truly, we are never alone.

JUST AS I AM WITHOUT ONE PLEA

CHARLOTTE ELLIOTT, 1835

The latest hymn to inspire me is the one I know best.

Just as I am, without one plea,
But that thy blood was shed for me,
And that thou bidst me come to thee,
O Lamb of God, I come, I come.

I have sung it so many times, but now in Iraq it suddenly means so much more. One of my very closest friends is the evangelist J John. We often go away together, and he is the only person who phones me even in Baghdad. I get his emailed newsletters every Monday, and in one of them he wrote about Charlotte Elliott, the writer of this hymn, and how she was challenged to come to true faith. I was amazed to read that she came from the corner of south London where I was once a minister. I was even more surprised when this hymn was chosen to end our service the following Sunday in the chapel in the Palace.

Just as I am, and waiting not
To rid my soul of one dark blot,
To thee whose blood can cleanse each spot,
O Lamb of God, I come, I come.

Just as I am, though tossed about
With many a conflict, many a doubt,

Fightings and fears within, without,
O Lamb of God, I come, I come.

Just as I am, poor, wretched, blind;
Sight, riches, healing of the mind,
Yea, all I need in thee to find,
O Lamb of God, I come, I come.

Just as I am, thou wilt receive,
Wilt welcome, pardon, cleanse, relieve;
Because thy promise I believe,
O Lamb of God, I come, I come.

Just as I am, thy love unknown
Hath broken every barrier down;
Now, to be thine, yea, thine alone,
O Lamb of God, I come, I come.

Just as I am, of that free love
The breadth, length, depth and height to prove,
Here for a season, then above,
O Lamb of God, I come, I come!

Every verse inspires me, but it is the third that speaks to me most deeply. Truly, in Baghdad we are "tossed about with many a conflict" – though I have to confess that I haven't experienced "many a doubt". I have never for even one moment doubted the power and love of my God. I realize that this makes me unusual, but maybe that is why God has sent me to Iraq. Though I spend much of my time meeting some of the most powerful people in the world, and seem always to be involved in very serious conversations, my trust in God is very simple.

Let me end this book with a fifth hymn, which I wrote myself as I was finishing this chapter. It can be sung to the tune of "Just As I Am", and it sums up my experience in Iraq.

OH, RECONCILE ME NOW TO YOU!

Into the darkness I do go.
I long to see my Saviour's peace,
To see his light shining through.
Oh, reconcile me now to you!

I love you, Lord, I love you so,
Though I do see such conflict now.
I know your peace is deep within.
Oh, reconcile me now to you!

The bullets fly, the rockets thud.
I long, O Lord, to see you here,
To see your peace breaking through.
Oh, reconcile me now to you!

In every circumstance of life,
I know your peace does come with me
Despite the rampage all around.
Oh, reconcile me now to you!

I see your glory shining through.
The darkness fades at your command.
The glory heals the brokenness.
Oh, reconcile me now to you!

In this spirit I continue to fight for peace in the Middle East, and I will go on doing so until my Lord tells me to stop.

PART 2

MY JOURNEY SO FAR

Acknowledgements

Whenever I attempt to thank all the people who deserve to be acknowledged, who have helped in the writing of one of my books, there are always far too many – but I want, at least, to list the bare minimum.

I have to mention my family. First of all, the people who have put up with me the longest: my wonderful mother, Pauline White, my wonderful wife, Caroline, and my dear sons, Josiah and Jacob.

In addition to my children are my godchildren and especially those closest to me: Alexander Muir, Hannah-Rivkah Martin-Thomas, and Alice Cross. I thank God for these people every day – each is an inspiration in my life.

Thank you to all my staff in the UK, Israel, Iraq, Jordan, and the US. Special thanks go to Lesley Kent and Phillip Rowdan, my assistants in the UK, and Hanna Ishaq, my assistant in Israel.

I also acknowledge those who have been closest to me in Baghdad: my unofficial adopted children, Dawood, his wife, Sandy, and their baby, Andrew, dear Fulla, who now lives in Chicago, and Sally Multi, who is still in Baghdad.

One other person I must mention is Dr Sarah Ahmed, who essentially runs my life.

Finally, I cannot thank enough those who made this book possible: my publisher, Tony Collins, and his team at Lion Hudson, and my wonderful editor, Tim Pettingale. Thank you so much. You are all the greatest.

Foreword

I have known Andrew for a long time, especially as his mother lived in my former diocese of Rochester. It was, however, not until he asked me to visit him in Baghdad that I began to realize what a remarkable person he is. In this book he mentions the need religious leaders have for comfortable accommodation at conferences. This is certainly not the case with him! He lived, as he says, in the simplest possible way in one room in a small house next to St George's Church. I have stayed with him there and I do not know how he managed it, particularly with his debilitating illness.

Andrew has a talent for being in the wrong place at the wrong time – at least from a human point of view! Whether it is the intifada in Israel/Palestine or terrorism in Baghdad, there he is! This may be frustrating for security-wallahs, diplomats, and policy makers but for Andrew it is because of his obedience to divine direction.

His ministry at St George's has been nothing short of miraculous and we must pray that it will continue with the most remarkable Iraqi Christians there, now that Andrew no longer is. It has been, and is, an example of holistic mission with worship, prayer, healing (medical and spiritual), feeding, witnessing, and loving all going on side by side.

Andrew has been driven by his own Isaiah Vision, drawn from Isaiah 61:1–4. This has led him to love the unlovely, to befriend the friendless, to bring enemies face to face so they can become friends and to hold together reconciliation and relief for the hungry, the homeless, and the sick. The results are there for all to see.

Although the world has seen him, most recently, as the

"Vicar of Baghdad", in fact his vision is for the whole of the Middle East. It may be that he is being led back to addressing the wider task of reconciliation and peace in that violent part of the world.

It is not just Andrew's work, of course, that deserves notice, but the miracle of his personal story. The immediacy of his walk and his talk with his God is obvious to anyone who is with him for any length of time. He is himself the "wounded healer" bringing healing to others, while being seriously ill himself. In this, he is a witness to the crucified Christ, the One he serves with heart, mind, and body. We need also to note the sacrifices made by his family in releasing him for this ministry. Let us hope that they will now see a little more of him.

I am glad he has written this book so that we can better understand his passionate commitments and his strong faith in the One who continues to sustain him.

The Rt Revd Dr Michael Nazir-Ali,
former Bishop of Rochester

With Pope John Paul II in 1992. My vicar at the time was rather taken aback that his curate received so many summonses to the Vatican.

Presenting a replica of Coventry's Cross of Nails to the late Raphael I Bidawid in the ruins of the old cathedral in 1999. Also in the picture are two men who were to become crucial allies in the cause of peace in Iraq: the wise and holy Ayatollah Hussein al-Sadr and the delightful Sheikh Dr Abdel Latif Humayem.

Archbishop Aristichos signing the Alexandria Declaration in 2002, watched by the Grand Imam of al-Azhar (seated) and two great men of peace: the late Sheikh Talal Sidr (standing, left) and Rabbi Michael Melchior (standing, right). In between them is Sheikh Tantawi's interfaith adviser.

Hanna Ishaq, my man in Jerusalem, who has worked with me longer than anyone. This picture was taken in Tel Aviv.

Visiting Yasser Arafat in the Muqata in 2003. The outcome of meetings with him often depended on his mood.

Talking to an American soldier in Baghdad. The statue of Saddam Hussein is one of four huge bronzes of him that used to adorn his Republican Palace.

Standing in al-Khadamiya in the short period after the liberation of Baghdad when it was still safe to venture outside the Green Zone. And we thought it was dangerous then…

A typical view in the Green Zone two years later. By this time, all our movements were controlled by concrete and plastic – as in the passes round our necks. Immediately behind me is Fadel Alfatlawi.

When Saddam's Palace became the headquarters of the Coalition Provisional Authority, his throne room was used as the chapel and whoever was leading the service would sit on his gold-plated throne. Here I am relaxing with two friends from the US Army.

Attending a gathering of Muslim religious leaders from Israel and Palestine in Cairo in 2005, to follow up the Alexandria Declaration. On my right is the chief justice of the Palestinian *shari'a* courts, Sheikh Taysir al-Tamimi.

With the then British Prime Minister, Tony Blair, and my great friend and co-worker for peace Lord Carey, early in 2007.

With Paul Bremer, ex-'king' of Iraq, at a dinner given in my honour at the Pentagon in 2007.

With General David Petraeus in 2007. On my left stands Samir; on the general's right stands Colonel Mike Hoyt and, beyond him, Peter Maki and another general. Unlike this picture, the US military is very focused!

With Ibrahim Ja'fari outside his prime ministerial residence, before his fall from power in May 2007.

With the current Prime Minister of Iraq, Nuri al-Maliki. Also pictured are (left to right) Peter Maki, Colonel Hoyt, Dr Mowaffak al-Rubaie and Samir.

Iraqi Shia and Sunni leaders meeting with the Grand Imam of al-Azhar (right) in Cairo early in 2007.

Enjoying the hospitality of my dear friend Ayatollah al-Sadr in November 2007. On his right stands Samir, and next to him the Danish pastor Niels Eriksen.

With my close friend and ally Dr Mowaffak (second from right), conversing with the Armenian Orthodox Archbishop of Baghdad, Avak Asadorian, in Copenhagen.

Listening intently in Copenhagen: left to right, a Kurdish sheikh, Sheikh Dr Abdel Latif, Sheikh Abdel Halimjawad Kadhum al-Zuhairi, Mrs Samia Aziz Mohamed and Yonadam Kana, the leader of the Assyrian Christian democrats.

With the former British prime minister Sir John Major and our respective wives (Caroline is on the left) the day I received the Woolf Institute's 2007 Pursuer of Peace Prize at Middle Temple in London.

Standing shoulder-to-shoulder with Gordon England, America's Deputy Secretary of Defense, in his office at the Pentagon in April 2008.

Below: With my great friend Sheikh Dr Ahmed al-Kubaisi outside his home in Dubai. Samir is with me, as always.

Sheikh Dr Abdel Latif feeling at home in the Cairo Marriott Hotel. The beads he is holding represent the 99 names of God.

Getting down to business in Beirut in 2008 Arab-style, four of Iraq's most senior religious leaders: (clockwise from left) Sheikh Dr al-Kubaisi, Sheikh Dr Abdel Latif, Sheikh al-Zuhairi and Ayatollah Ammar Abu Ragif.

Ayatollah Abu Ragif with Samir, signing the first ever *fatwa* against violence issued jointly by Sunna and Shia.

With Lord Hylton (left), when he presented my foundation's 2008 Prize for Peace in the Middle East to Dr Mowaffak (right) in Baghdad.

The 'most wonderful church in the world' is the congregation, certainly not the building! Since the end of 2004, the latter has been surrounded by concrete blocks, concrete-filled oil drums and razor wire.

Waiting to leave St George's with a few of my people and four of my bodyguards from the Iraqi special forces.

With Majid (on my right), then lay pastor of St George's, and his family at the baptism of his daughter in 2006. He was kidnapped shortly after. On my left stands Colonel Hoyt.

Showing Michael Lewis, our new bishop, around the church on his first ever visit to Baghdad.

With little Vivian
in Amman on the
joyful day when she
came out of hospital
after major surgery.

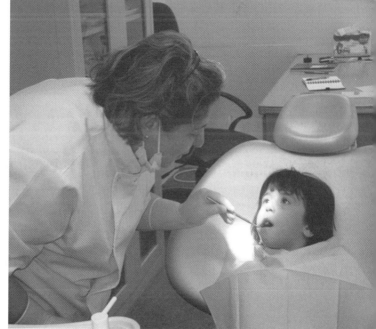

The first patient
in the new
dental clinic at
St George's. The
local American
commander said
its facilities were
the best he had
seen in Iraq.

Six young people from St George's on a visit to heaven – or, at least, Coventry Cathedral – in 2008: with Samir, me and my son Jacob are (left to right) Osama, David, Sally (holding a replica of the Cross of Nails), Lina, Fulla and Mabel.

With the distinguished British-Somali reporter Rageh Omar outside the door to my home in the Green Zone. He presented a one-hour documentary about me for ITV at the beginning of 2008, titled *The Vicar of Baghdad*.

CHAPTER 1

An Unusual Beginning

My earliest memory is of being told how much Jesus loved me. I was brought up in a Christian household and my parents took every opportunity to reveal the love of God to me. Consequently, I cannot remember a time when I didn't know about Jesus: He was part of my life right from the beginning, and I loved Him just as much as He loved me.

Even without being told, I guessed that I should speak to Jesus every day, so I did. My parents would pray with me every night while settling me into bed, and then I knew that it was my time to talk with Him. My childlike prayer ran the same way each night:

Dear Lord Jesus, I love you so much. Thank you for loving me so much too. Thank you for hearing and answering my prayers.

To this day, I begin my night-time prayers with these same words. Until now I have never written them down, and doing so makes me feel like bursting into tears. I'm trying hard to avoid doing this, however, since I'm writing on an aeroplane!

I can't have been much older than two when I began praying that prayer – essentially, as soon as I could talk – but this is how real Jesus has been to me for my entire life. I hope this will explain why I cannot recall a single moment when I had what most people call a "conversion experience". I had always loved Jesus and I knew in my heart that He loved me, so there was no "before and after" Jesus for me; there was just Jesus, ever present.

I have, however, never doubted the reality of my salvation. Even when I was studying theology at Cambridge, and was surrounded by a great number of doubting people, my faith was secure.

When I speak in churches, I like to tease the congregation by telling them that I have never been converted. People tend to react with a mixture of disbelief, shock, and horror!

Our household was a Christian one, but not Anglican. My father, Maurice White, was a staunch Calvinist, and my mother, Pauline, came from a classical Assemblies of God Pentecostal background. As a result, my faith was formed in a melting pot of church cultures. The act of coming to faith in the Pentecostal Church stream tends to emphasize "giving one's heart to Christ". There are lots of altar calls in Pentecostal churches, which focus on encouraging people to "make a decision to follow Jesus". As a child, I was slightly concerned for a while that I had never officially "given my heart to Jesus" and I wasn't entirely sure what it meant. In my childlike way, I tried to work out how one might do this, so I literally cut a heart shape out of paper in order somehow to give it to Him!

A CONTENTED CHILDHOOD

I have only wonderful memories of the vast majority of my childhood, and I was an exceptionally happy child. With me were my sister, Joanna, two years older than me, and Mark, my younger brother by just eleven months. We were not a wealthy household – in fact, quite a poor one – but we were very content. Though poor, one thing we didn't lack were toys, of which there was an abundance because most of them were made by my father.

My father was of Anglo-Indian descent, coming from a somewhat strange tribe of British Indians who were a product of the Raj. He had grown up in a very distinguished, influential family, but had chosen to marry my mother, much to his family's disapproval. His parents didn't view her as having the "right" social background, since she came from humble, working-class stock. In due course my father was disinherited and he and my mother ended up living a simple life in a poorer part of London.

Yet Mother had a rich spiritual heritage. Her father had studied at one of the first Assemblies of God Bible colleges in the UK and, after graduation, went to work alongside Smith Wigglesworth, one of the greatest Pentecostal leaders of all time. Today I am good friends with Henry Fardell, Wigglesworth's great-grandson, and the Pentecostal pioneer's influence continues to reverberate down the generations.

My father was an exceptionally bright man. He had degrees in biological sciences, civil engineering, and theology. He knew all the classical languages and could write fluently in both Latin and Classical Greek. But it was his grasp of mathematics that totally baffled me. He would try to teach me maths and I could never understand it. Of his three children, I was considered the one with the nicest personality, but not the brightest.

Of the many toys that my father made for us, two in particular were very important to me. The first was a little wooden farmyard. It had authentic wooden outbuildings surrounded by a cluster of wooden trees. I would populate my farm with an array of plastic farm animals and spend hours just moving them around, acting out what I thought farm life must be like. One thing that was slightly different about my farm was that my favourite animal was a kangaroo! I don't know why, but I had a fondness for kangaroos. I also had a soft one, knitted by my mother, complete with a baby roo in its pouch.

My other memorable toy came when I was older and lasted for several years. It was the most amazing wooden go-cart. It was constructed mainly from wood, but my father built it like a vintage Rolls-Royce, with a properly functioning steering wheel, highly effective suspension, and a metal "bonnet" fashioned after the house-shaped angles of the Silver Ghost. It was simply an amazing piece of work, and I cherished it.

My pseudo-Rolls go-cart had one other interesting feature: the bonnet could be lifted up to reveal a storage compartment. Inside this I kept an extensive first-aid kit. As with my ever-present faith, I have always had a fascination with medicine. It is hard to say when this began, but during my go-carting years first aid was a major interest of mine.

It was no surprise to anyone that, aged nine, I decided to join the St John Ambulance Brigade. St John had the wonderful foresight to provide training for young boys and girls, thereby ensuring their legacy would continue into the future.

Thursday evenings were Brigade meetings and the highlight of my week, when we would come together for first-aid lessons and to practise the techniques we had already been taught. As I look back, forty years on, I am amazed by just how much I was taught, despite the fact that I was a child. But, for me, being taught something wasn't enough; I wanted to practise! So I began treating all the children in my neighbourhood whenever they had minor accidents. I know it sounds strange now, but if I heard that anyone had been hurt, I would go in my go-cart to find them, get my first-aid kit out, and treat them. My go-cart was like an unofficial junior ambulance. Eventually even the local doctor heard about and complimented me on my first-aid skills!

SPIRITUAL FORMATION

The majority of my formative years were spent soaking up information like a sponge. While other boys were out playing football, I was on a steep learning curve, taking in equal measures of information about medicine and spirituality.

I remember that one of the first books that was ever read to me was Bunyan's *The Holy War*, which he wrote in 1682 while serving a twelve-year sentence in prison for preaching without a licence. Yes, my experiences were very different from those that most children had. I also recall being taught what were, in essence, complex theological concepts, so that by the age of six I could recite the five points of Calvinism with the acronym TULIP:

T*otal Depravity*
U*nconditional Election*
L*imited Atonement*
I*rresistible Grace*
P*erseverance of the Saints*

This I didn't just repeat parrot-fashion – I could actually say what each point meant.

Sundays were a mix of spiritual traditions. In the morning the whole family would attend a Strict Baptist Sunday school, followed by their morning service. Then we would rush home for our Sunday lunch, before heading to the large Assemblies of God church nearby for their afternoon Sunday school. We would take a packed tea with us and stay on for their evening service.

Just to add yet another dimension to my spiritual education, my father had an unusually philo-Semitic understanding of his faith, and therefore taught me not only about Christianity but also about Judaism. He showed me that Judaism was in fact the foundation of the Christian faith. I also became aware of the evils of anti-Semitism and learned about the Holocaust. Our family lived in an area of London that had traditionally been a Jewish neighbourhood and therefore had one of the largest Jewish cemeteries. As a young boy I took the issue of anti-Semitism very seriously, and though I had never seen the cemetery being attacked I was aware that it could be, so I would regularly go and stand outside its gates to "guard" it.

While other children were reading *The Beano* or *The Dandy*,[1] I spent my time reading about Judaism and medicine. By the age of ten my main reading material was *A Jewish Theology* by Rabbi Louis Jacobs[2] and *An Introduction to Surgery*. Alongside these I would read many complementary works, spending hours in the local library searching out the right kind of books to take home and devour.

WHAT DO YOU WANT TO BE WHEN YOU GROW UP?

I remember one day at school when our form teacher informed us that we all needed to consider what we wanted to do when we grew up. Many of my peers had no idea what they wanted to do, but I was always very clear about it, if rather unconventional.

---

1   *The Beano* is a British children's comic, published by D. C. Thomson & Co., which first appeared in 1938. *The Dandy* was published by the same company from 1937 to 2012.
2   Published by Behrman House Publishing, 1973.

I was keen to pursue my twin passions of faith and medicine. I knew enough about the latter to have established a specific area of interest: anaesthetics. I wanted to be both a priest and an anaesthetist, and told my teacher so. I was told that I could do one or the other, but not both.

I had a similar conversation with my parents. This time I was told that I could go into medicine if I wanted to, but I couldn't be a "priest" since I was a Strict Baptist and they didn't have priests. None of this deterred me, though. I felt that God had put this twin calling on my life and that, somehow, Jesus was going to help me to do all that I was supposed to do in life.

Around this time I made an unlikely friend who was to have a profound effect on my spiritual formation and help put me on the path towards becoming a priest. Living on the same road as our family was an old lady who was bedridden. No one ever laid eyes on her, but we often heard about "Miss Davis", especially from her sister, who lived right next door to us. One day I asked our neighbour if I would be allowed to go and see Miss Davis, her sister. I was assured that she would love to meet me and the same day I was invited round to her house.

Immediately we became firm friends, and from that day forward Miss Davis became "Aunty Hilda" to me. I visited her almost every day and discovered that she had a profoundly deep faith in and love for Jesus. We would pray together about all manner of things; she was a wonderful lady. There was just one problem: Aunty Hilda was not a Baptist, or even a Pentecostal; she was a member of the Church of England. Sad to say, in the Baptist/Pentecostal circles I moved in during the seventies, Anglicans were not even considered "real" Christians. Yet it was clear to me that here was a lady of authentic faith, who knew God and loved Him deeply.

Because Aunty Hilda was unable to leave her house owing

to ill health, her local priest would visit every week to minister Holy Communion. This same priest visited our school each week. Before long he invited me to go and visit Aunty Hilda's church and I was most curious to see what it might be like, so I asked my parents' permission and arranged to go.

In due course I entered a different world – church as I had never experienced it before. It was smells and bells and high-church Anglo-Catholic liturgy. To me as a ten-year-old boy, it seemed like a glimpse into what I imagined heaven was like, and I immediately fell in love with it.

This meant that my churchgoing activities were about to become considerably more complicated, with my Sundays spent dashing from one place to the next. My morning would begin with the Anglicans at 7 a.m., followed by a rush to get to the Strict Baptist service and later the Assemblies of God service.

It was a clash of church cultures but I was drawn to the Anglican model of church and began attending more of Aunty Hilda's church's services. Each day after school, I would run out of the door in order to get to church in time for their Evensong service, which would be conducted according to the 1662 Book of Common Prayer. On Saturdays I would also attend their Communion service. After a while I was asked if I would be a server. I was delighted to do so and greatly enjoyed dressing up in a robe. I recall walking to the church with the priest one Sunday morning and mentioning to him all the services I would be attending that day. He said to me, "Andrew, don't you get indigestion with all this church?"

I admit it was strange, but I loved it.

CHAPTER 2

Turbulence

Having enjoyed a blissfully happy existence up to the end of my pre-teen years, I suddenly began to experience some personal health problems and, around the same time, some family turmoil.

I had suffered with minor ear and throat troubles for a few years, but these hadn't bothered me much to begin with. When I was eleven, however, they became a lot worse and persisted to the point where they were causing me chronic problems. It was decided that I needed both a tonsillectomy and a myringotomy, the latter to relieve pressure in my eardrum caused by the build-up of excess fluid, so I was admitted to hospital. Some children would have found this an ordeal, but to me it was an adventure.

My first experience of entering an operating theatre is indelibly printed on my mind. By now I was well read in the theory of anaesthetics and was very pleased to be meeting a real-life anaesthetist. It must have been strange for him, I'm sure, to have an eleven-year-old boy asking him why he was still using cyclopropane in his anaesthetic machine, and did he not consider it dangerous to do so? (At the time, questions were being asked about its safety and today cyclopropane is no longer used.) I remember him telling me that it was a very good induction agent for children because of its sweet smell. I had to agree, and thoroughly enjoyed the sensation of being anaesthetized!

The next sensation I became aware of was not so pleasant, however. I came round to find myself vomiting blood. It wasn't just a little, and the doctors bustled around me, clearly very worried. They set up a blood transfusion and I was admitted to a ward to recover. I had entered hospital early that morning and it was almost midnight by the time they were satisfied that it was safe for me to have my operation. I was taken back to theatre and saw the same consultant anaesthetist, still on duty. I managed to have another conversation with him and asked another unlikely question for a young boy: "Are you going to use cricoid pressure?" (an emergency procedure used whenever there is a risk of the stomach filling with blood). He assured me that he would, if it became necessary.

After the operation my recovery was slow, but as soon as I was feeling well enough to go out I was taken on one of my father's trips into central London. These were regular excursions and, whatever else happened, always featured certain events. Lunch would be taken in my father's favourite Indian restaurant, Anwar's in Gower Street, off the Tottenham Court Road. I loved this place. I first visited Anwar's at the age of four and I was very sad when it closed recently.

Another regular feature was a visit to Charing Cross Road, to one of the many bookshops for which my father and I shared a passion. Our favourite was Foyles, the largest bookstore in Europe at that time. Downstairs, on the lower ground floor, was a huge medical department. On this trip I was allowed to select a book of my choice for having endured my surgery. I headed straight for the anaesthetics section and picked out *Lee's Synopsis of Anaesthesia*, still widely regarded as a comprehensive classic on the subject. Today, this volume has pride of place on the bookshelf of my study at home in England.

I suppose one could say that before I'd entered my teens, the foundation of my life was set: a love for the church, both Anglican and Pentecostal branches, a passion for medicine, particularly anaesthetics, and an interest in Judaism.

FAMILY TRIBULATIONS

After I recovered from surgery, life returned to normal for a while, but it was about to change radically. My dear sister, Joanna, was becoming increasingly ill and no one could find out exactly what was wrong with her. She had stopped eating and was clearly mentally distressed. She went from doctor to doctor, hospital to hospital, all to no avail. My parents took her to see private doctors in Harley Street, which evidently they couldn't afford, but it was a long time before any conclusions were reached.

Eventually, it was established that she was suffering from a mental illness, which manifested itself as anorexia nervosa. This was at a time when very little was known about the condition. Joanna spent hours crying and screaming and life became intolerable for her. This had a dramatic effect on the rest of the family and we all lived in fear of her extreme behaviour. She would often be taken into a psychiatric unit for long periods and, sad to say, these were the only times when it was bearable to be at home.

I found it very difficult to cope with Joanna's sickness. I remember walking home from school with my brother, Mark, both of us praying that when we arrived Joanna would not be in her "crazy" state. Most of the time, however, she was. As a result, I spent more and more time with Aunty Hilda. Sadly, though, it wasn't long before Hilda was too frail to continue living on her own and she was taken into a Christian convent hospital on the other side of London. This caused me considerable pain and distress.

Time during the school holidays was spent out of the house as much as possible. A typical day would see Mark and me travelling by bus all over London on a "Red Rover" unlimited travel ticket, as we took in the capital's bookstores, libraries, and museums.

It soon became clear to us boys that my parents wanted to relocate out of the city, so that we could grow up in a better area, attend better schools, and perhaps provide Joanna with a more peaceful environment. They were thinking of moving to Kent, known as the Garden of England, and were interested in going to Bexley. I knew the area fairly well – it was where my maternal grandparents lived and where my mother had grown up.

At the grand old age of twelve I thought that I was mature enough to do the house hunting on behalf of the family, and this I did quite successfully. I found a good house in the right area, which my parents subsequently bought. It was much larger and far nicer than the one we'd been used to in London. We started attending excellent new schools and really appreciated the new area. But my sister continued to have serious health challenges and was constantly in and out of hospital. Her anorexia was so severe that at one point she weighed a mere four stone, and she was five foot two inches tall. So, in this regard, life remained difficult.

Church continued to play a major role in my life. We attended a local Strict Baptist chapel and also found a local Assemblies of God church. I found an Anglican church to attend, but it was nothing like the Anglo-Catholic one I had been a member of in London, and consequently I never joined it.

Around this time I made a close friend for the first time in my life. Brian Heath went to a local United Reformed church and attended the same school as me. We would often do our homework/prep together. The other thing we used to love doing was looking for frogs in a local stream. We gathered such an impressive collection of frogs that we had to create a pond especially for them in my back garden at home. We gave them all biblical names. I can remember Obadiah, Malachi and, from the New Testament, Bartholomew! The rest of my time was spent attending church meetings and visiting older people.

I became very friendly with one particular couple. Retired Colonel Watson was British, but had formerly served in the Indian Army Ordnance Corps. Like much of my family, Col and Mrs Watson were products of the British Raj, and lived in India until independence in 1947. At that time Col Watson had returned to England and spent the rest of his career in the British military as a Brigadier General. (It puzzled me that he was always referred to as "the Colonel", but I never did get to the bottom of it.) I would spend hours in conversation with both of them at the front gate of their house. Eventually the Colonel died and thereafter I became very close to Mrs Watson, who was a surrogate "Aunty Hilda" to me. I visited her regularly after school and often did my homework at her house. The other thing about going to Mrs Watson's bungalow was that she had a television – an item that was forbidden in our house while we remained of school age – so I became a secret TV watcher!

SERIOUS ILLNESS

During my first summer vacation in Kent I realized that I wanted to do something to help other people in our community.

I went to the local volunteer centre and they sent me to visit a place called the Pop-in Parlour, or PIP as it was known, a place where elderly people could meet, drink tea, and chat with one another.

I liked the PIP and immediately became wholeheartedly involved. It was normal to give about two hours of your time to serving there, but I tended to stay all day – not just chatting with the many diverse visitors, as was expected, but also cleaning the centre from top to bottom. I got to know the people who came along quite well and they told me about the various needs they had at home, so increasingly I began to visit their homes to help them. Life soon became centred on the PIP and this continued after the summer holidays. I would spend my Saturdays working there and I loved it. Then, a seemingly innocuous accident had a very dramatic effect on my life.

I travelled everywhere on my bike. One weekend, cycling home from the PIP, I hit a bump in the road and fell off, cutting my right knee quite badly on the gravel. Being St John-trained, I cleaned and dressed the wound myself, then took myself off to the local hospital. The A&E staff were quite concerned because there still seemed to be some gravel embedded deep within the wound. They cleaned and re-dressed the wound and I was sent home.

The wound did not heal properly, however, and soon became badly infected. The hospital doctors decided that I would need an operation, which in due course I had, but soon afterwards the wound broke down and became infected again. Thus began a series of operations and recurrent infections. Post-operation I was usually in absolute agony, and I recall much time spent in bed crying with pain.

During this time one person was a tremendous comfort to me – Jim Palmer, pastor of our local Assemblies of God church. He would come and visit regularly to pray for me. I remember how he ministered to me patiently and compassionately, praying for healing. He was very much like Jesus for me, a constant comfort.

After many more operations my wound eventually healed, but my problems were far from over. My leg became increasingly swollen and the doctors suspected this was probably lymphoedema – a serious swelling caused by occlusion of the lymphatic system. From my ongoing medical studies I knew that there was only really one surgeon in the UK who was an expert in lymphatics – Professor John B. Kinmonth, author of a then famous book, *Lymphatics: Diseases, Lymphography and Surgery*. My local library tracked down a copy for me and it became my new favourite book. At those times when my leg was worse, I would regularly be taken to see a local surgeon. It became apparent that he knew a great deal less about the condition than I did, because he hadn't read the book and I had!

On 5 September 1979 I was fifteen years old and in London for the day to watch the funeral procession of the assassinated Earl Mountbatten of Burma. I stood for hours in a prominent position by Westminster Abbey. By the time the ceremony had finished, my leg had swollen up so much that I was in agony and could hardly walk. Across the Thames I could see St Thomas' Hospital, and I decided I should take myself over to its A&E department to see what they could do for me.

I made it with some effort and, after looking at me, the doctors decided I ought to be admitted. I phoned home to tell my parents and a few hours later my mother arrived, bringing everything I would need. I was placed under the care of the orthopaedic department. I lay on my hospital bed thinking, "Why on earth am I in the orthopaedic department?" The next day the orthopaedic consultant came to see me. I remember him well: his name was Fred Heatley, and in just a few years I would be working alongside him. He looked at my leg and said, "You are in the right hospital but the wrong department." I knew that already! But then I was told I was being transferred to the care of Professor J. B. Kinmonth. My eyes lit up – the right man! I recall saying, "At last, the person I really need to see."

I wish I could say that this solved all my problems and that I was shortly made better, but things didn't turn out that way and there ensued a long, complex process. Prof. Kinmonth decided that there was a problem with the lymph nodes in my groin and that they should operate. To cut a long story short, it turned out that the groin had many infected nodes and, once again, post-operation the wound broke down. Multiple operations followed and at one point I was in hospital for fourteen consecutive weeks.

This scenario continued, not just for months but for years. In between operations I would go home, resume my schooling, and try to live life as normally as possible. On one occasion I became very ill and was losing consciousness. It was discovered that I had developed septicaemia. My situation was so grave that the hospital was unsure if I would survive. The consultant stood at the end of my bed telling my mother that my condition was so serious, he didn't know if I would pull through, but he would do everything possible to help me. I had my eyes closed as if I were asleep, but I could hear every word. I remember the occasion well, as it happened on 29 July 1981 and coincided with the marriage of Prince Charles to Lady Diana Spencer.

Eventually, I returned home and each day the district nurse came to dress my wounds before I left for school. Soon after this episode a surgeon decided to do a very radical procedure which involved removing a large section of the bottom of my abdomen and much of the top of my right leg. It was painful surgery, but it worked.

HOPE DASHED AND REBORN

Finally free of infection and back at school, I had to take my final exams. I was studying biology, chemistry, religious studies, and politics. A lot of the studying for these subjects I'd had to do on my own from my hospital bed. At this stage it was also time to apply to a university for further study.

There was no doubt about what I wanted to do – study anaesthetics and surgery. During my extensive reading I had obtained some valuable information. If one were to take the normal route for doing this, it would take years before one got to work in an operating theatre. But there was a way that would get you into the heart of the action very quickly, and that was training as an Operating Department Practitioner. Most of the teaching hospitals had training schools for this profession, so I applied to many prestigious establishments, but truly there was only one that I was really passionate about: St Thomas' Hospital, where I had spent a great deal of time as a patient. It was the oldest hospital in the country, with its roots dating back as far as 1106, and I loved its ethos. I prayed very hard that I might be able to train there.

I was eventually called for an interview at St Thomas'. When the day came I felt that the interview had gone wonderfully well and I loved my short time there. From then on, I monitored our letter box daily, waiting for a reply. Eventually a letter arrived, but to my utter dismay it said that unfortunately I had not been selected. Having prayed a great deal about it, I was certain that God had told me I would go there, so I couldn't understand why I'd been turned down. I was in despair and cried out to Him asking why.

At this time the head of sixth form at my school was a wonderful man called Michael Amos. I knew him fairly well, as I was the chair of the sixth-form committee. I had already told him of my desire to study at St Thomas' and so I shared with him my disappointment at being turned down. He was very encouraging and assured me that I would end up in the best place for me.

Just a few days later, as I was about to go out for the day, the postman arrived and handed me a letter. It was another piece of correspondence from St Thomas' Hospital, which was puzzling. I opened it and to my shock and delight it said that their previous letter had been an administrative error and I had in fact been selected for training, which would begin in September, subject to the successful completion of my exams. It was the happiest day of my life.

I showed the letter to Mr Amos the following Monday morning and he was thrilled. He hugged me and told me, "You are going to go very far and no one will be able to stop you."

Michael Amos was an inspirational man. I saw him again, just a few years ago, when I was awarded a major peace prize by the Wolf Institute at Cambridge University. The prize was presented to me by Baroness Valerie Amos, a senior member of the House of Lords and the current UN Under-Secretary-General for Humanitarian Affairs and Emergency Relief Coordinator. Baroness Amos is Michael's daughter and he was there to see me receive the prize. It gave me so much joy to see him, all these years later, and to be able to tell him what an inspiration he'd been to me.

Just a few weeks after the event, Baroness Amos contacted me to say her father was critically ill and dying. I returned from Iraq and was by his side in the UK until he died. Then I had the privilege of taking his funeral service. I can honestly say that, to me, it was one of the most important services I have ever taken.

CHAPTER 3

Just Like Heaven

I eventually took my exams and passed them well. September arrived with much anticipation and excitement on my part and I began my training at St Thomas' Hospital.

Being a student there was wonderful. My greatest dream had come true and there was no aspect of my study that I did not enjoy. During my early days at St Thomas' I lived at home and took an early train into London each morning.

To begin with, my time was spent only in the lecture theatre, but eventually the day came when we were allowed to pay a visit to the operating theatre and, for me at least, the really exciting part began. Special provision had to be made for my large size-sixteen feet. None of the available theatre boots would fit me and it took the hospital several months to track down a suitable pair for me. They had been specially made. I will never forget the first day I stepped into the theatre: the smell, the intense atmosphere... I always say it was like being in heaven, except that I'm sure heaven does not have all that blood.

Before I go further, I would point out that this chapter contains references to the medical procedures I was involved in performing – some of which are not for the squeamish. You have been warned!

* * *

My first six-week placement was working in anaesthesia, an area which continued to fascinate me, but my first proper theatre training was in urology and gynaecology – to my mind not the most interesting type of surgery. However, I loved being in the theatre. I was so enthusiastic to learn that in between cases I went off into the other theatres to observe the more dramatic procedures – orthopaedic, cardiac, or general surgery. Apparently this was not allowed, and it wasn't long until I was found out. I was severely reprimanded and told that students were not allowed to do this kind of thing!

So I spent a good deal of my time sitting in the dark, wet room that was the urology theatre. Most of the surgery was transurethral and was carried out with the surgeon sitting between the patient's legs with one eye glued to a uroscope. The person's bladder would be completely filled with water, then emptied again and again. The water came straight out onto the floor and was constantly mopped into the theatre's drains. Now you understand why it was both dark and wet. Eventually I would change to orthopaedic surgery, which was so much more enjoyable. Replacing a person's hip joint involved a lot of hammering and chiselling – much noisier than urology, but certainly a lot more fun (for me, not the patient). Meanwhile, I was learning much about the practical application of anaesthetics, though I already knew the theory inside out.

A regular visitor to the theatre was Suzy Lupton (now Knight), who was a student nurse on the men's urology ward and regularly brought down patients for their operations. Suzy was a Christian and we would also see each other at the hospital's Christian Union (CU) meetings. We became firm friends and over thirty years later our friendship remains as strong as it was then.

The CU was the major focal point for Christians studying at the hospital. It was almost, but not quite, entirely made up of students. They were a diverse bunch from across the hospital's many departments – medical students, student nurses at the Nightingale School of Nursing, students of pharmacy, radiology, physiotherapy, laboratory science, and phlebotomy, and Operating Department Practitioners like me.

The CU was very dynamic. We prayed, we sang, we had regular house parties and a whole series of excellent speakers. We were so much more than a group of Christians who met each week for a kind of service – deep friendships were forged and we continued to meet throughout the week in the library or staff restaurant. Many of us also attended the same churches.

It was in the CU that I met the closest male friend I have ever had, Malcolm Mathew. Malcolm was a medical student and we would see each other regularly at CU and around the hospital. Each Sunday Malcolm and I would go into the hospital again in order to take people in wheelchairs or beds to the chapel. It was a wonderful opportunity for us to have some meaningful contact with the patients and to take them to share in worship in the beautiful, traditional old Anglican chapel, which was the size of most decent parish churches.

The chaplain, Michael Stevens, was a real friend to us and was widely loved and respected. Once a month he would invite the CU to take the chapel service and we students would lead the meeting. It was at one such service that I preached my first ever sermon. I confess it was a pretty awful sermon, but it was the beginning of what would turn into a lifetime of preaching. I immediately realized I needed much more public-speaking experience, so after chapel and lunch Malcolm and I would often go to Speakers' Corner in Hyde Park and I would speak on a mixture of faith and politics.

Most Sundays, a stint at Speakers' Corner was followed by a Tube ride to the church that many of our fellow CU members attended, St Mark's, Kennington. St Mark's was a powerhouse of a church, where the charismatic community met the established church, resulting in a vibrant atmosphere. The vicar was Nicholas Rivett-Carnac, a man full to overflowing with the Holy Spirit and the love of God, as was his lovely wife, Marigold. They were both adored by the congregation.

AN EXPERIENCE OF GOD'S SPIRIT

Attending St Mark's was a great experience for all of us students. It was like a machine that recharged our batteries at the end of each week. Though I had grown up with some experience of the Pentecostal Church, I had never before spent a long time in a dynamic, Spirit-filled environment. I was aware of the experience of the "infilling of the Holy Spirit" that is at the heart of Pentecostal Christian teaching, but I had not experienced this myself.

In our old Assemblies of God church we would regularly have "waiting meetings" in which we would sit, pray, and wait to be filled with the Holy Spirit – the evidence of which would be the gift of speaking in tongues. I confess that these were among the most boring meetings I have ever attended. They were certainly about waiting – we waited and waited and did little else. I do not want to generalize, of course, but the small part of the Pentecostal Church that I knew personally had changed much since the days of Smith Wigglesworth and become set in its ways. At St Mark's, however, I experienced a taste of the glory and power of God as never before.

The day came when I realized that I needed someone to pray for me, in order for me to experience the Holy Spirit in this new way. At one particular meeting I went and knelt at the altar, and a dear lady called Anthea Demitri prayed for me. That day my life was changed for ever. The presence of the Holy Spirit hit me like a thunderbolt. Although I wasn't expecting it, I received the gift of speaking in tongues, and from that moment on I was a new man. That night I went home singing and glorifying God loudly in tongues.

I noticed the difference the next day when I went into St Thomas'. It was a theatre training day, rather than lectures, and as I entered the theatre I was aware, as never before, of the glory and presence of God. It was quite amazing.

My physiology lecturer was the very interesting and totally eccentric Louis Cronje. If a student answered a question correctly during his lecture he would give them a Jelly Baby™. This day he came right up to me during class, planted his hands on my desk, looked me in the eyes, and said, "Andrew, you are going to do very well here, but this is not where you are meant to be. You are going to change the world." This was remarkable in itself, but he went on to repeat this mantra to me week in and week out for months to come. I didn't want to change the world. I just wanted to become a good "gas man", as anaesthetists are known.

One of the surgeons I had the privilege of assisting was Ian Fergusson. I helped him with a number of caesarean section births and he told me that I was his favourite student for such tasks, since I had such large hands and was best at helping the baby out. Until he'd said that, I hadn't realized I had such big hands; I just knew I had big feet!

It was a huge responsibility to help bring a new life into the world, but I now knew the constant reassuring presence of the Holy Spirit and this helped me to cope with potentially difficult or stressful situations. On another occasion, I was assigned to help a visiting surgeon from India in the cardiac theatre. The patient was having a new aortic valve fitted, but the surgeon put it in the wrong way. As a result I spent the next four hours holding a retractor in the heart while the mistake was corrected, and it meant I had to keep as steady as a rock. Before long I was in agony, but I just could not move and jeopardize the procedure. I silently praised and worshipped God and, somehow, He sustained me and got me through it.

It was a wonder to me how intertwined my spiritual life was with my medical life and I had many wonderful times of praise and worship on my own in operating theatres while I was doing the set-up and preparation. Anyone looking in on me may well have thought I was mad!

A BUMP IN THE ROAD

I was well into my training when suddenly I developed some pain and swelling in my right groin. Within a day my old wound had totally broken down and I was in a bad way. I was admitted to St Thomas' as a patient and placed on a staff ward. This was very different from being a "normal" patient, since I knew all the staff and had worked with many of them.

By this time I had a great deal more knowledge and knew enough to understand how complex and dangerous my situation was. A date was set for surgery, this time carried out by friends/ colleagues. I had the surgery and we waited to see the outcome, but it was only a matter of days before the wound broke down and became infected again. Several more operations followed and I began to worry about all the study time I was missing. Eventually I was sent home to my parents and told to allow enough time to recuperate properly.

By now I had moved out of the family home and a couple of fellow students and I were living in rented accommodation. Returning home was not easy. My sister, Joanna, though now engaged, was still suffering very much and was extremely hard to be around. My brother, Mark, who was by far the most intelligent of all of us, had finished school but opted out of going to university. Instead, his only interests seemed to be football and hanging out with a crowd of very unsavoury characters. His behaviour was erratic and I became convinced that he was taking drugs. Increasingly, he was getting into trouble with the police.

After a period of rest I was well enough to return to St Thomas' and found it difficult to leave such a complex family situation behind. Given my brother's and sister's situations, I was profoundly conscious, despite my health problems, of how blessed I was to be thriving in an environment I loved, and keenly aware of God's presence with me. I did not take it for granted. But I also wondered why it was that both my brother and my sister were suffering with their mental well-being and I was not. It's something that I still do not understand.

On my return to St Thomas' I decided to become as fit as I could and so became a vegetarian and began running several miles every day. Within a short while I felt the healthiest I had ever been and, of course, loved being back at the hospital. My academic work was going well, but the teaching staff came to the conclusion that, because of all the time I'd lost while I'd been hospitalized and then recuperating, my training would have to be extended, and my finals were put back three months. But, once again, I knew God's help. I completed my thesis in obstetric problems and, when I eventually took my exams, I got excellent results.

TO THE NORTH AND BACK

After qualifying I was appointed to my first proper role in obstetric anaesthetics at Derby City Hospital, and headed north into a very different world from that which I'd known in London.

Here my work spanned both the operating theatre and the labour ward, and so involved epidurals as much as caesarean sections. The hospital was radically different from St Thomas' and I longed to be back in London. At the earliest opportunity I applied for a new job there and to my delight I was accepted. After my brief foray to the north I was soon back in my beloved St Thomas' and working in my favourite theatres again.

I was tasked with dealing with three main areas. The first was any emergency surgery that needed doing. Emergencies occurred daily, but we dealt with the issues that were too complex to be handled by other hospitals. Second was vascular surgery – venous, arterial, and lymphatic – dealing with radical problems such as aortic aneurisms. Third, there was ear, nose, and throat surgery (ENT). ENT probably doesn't sound very challenging to most people, but from an anaesthetic and surgical point of view it can be very demanding indeed, including as it does such procedures as laryngectomy (removing the voice box in cancer patients). There were also many paediatric cases, and anaesthetizing children is always very difficult.

These were the delights I faced on a daily basis, but increasingly I was asked to become involved in the hospital's "crash team" as well. This is essentially the cardiac arrest team, but they are usually called on to assist with other major crises in the A&E department. The crash team were a full-time unit, but I was seconded to the team whenever they needed extra capacity. I soon found myself volunteering for them, even when I was not on duty, and would come in to support them at weekends. It meant carrying around a crash bleeper and, when an emergency occurred, the miniature screen flashed up "Crash call" with the location of the event. One would then run there as fast as possible and try to resuscitate the patient. When I tell people about these events today I like to say that I didn't just put people to sleep, I also raised the dead!

During my training one lecturer uttered a phrase that has always stayed with me: "Medicine," he said, "must never become torture." There were times when I wondered whether our treatment of patients was indeed treatment or torture. Sometimes the "treatment" could be radical and painful. If the damage didn't cause long-term problems, then this was acceptable. But, at times, saving a person's life meant leaving them in a terrible state for the rest of that life.

Don't read on unless you can cope with something seriously gruesome, but the worst case I ever dealt with was when we were called to assist a man who had been crushed under a stage lift at the National Theatre in London. After he was extracted, his treatment meant almost daily surgery, which included amputating both his legs. Then, one day, it was decided that he needed a hemicorporectomy – the complete amputation of the lower half of the body from above the pelvis. It was the most horrendous operation I have ever seen and I admit to praying that he would not survive. Towards the end of his surgery he went into cardiac arrest and my colleagues and I agreed that we could not resuscitate him. Medicine had become torture, rather than the healing and restoring process it was meant to be. The Lord gives and the Lord takes away, but sometimes we try to stop Him. Medical ethics, I believe, are as much about not going too far as about not going far enough.

So life at St Thomas' was busy and demanding, but I thrived in that environment. "This is it," I thought. "I'll probably spend the rest of my career right here." But I was wrong.

CHAPTER 4

Called by God

One day, between crash calls, I was standing in the hospital gardens opposite Big Ben and praying. I began to thank God for everything He had done for me. He had enabled me to both train and now work at St Thomas'. He had built a wonderful spiritual foundation in my life and filled me with His presence. Then I said to Him, "What next, Lord?" and presumed He would say I should stay right where I was and that one day I would become the crash team director. But He did not. Instead, He said very clearly, "I want you to go into the Church of England."

Immediately I protested: "But I love it here. You sent me here and I'm good at what I do. Besides, they are not even all saved in the Church of England!"

But when God calls you to do something, you cannot fight it for long. He always gets His own way and He spent the following day changing my mind.

The next morning I was preparing for that day's cases in theatre and entered into what was now my regular time of praise and worship. As I did so, I became increasingly aware of the fact that all I actually wanted to do with my life was to serve God. I wanted to do what He wanted me to do – even if it meant training for ministry in the Church of England. As the day wore on, I felt more and more that, in fact, I did want to go into the church.

Near the end of the day we performed a procedure on a patient to bypass a blocked artery in their leg and, by the end of it, I wanted nothing more than to serve God through His church. Then the Lord brought to my mind the question I'd been asked as a ten-year-old boy: "What do you want to do when you grow up?", to which I had responded, "Work in anaesthetics and be a priest." I had done the first; maybe now I was going to do the second.

It was clear that all this was from God. He had given me the desires of my heart in the first place. I needed to talk to someone about all this and so went to my vicar at St Mark's, Nicholas, and earnestly told him what I felt God was saying. I didn't realize at the time that vicars are regularly accosted by people telling them they think they are being called to ministry, so I didn't quite get the reaction I was hoping for. Instead, he graciously passed me over to Mike Marshall, his new curate, to talk me through the process.

I met with Mike to discuss things. He began by asking if I was really qualified enough to cope with training for ministry. Had I been to university? Did I have a degree in anything? I assured him that I had a degree in surgery and anaesthetics from St Thomas' Hospital. He told me that selection for ministry was a long process that began with a meeting with the director of ordinands and could last for up to two years. In due course this would culminate in a three-day residential selection conference, from which recommendations would be given to the diocesan bishop regarding who should train for ordination.

Undeterred by the length of the process or the fact that I might be turned down at the end, I pressed ahead and had a series of meetings with Canon John Cox. He could see how much I loved my present job, but that I was also very committed to wanting to serve God and His people. I was rightly pushed hard to consider the tension between my intense love for the medical world and the major sacrifice it would be to leave that way of life. But things progressed well and it was not long before I was told I needed to begin thinking about where I would study theology. I was informed that I should consider Oxford or Cambridge. I was excited by this. In my heart I would always have loved to be an Oxbridge scholar, and here was my chance.

I thought that Oxford was perhaps the better place and began to investigate some of the Oxford colleges. But another of my close friends at St Thomas' was a student nurse called Maria and she was from Cambridge – her father was a Methodist minister who had trained there. Maria decided she was taking me to Cambridge and I immediately fell in love with both the city and its university.

While there, I recalled a school trip to Cambridge years before, when I was a small boy. I'd walked down King's Parade and said to myself, "Oh, I wish I could come and study here one day." It seemed destined that God would bring me here.

I was very blessed while at St Mark's, Kennington, to be in a wonderful home group led by Ray and Carol Austin. I had first met Ray on the cardiothoracic operating table. He had an inoperable bronchial tumour. He was a young man and it was an issue of major concern to the thoracic team. To cut a very long story short, his wife got him back home from hospital and Nicholas, the vicar of St Mark's, came round to pray for him. Ray returned to hospital for checks a completely healed man. Ray and Carol were a massive encouragement and support to me as I toiled through the laborious selection process.

Finally, I was put forward for the selection conference known as ACCM (the Advisory Council for the Church's Ministry). As I began to prepare for the conference, I had a sudden revelation: I was not actually an Anglican! I had never been confirmed as a member of the Church of England. So it was swiftly arranged for me to have an emergency confirmation at a church in Croydon. I became an Anglican just four days before I went to the selection conference!

Once I had got to this stage I had to be honest with the hospital about the possibility of my moving to Cambridge to study theology in preparation for going into the Church of England. All my colleagues were shocked by this news, but every one of them was very supportive. It was interesting to see that the response from my family was quite different. They could not understand how I could turn my back on my wonderful training and the place where I had always wanted to work, especially to go into the Church of England. They were ardent Nonconformists; was their son joining the opposition?

The day came for the final selection conference. It was at Bishop Woodford House in Ely – a wonderful setting for probably the most important interview of my life. There were sixteen people being interviewed from all over the UK. None of us knew each other. Then there was a considerable interviewing panel with each person looking at a different aspect of ministry. The chair was an archdeacon from Leicestershire and, to my surprise, I discovered that he had also been a Strict Baptist, like me. I remember one question he asked: "What is the most inspirational book you have read recently?" I had just read William Temple's *Philosophy of Religion*, which was excellent, but was not the book that had really inspired me. The book that had challenged and motivated me most was a little book by Colin Urquhart, who regularly preached at St Mark's, called *Anything You Ask*. It was simply about putting faith into action. I mentioned this and we had a brief discussion about living in the dimension of God's miraculous power. It was an unusual line to take for one wanting to be a part of the state church.

I returned to London full of expectation and waited impatiently for a response. My operating theatre colleagues seemed as keen to hear the answer as I was. Eventually the letter arrived at my flat in Kennington and it said that the bishop was recommending me for training for ordination. I looked at my diary and planned to use some of my holiday leave for spiritual preparation for my training. I was scheduled to spend a week at Colin Urquhart's Kingdom Faith Conference, where I had pledged my services to look after the on-site medical centre. After that I thought I would go and spend some time in a monastery. The Kingdom Faith week was outstanding and in both the ministry times and the medical clinic we saw lots of miracles. It was a wonderful time – apart from the camping. I have never had the calling to be a camper!

Afterwards I went home to visit my parents before returning to work, and found them in a frenzy. They had been trying to contact me for three days (this was long before the ubiquity of mobile phones). The hospital wanted me urgently. They had major problems with their crash team: a member of staff had been suspended, and I was to be appointed temporary director.

I returned to St Thomas' and threw myself into this task. I loved every minute of it. I had wanted to be director of the crash team one day and here I was, being given a taste of what it was like. I was given accommodation in the hospital itself because of the importance of the role. Here I was experiencing another taste of heaven, but, of course, it could not continue. In due course I would leave and train to be a priest. Through this, however, God helped me to realize something very important.

What was it that I loved most about the crash team? It was rising to the occasion of dealing with a crisis. One day, all this training in dealing with crises under pressure would be immensely valuable to me – as valuable as my spiritual training.

I had thought I might take a few days' break between finishing at St Thomas' and going to Cambridge, but this was not to be. Until the very day before I left for Cambridge I was working – and that day was as busy as ever. My bleeper went off and I was called to a cardiac arrest in the psychiatric outpatients department.

It was not an area of the hospital the crash team expected to visit frequently and I knew that the resuscitation equipment there would be very limited, so I grabbed the nearest anaesthetic machine and ran with it down the corridor to the psychiatric unit. Just then, one of the senior nursing officers got in my way and I swerved to avoid knocking her flying. As I did so, the anaesthetic machine hit me in the face, chipping my teeth, and blood began pouring down my chin. Fortunately, we managed to resuscitate the patient and all was well – apart from my smashed-up face. The next day I took the train to Cambridge and began my training for ordination looking as if I had just lost a fist fight. Whoever would believe what had happened to me?

CHAPTER 5

The Academic Hothouse

I arrived in Cambridge with my battered face (to more than a few bemused stares) and found my accommodation. I liked my room off H staircase at Ridley Hall. I was shocked when I opened the wardrobe in the study and discovered a list, to which each of the room's former occupants had added their name. It included many of the great leaders of our faith tradition, such as John Stott and David Watson, and now here I was too.

I joined the other new students to attend an induction talk and was pleased to hear that I would be learning not just theology, but also philosophy, church history, Greek, liturgy, and much more. Then we had our pre-term lecture. This was a special event at which a significant visiting speaker would address all the new students. We had the privilege of listening to Bishop Lesslie Newbigin, who had spent much of his ministry serving as a missionary in India. I remember thinking what a tremendous sacrifice he had made to do this.

Soon the term proper began and I was surprised to find that the academic discipline required was much more demanding than I'd expected. I found the study very difficult, but nonetheless pursued it with joy. I suppose I was experiencing the phenomenon common to postgraduates: the discomfort of being "deskilled". Most of the students had come from places where they had been pretty good at something – perhaps even expert at it. My discipline had been medicine and surgery. But, now, whatever we'd previously been very good at didn't matter. We were nobodies! I guess the undergraduates experienced this too, but in a different way. Most of them would have been the outstanding students in their former institutions, and suddenly they were among hundreds of other students who were just as brilliant. Such paradoxes exist at places like Oxford and Cambridge, where everybody is very gifted.

In parallel with our academic work, we learned about the pastoral side of ministry. Each of us was assigned to a parish. I was blessed to be attached to one of the most significant, historic churches in Cambridge, Holy Trinity. It was the church where the famous English evangelical Charles Simeon had been vicar. Simeon had also been the Dean of King's College and was hailed as one of the great early evangelical preachers. For me, being a part of Simeon's church was one of the best things about being in Cambridge.

There have been many books written about Simeon, but one of his recorded discussions with John Wesley best sums up the man and his beliefs:

> *[Speaking to an elderly John Wesley] Sir, I understand that you are called an Arminian; and I have been sometimes called a Calvinist; and therefore I suppose we are to draw daggers. But before I consent to begin the combat, with your permission I will ask you a few questions. Pray, Sir, do you feel yourself a depraved creature, so depraved that you would never have thought of turning to God, if God had not first put it into your heart?*

Yes, I do indeed.

And do you utterly despair of recommending yourself to God by anything you can do; and look for salvation solely through the blood and righteousness of Christ?

Yes, solely through Christ.

But, Sir, supposing you were at first saved by Christ, are you not somehow or other to save yourself afterwards by your own works?

No, I must be saved by Christ from first to last.

Allowing, then, that you were first turned by the grace of God, are you not in some way or other to keep yourself by your own power?

No.

What then, are you to be upheld every hour and every moment by God, as much as an infant in its mother's arms?

Yes, altogether.

And is all your hope in the grace and mercy of God to preserve you unto His heavenly kingdom?

Yes, I have no hope but in Him.

Then, Sir, with your leave I will put up my dagger again; for this is all my Calvinism; this is my election, my justification by faith, my final perseverance: it is in substance all that I hold, and as I hold it; and therefore, if you please, instead of searching out terms and phrases to be a ground of contention between us, we will cordially unite in those things where in we agree.[3]

As one formed very much within the Calvinist tradition, I have a great affinity with all that Simeon stood for. I was simply awed to be able to serve in the same parish in which he served.

THE DAWNING OF MY RECONCILIATION WORK

Along with the inspiration I drew from Simeon, and the history of his former church, I was also impressed and inspired by its new curate. David Armstrong from Northern Ireland had just been installed after being a Presbyterian minister for many years. During his time in Northern Ireland he had steadfastly refused to be drawn into the sectarian divide between Catholics and Protestants.

In his book, *Road Too Wide*,[4] he tells the story of how, one Christmas, he walked across a road that marked the religious territorial divide, just to say happy Christmas to some Catholics. The resulting fallout was unbelievably horrendous. David's example was my first introduction to the concept of the ministry of reconciliation. I learned so much from him about the value of taking risks and showing love to others for the sake of peace. Little did I know that one day this would be the all-consuming focus of my work and life.

After three years David moved to be vicar of another church in the poorer end of Cambridge, and I decided to go with him. I was with him throughout my four years in Cambridge and he

---

3   Moule, Handley, *Charles Simeon – Pastor of a Generation*, Christian Focus Publications, 2005, page 79 ff.
4   Armstrong, David, *Road Too Wide*, Marshall Pickering, 1985.

imparted much wisdom to me. One extremely useful piece of advice he gave me was this: "Don't ever read your sermons or use notes; look at the people." To this day I have always observed this practice. During my time at college and also through my curacy I was forced to use notes, mainly because they were checked by our superiors, but once I was a free man I never used them again. It is so important to look into people's eyes, engage with them, read their reactions, and respond accordingly.

A GROWING INTEREST IN JUDAISM

My studies continued to challenge me so much more than my medical studies had, but two subjects that I found thoroughly enjoyable were Judaism and the philosophy of religion. In addition to my compulsory lectures I would often go and listen to one of the most inspiring lecturers at Cambridge at that time, Rabbi Professor Nicholas de Lange. I learned a great deal from him. I admired the fact that he didn't just "lecture", but taught like a real rabbi.

My interest in Judaism continued to grow such that in due course I became a member of Cambridge's Jewish Society. I wanted to deepen my understanding of how the Jewish faith supplied the foundation of our Christian faith. I even began attending the weekly Friday evening service at the local Orthodox synagogue and stayed on for the meal after the service. The Jewish community became as much "my community" as the Christian church.

I continued to feel somewhat deskilled and missed my medical career. Once I could do practical things that had an immediate, positive effect on people and often radically changed their life. Now I would study, attend lectures, and write, write, write! It was a challenge, but I told myself I was working towards something bigger.

Then life changed drastically for me again when I started to become quite ill. Gradually at first, then increasingly, I noticed that I had multiple troubling symptoms of some form of illness, including a number of quite serious neurological symptoms. These began to worsen and I was eventually admitted to Addenbrooke's Hospital. I stayed there for two weeks, feeling very ill, before I was moved into the Principal's Lodge for a short time until it could be arranged to send me home to my parents. I can't describe how awful I felt. A number of consultations ensued and it was thought that I had myalgic encephalomyelitis, commonly known simply as ME.

At my parents', I lay in bed for the next two weeks, feeling so ill that I could hardly get up to go to the bathroom. Long before I was really ready, I returned to Cambridge, determined to get on with my studies. Back at Cambridge I was not well enough to sit through an entire lecture, so my lecturers would come to me each day, courtesy of the Cambridge system in which much of the important work is carried out by means of one-to-one supervisions.

At the time, if someone had told me that these symptoms would remain with me for the majority of my foreseeable life and ministry, I would not have believed them – but that was to be the case. And yet, through God's grace and His strength, I have never been unable to do anything I have needed to do. There were certainly those around me who wondered if I would ever be well enough to fulfil the duties of a curate, but I remain grateful to the then Bishop of Kingston, Peter Selby, who insisted I could do all I would ever need to do.

Meanwhile, the single most significant event of my time in Cambridge was about to happen.

PEACEMAKER

The Christian presence in Cambridge has always been very strong, and was led by the Cambridge Inter-Collegiate Christian Union (CICCU). Every three years CICCU had a big mission. In 1988 the mission was chaired by a good friend of mine, Richard Coombs. Richard lived in the room next to mine and, in years to come, would be best man at my wedding. This year, the mission committee decided to invite Jews for Jesus to participate in order to "target" as many Jewish students as possible. At this point the whole venture began to go horribly wrong, as the Jewish community learned about the plans and was up in arms about it.

As the only Christian who was also a member of a synagogue, I was asked if I would intervene in this crisis. As a measure of just how serious the matter was, the headline of the *Jewish Chronicle* read, "Holy War in Cambridge". How was the situation going to be resolved? What was clear was that we had to get the Jews and Christians talking to one another. This was a lot more complex than it sounds. I took on responsibility for dealing with the issue.

I spent a long time talking to the CICCU leadership about the fears of the Jewish community. They didn't really understand. In their eyes, their priority was simply to get people saved and keep them out of hell. They could not grapple with the many theological questions about the role of the Jews in soteriology.

When I sat down with the Jews, their attitude was very different. They expressed their awareness of the history of their people, not least of how, in the past, they had suffered forced conversion at the hands of "militant Christians". They were particularly anxious about this group, Jews for Jesus – who came from the Christian understanding of Messianic Judaism.

Classical Judaism is messianic at its heart, but always rooted in the future.

What was clear from my meetings with both parties was the possibility of a complete breakdown of relationship between the two. What needed to happen was a meeting of representatives from the two communities who were willing to engage with one another. I managed to call together a meeting of those Jews and Christians who were willing to start a dialogue.

I found that whereas many Orthodox Jewish students were willing to participate, far fewer evangelical Christians were keen to engage, so I reached out to students from a more liberal theological college, Westcott House, and some students from there became involved. In due course, it seemed appropriate to strengthen the foundations of this initial gathering and formalize it by starting a new society in the university. So began a group called Cambridge University Jews and Christians (CUJAC). The founding meeting was held at King's College, Cambridge and the speaker was Rabbi Jeremy Rosen, who was Chief Rabbi Jakobovits's cabinet member for interfaith affairs. It was a great meeting attended by over 100 people – Jews and Christians drawn from undergraduates and postgraduates as well as college fellows.

What we had begun was a unique process of reconciliation. Here was something that had no official place in my study programme at Cambridge, yet it was foundational in preparing me for the bulk of my work in years to come – where I would spend the majority of my time seeking reconciliation between opposing groups. CUJAC went from strength to strength, meeting not just occasionally but up to three times each week during term time. Lectures, text studies, visits to different places of worship, and visiting speakers were all part of our regular routine.

It was only a matter of weeks before CUJAC was asked to become involved with the Council of Christians and Jews (CCJ). The oldest interfaith organization in the UK, it was established during the Second World War by the then Archbishop of Canterbury, William Temple, and Chief Rabbi, Joseph H. Hertz. I decided I should get involved with them and a short while later was offered an honorary role on their executive. That summer the international branch of the CCJ, based in Heppenheim, Germany, was to hold its annual meeting in England. This included a meeting of its young leadership section. Each year, young people from around the world who were committed to Jewish–Christian relations would come together to discuss the issue. Somehow I found myself dragged into organizing a somewhat badly planned meeting at the last minute. I rather enjoyed this, bringing order out of chaos at the drop of a hat.

The ICCJ's young leadership section had an international committee and, towards the end of the conference, they elected people to be committee members for the next two years. To my utter surprise, since I was very new to the movement, I was elected. To my even greater surprise, I was then unanimously voted in as chairman. It was an important step that would set me on the road to my ultimate destiny.

CHAPTER 6

A Prophetic Word

FORMER ARCHBISHOP'S INFLUENCE

My new role as Chairman of the ICCJ was very high-profile. It carried with it a seat on the board of the organization's international council. By virtue of becoming chairman I also got to know one of the most inspirational people I've ever known: Donald, Lord Coggan, former Archbishop of Canterbury and the Honorary President of the movement. He quickly became my teacher and mentor.

I would see Lord Coggan at ICCJ meetings around the world and also visit him regularly in the UK, in Cambridge or London or at his home in Winchester, where he lived with his dear wife, Jean. When in London, we would often meet at the home of two other great friends, Sidney and Elizabeth Corob. Sidney was a statesman of the Jewish community and a great businessman and philanthropist. Lord Coggan and I would often sit talking with Sidney and Elizabeth in their Mayfair home. I frequently wondered why on earth these two men should invest so much of their valuable time in a young man like me, who hadn't really achieved anything. Thankfully, they saw something bigger – they were investing in a future generation.

As I left the house in Hill Street, Mayfair, Lord Coggan

would always take my hand and hold it tight in order to get my full attention. He would tell me how radical leaders of the church needed to be and how I must never compromise in my leadership of our Lord's church. I pray that I have never compromised and I have always tried to keep my promise to Lord Coggan – and, more importantly, to the Lord Himself.

VISITS TO ST THOMAS'

When I was not attending ICCJ events, and despite having continuing health problems, I would return to help at St Thomas's Hospital. I was not well enough to cope with the rigours of the crash team, running around the hospital resuscitating the dead, but I could work in anaesthetics in the operating theatre. Acting as a medical locum meant that I managed to earn quite a lot of money during my Cambridge days and thus didn't have to be a poor student.

During the summer I worked through a well-respected agency. I knew little about the company other than that the CEO was someone called Dr Baker. Many years later, this "Dr Baker" would become one of my closest colleagues in the war zone of Baghdad. It turned out he was none other than Dr Mowaffak Baqer al-Rubaie, who lived and worked in the UK until 2003, when he was appointed to the Iraqi Governing Council, and later to the role of National Security Advisor. In 2003 he contacted me to discuss his return to Iraq, knowing that I was involved there, but with no idea of our past link. I would eventually move into his house in Baghdad and over a decade later we are still close colleagues and see each other at least once each week.

After the summer break I would return to Cambridge, inspired to face the challenges of the coming year. Each new academic year began with a Freshers' Fair. It was here that the many university societies would do their best to recruit new members. In 1989, the beginning of my final year, I was promoting CUJAC and had a great conversation with a young law student, Melanie Wright. She clearly had a huge interest in Jewish–Christian relations and ended up getting involved with us. In a matter of weeks she switched course from law to theology and in time she would become the president of CUJAC.

By now I was involved in some serious research and my subject was "The Role of Israel in Christian Theology". It was an area that brought together all of my major interests: Christianity, Judaism, and Israel. My three years of study at Cambridge had been extended, so I had the opportunity to go to spend some time in Israel, where I studied at the Hebrew University in Jerusalem. At the same time I was interviewing large numbers of Christians about their theological approach to Israel. It was a non-stop learning experience.

Apart from my general interest in Judaism, I had a specific interest in Hasidism, or "ultra-Orthodoxy". The followers of Hasidism are the most recognizable Jews – the men with the big fur hats and ringlets of hair hanging from their heads. Hasidic Jews, however, form a very closed community. Outsiders cannot easily engage with them in order to find out about their ideology. Hasidism was founded in eighteenth-century Eastern Europe by Rabbi Israel Baal Shem Tov in response to the *Haskalah* (the Jewish Enlightenment), when many Jews moved away from their traditional way of life, based on the traditional study of the Torah (Scripture), Talmud, and Mishnah (traditional Jewish writings).

I became friends with an ultra-Orthodox rabbi who expressed his concern about my studying Hasidism at the Hebrew University, which he viewed as being very liberal. He recognized my love of Judaism and wanted me to understand it really thoroughly. To my surprise, he offered to let me join his ultra-Orthodox yeshiva (seminary) in Mea Shearim, the Hasidic part of Jerusalem. I often say that going to yeshiva and marrying Caroline were the two most important things in my life. That is not to say that Cambridge was not influential – it was – but it was at Mea Shearim that I developed my immense love for Hasidism.

During my studies I lived with the Hasidic community and realized how diverse they are. Though the people look similar in appearance, each community grouping has its own name, usually linked to where it originated in Eastern Europe. There are at least fifty different groups, but among the ultra-Orthodox there is a major division between the Hasidim and the Misnagdim, which literally means "the opponents" of the Hasidim. The Misnagdim are also known as the Litvaks because they originate from Lithuania.

While the practice of Hasidism tends to look very serious and formal to outsiders, on Friday night after Shabbat the chief rabbis of each group host a celebration called the Tish (which literally means "table"). The men who attend these events sing and dance like most people could not comprehend! These events are never filmed because they happen on Shabbat, when it is forbidden to use cameras.

So, in this enclosed environment I literally lived Judaism. We could not speak Hebrew because it was seen as too holy to use as an everyday language for communication, so the old Jewish language of Eastern Europe was used, combining German, Russian, and some Hebrew, but the latter only in written form. This was not seen as a kosher community, but as a *glatt kosher* one. In other words, "extra-special kosher". When I finally got back to Cambridge I was appointed as the *kashrut* (kosher) officer to the Cambridge University Jewish Society. It was unheard of to have a *goy* (a non-Jew) overseeing *kashrut*.

But then the Jewish students complained that I was too strict with them. Glatt kosher I was!

I remember the college principal approaching me one day and telling me not to be too Jewish and to remember that I was a Christian. I hadn't forgotten that I was, first and foremost, a Christian, but I was also very aware that my Master and Messiah, Jesus, was not a Christian but a Jew.

As I entered my final year at Cambridge plans had to be made for where I would serve my title. There seemed to be only one serious option: St Mark's Church in Battersea Rise. This was a church plant from Holy Trinity Church, Brompton, just over the river in central London, by far one of the most dynamic churches in the country. I very much wanted to go to St Mark's, but there were questions over whether I would be fit enough, on account of my health. Bishop Peter Selby intervened and said he felt I was the right person for the post, and so I was assigned there.

By God's grace I passed all my exams and I was scheduled for ordination. I was sad to be leaving Cambridge, but at the same time excited, because I planned to spend my summer back in Israel.

Two people wanted to accompany me that summer. The first was Melanie Wright, the former law student from the Freshers' Fair. The other was a friend from St Thomas' Christian Union, Alison Boyle. We went to Israel together and had a wonderful time. It was so different from what my days in Israel would be like in just a few years' time. We stayed in the Maronite Hostel and lived on fruit and vegetables, travelled around Israel by bus, and spent a bit of time lying on the beach in Galilee.

We visited Jerusalem, where we met my ultra-Orthodox rabbi friend. As we stood chatting in the cobbled streets I was very surprised when he told me that he wanted me to meet someone very important, someone who, as he put it, was full of the glory of Adonai (the Lord).

"This person can speak the words of God to you," he told me. I could see that the rabbi was totally inspired by this person and I listened intently, expecting to hear the name of another prominent rabbi. Instead, he told me of a Christian who, like me, had a love and reverence for Judaism. More of a shock than that, this person was a woman, not a man. So this ultra-Orthodox rabbi sent me to meet a Christian lady called Ruth Heflin.

I didn't know who Ruth was, so I tried to find out. My circles in Jerusalem tended to be very Jewish, but I made contact with Christ Church, Jaffa Gate, an evangelical Anglican church. The people there gave me a very different impression. Ruth Heflin was described to me as "powerful and scary"! It turned out that she led a ministry called the Mount Zion Fellowship. They were based on the east side of Jerusalem, the predominantly Arab side, and every Saturday evening they held a meeting. That Saturday night my friends and I decided to go and visit this house in Nashashibi Street in east Jerusalem.

Having attended many charismatic services, I had seen a few things that more-conservative believers might consider "wacky", but this meeting was in a completely different league. The service was powerful, however, and there was a tangible sense of God's presence there. The "powerful and scary" lady was certainly present in force. She led with power. She sang her own songs, prophesied, and preached on the glory of God. Many of those present had flown in from all over the world to attend and many had come simply to receive prayer for healing.

Suddenly, in the midst of all the action, Ruth stopped what she was doing and approached me and my friends. She pointed at me and actually shouted, "The Lord has called and chosen you to spend your life working for peace in the Middle East. Through you the Lord will do great things in this region."

That was it. I can remember thinking, "That's a nice prophetic word for a Saturday evening." Ruth then approached Melanie, who by nature was quite reserved, pointed at her, and said, "The Lord has chosen you to be a great academic leader in Jewish–Christian relations."

It was a remarkable evening and I thought much about what had happened. An ultra-Orthodox rabbi introducing me to a scary prophetic lady who had a razor-sharp word from the Lord could only have been orchestrated by the Lord Himself.

You may have noticed that I have not mentioned my rabbi friend's name. It is because our close friendship would not be understood by the Hasidic community and if this became public it could be very unhelpful for him. Before leaving Israel we visited him again and I told him what Ruth had said to me. I was really intrigued to know how he himself had come to know her. He told me that the reason for their friendship was simple: at heart, Ruth held to many of the Hasidic virtues of dynamism and mysticism. Suddenly I began to see the connection.

As I think about that meeting now, many years later, I am humbled by how Ruth's words have come to pass, for me and for my friend. Melanie did become a great academic on the subject of Jewish–Christian relations. She studied for her DPhil at Oxford, wrote a number of books, and returned to Cambridge to teach. I always maintained contact with her. Latterly, she became ill and was diagnosed with cancer. When she was terminally ill we kept in contact daily between Iraq and Cambridge via email. In the days before she died we suddenly started communicating about that crazy day in Jerusalem. She had never forgotten it either. Melanie reminded me that Ruth did not say I was to spend my life working for peace in "Israel" but "the Middle East". Today I am still involved in Israel but based in Arab Iraq. God knows what He is doing even if we do not! My dear Melanie passed to glory while still very young, but I will never forget her.

CHAPTER 7

Life-defining Events

My years of learning in the ivory tower of Cambridge were over and I entered the real world and began serving my title at St Mark's, Battersea Rise, sponsored by the Diocese of Southwark. Back in familiar territory, I took up this role with a great sense of joy and anticipation. I had roots in this area of south London, having worshipped at St Mark's, Kennington, during my student days at St Thomas' Hospital.

St Mark's, Battersea Rise, was one of three church plants out of Holy Trinity, Brompton, the others being St Paul's, Onslow Square and St Barnabas, Kensington. Our vicar at St Mark's was Paul Perkin, a highly respected man who had been sent out to pioneer the church plant. Church planting in the Anglican Church tends to be different from other church streams. Whereas many churches aim to plant in areas where there is no church, and will meet in school halls and the like, C of E "plants" were all existing Anglican churches with significant buildings, but with seriously dwindling congregations. Members of HTB committed to move to these almost non-existent churches and subsequently the churches came alive again.

As curate of St Mark's I moved into a house on the edge of Clapham Common. I'd never had my own home before so it was a new experience for me. I had always shared accommodation with fellow students or work colleagues and consequently had virtually no furniture, although I had plenty of books. Setting up home was an exciting venture, however. The first piece of furniture I bought was a very substantial desk from the 1920s, which I still have sitting at home in my UK office.

ORDINATION

Besides settling in to my new home, I spent my time getting to know who was who in the church, and before long was heading off to the diocesan retreat house in preparation for my ordination.

The retreat house was in Bletchingley, Surrey. St Mary's, Bletchingley, was the church where Archbishop Desmond Tutu famously served as a curate. I write this paragraph on the day that the great President Nelson Mandela died. I can never think of Archbishop Tutu without thinking of his great brother in reconciliation, Nelson Mandela. Looking back, it seems to me that the place of my final preparation for a life of ministry in reconciliation was no accident. It was the starting point for a great priest of reconciliation and it is utterly humbling to think that I began my service in the same place. Years later I would be honoured to spend time in the presence of both these great men.

The focus of the retreat was private prayer and I remember being inspired and uplifted by the words of the famous ordination hymn, "Veni, creator Spiritus".[5] After the retreat I travelled to Southwark Cathedral where the ordination itself would take place, carried out by the then Bishop of Southwark, Ronald Bowlby.

---

5   Believed to have been written by Rabanus Maurus in the ninth century.

The fact that the ordination would take place at Southwark was also significant to me. It was here, at The Cathedral and Collegiate Church of St Saviour and St Mary Overie, to give it its full title, that the first British hospital was established in 1106 – my beloved St Thomas'.

Around a hundred of my friends came together for the event – former colleagues from St Thomas' and both Christian and Jewish friends from Cambridge. I was fairly certain that I was the only person being ordained that day who would have a kosher reception afterwards! The day sped by and, apart from the ordination ceremony itself, I most remember singing the old Charles Wesley hymn "Come, Holy Ghost, Our Hearts Inspire" and being flooded with God's presence. The Holy Ghost did indeed come that day and inspired me in a new way.

I returned home to Clapham for our kosher reception and everyone was so kind and encouraging. That evening I attended my first service at St Mark's as a member of the clergy and experienced the wonderful, genuine warmth of the congregation.

PARISH LIFE

My vicar, Paul Perkin, was obviously a man of substantial intellectual capacity. I soon noticed that all his sermons were immaculately prepared and presented. As well as being a respected charismatic church leader, he was equally respected among the scholarly evangelical tradition, which had produced such great men as John Stott and Dick Lucas.

I felt very much the student again as I watched Paul go about his ministry with diligence and excellence, and I felt that I needed to aspire to his standard. I had much to learn in a short space of time, but Paul provided me with an outstanding grounding in ministry for which I will be forever grateful. I spent hours in sermon preparation, studying appropriate theological texts and commentaries. Frequently, I would become stuck and frustrated, and at these times I would phone my father in desperation. He was nearly always able to come to my aid.

I loved dealing with the pastoral needs of the congregation – visiting people, preparing for and taking funerals when necessary, and performing other parish duties. We had a diverse congregation that was split between the group of mainly young professionals who had moved from HTB and the local, predominantly working-class African-Caribbean community. But this apparent clash of cultures actually created a wonderful dynamic and I loved being at the church.

On my first night at St Mark's I met a man called Sergio who had come to the UK from Mozambique. It was clear to me that he had some mental health problems, but he had a great personality and I took a liking to him. Sergio was not depressed but schizophrenic and, at times, paranoid. I spent a great deal of time with him and often invited him round for meals.

Sergio was always reticent about telling me where he was living, but one day I persuaded him to show me where he was based. On arrival, I couldn't believe my eyes. He was in essence squatting in a derelict house. There was no water, no electricity, and very few floorboards – a complete hovel. It was also clear that Sergio had no means of supporting himself and received no help from anyone else, financial or otherwise. So that day I took him into my home to live with me.

I would like to say that he settled down at that point, but he didn't. One day I gave him some money to go out and buy food, and when he returned all he had bought were multiple boxes of bird seed. On another occasion I left Sergio alone in the house while I was away on an Alpha Course weekend, and when I returned I found that he had taken my front door off and put it back on the other way around. I eventually managed to persuade him to put it back how it was!

Lots of people thought I was mad to take someone like Sergio into my home, but God gave me such compassion for him that I had to do something – and this was just the beginning of people thinking that my actions were mad: there was more to come!

CAROLINE

I was involved in helping to organize a major mission in the parish that would host Britain's foremost evangelist, J. John. Previously I had heard him speak at a mission at Cambridge University and he was by far the most dynamic, entertaining, and funny speaker I'd ever heard, so I was looking forward to the mission and the plans were coming together well.

One night, as I was preaching at St Mark's, encouraging people to attend the mission and bring their friends, I noticed, sitting in the second row, the most beautiful young lady I'd ever seen. I thought to myself, "Wow! I like what I see", and I did! Immediately after the service I went over to greet her. We got chatting and I discovered that she was there with her sister. Caroline had previously been at St Helen's, Bishopsgate, in the City of London, and had just begun attending St Mark's with her sister, Sarah.

Caroline was a lawyer at one of the best firms in the City. I knew I wanted to see her again and so, being very spiritual about it, I asked if she and her sister would like to assist me with the mission planning. They agreed and later that week they both came round to my house.

By then I knew that I wanted Caroline to be more than just a fellow labourer in God's vineyard; I was falling in love with her and wanted to be with her all the time. But I had a rather large problem: I already had a girlfriend! I dealt with that matter as swiftly and kindly as I could and then, as soon as I could, I invited Caroline out to dinner. I was both relieved and thrilled when she agreed.

I took Caroline to the best restaurant on the edge of Clapham Common. I cannot remember a thing we had to eat; I just kept thinking how fortunate I was to be sitting opposite this beautiful person. After dinner we went for a walk on the Common under a moonlit sky and the atmosphere was just perfect. I stopped suddenly, looked into her eyes, and said, "Caroline, I think I love you." We hugged each other and then walked on, now holding hands. That was the beginning of my relationship with my beloved Caroline.

During the next few days we met almost every day and the following Sunday she invited me to her flat in Clapham for lunch. Caroline cooked us a fish pie. It was a memorable meal owing to the fact that fish pie is about the worst food I could ever be given, but I tried hard to be nice about it.

Our relationship flourished quickly. Caroline came along to a course I was leading at St Mark's called "Landmarks", which provided an excellent introduction to the basics of the Christian faith. We had only been together for two weeks when I was invited to go to meet Caroline's family. Her parents lived on their family farm an hour outside London in a very affluent part of southern England. Their beautiful fifteenth-century farmhouse was stunning and the setting picturesque, with exquisite gardens and a full-size swimming pool. Also set inside the farm grounds was an ancient little chapel, which served the parish, since the village had a total of just five residences.

We spent a great weekend together and I had a wonderful time with Caroline's parents. I was delighted to see where

Caroline had come from. Her father, Peter, was the senior partner in a very significant local law firm. He'd had a radical conversion to Christianity when Caroline was in her teens. He was filled to overflowing with the Holy Spirit and, at first, his family, who were all involved in the little village church, could not understand what had happened to him. Caroline's mother, Mary, was a full-time homemaker who frequently had bed and breakfast guests staying. They were both committed Christians who served the Lord through a variety of ministries. Peter was involved in the Full Gospel Business Men's Fellowship and would eventually become its UK president. He was also latterly an Anglican lay reader.

During the weekend we went to visit Caroline's grandmother in the next town. I noticed that she lived in a very nice, clean area. All the houses were large, detached properties and everything looked perfect. I commented to Caroline that I would hate to live in a place like this, where the streets were more like parks. I was happy living in downtown London. Years later, however, I find myself living not only on this very estate, but in the very house that belonged to Caroline's grandparents!

WEDDING PLANS

When things became serious between Caroline and me, one of the first things I wanted to do was introduce her to my mentor, Lord Coggan, and his wife. It meant a lot to me that he would approve of her, which he clearly did. I therefore thought that I should waste no time in asking Caroline to marry me.

Since receiving my very first student grant, and from every subsequent pay cheque, I had taken the unusual step of putting aside some money for the day when I would need to buy an engagement ring. I set off for Hatton Garden, the renowned jewellery centre of London, to look for a ring and soon found exactly what I was looking for. As I left the jeweller's, in a very good mood, I was stopped on the street by the journalist and television presenter Esther Rantzen. She was making a programme about dancing and wanted to know if I was a dancing vicar. She managed to persuade me to dance down the street with one of the other presenters of *That's Life* and the clip featured in the opening credits of the show for a whole year. I became known as "the dancing vicar"!

I had not only planned ahead to save up for the engagement ring, but had also worked out exactly how I would propose when the time came. It was going to be while punting on the River Cam, between Clare College and King's College, Cambridge. I had been dating Caroline for less than a month, so it was extremely early in our relationship, but I knew without doubt that she was the one for me. I arranged the date and we went punting down the river on a perfect afternoon. Just after we had passed Clare College, I looked at her and said, "Caroline, will you marry me?" She looked up at me and said, "Maybe…" Still punting down the river, I said, "Please, my dear," and eventually she said, "Yes." I threw her the ring from where I was standing at the end of the punt.

The next day we visited her parents and I had the task of asking her father the big question: "May I marry your daughter?" Peter was a bit surprised. He said, "Well, I knew it would happen, but it is rather quick." I agreed with him that it was quick, but he had not said no, so I was nearly there, if not entirely!

Because I was a young cleric, I also needed to obtain permission from both my vicar and my bishop. Paul Perkin noted that Caroline had not been attending the church for very long, so he approved but with certain reservations. The bishop, however, approved totally and told me what he would say to my vicar, if he were in my position. I understood Paul's hesitation, though.

Meanwhile, while these events played out, we had the parish mission to carry out. I had heard J. John speak and now I was in the presence of the man himself. I introduced him to my dear Caroline and told him that we had got to know one another while planning for the mission. Little did I realize that, in due course, J. John and his wife, Killy, would become our closest friends. (Even this book has been written because J. John told me to get on with it!)

The mission was a great success and, once it was over, Caroline and I could begin planning our wedding. For me, the key thing was who would be the person to marry us. I dearly wanted it to be Lord Coggan, and I was delighted when he agreed. To preach we wanted David Armstrong from Holy Trinity, Cambridge. I had always had a strong belief in the ministry of the Word and Sacrament, so having the Word preached, followed by Holy Communion, was very important to us.

The wedding was due to take place at Caroline's family home, with the service held in the little chapel and the reception on the farm – all on the same site. The only slight problem with this arrangement was that the chapel was small and could hold only about 130 people. This obviously reduced the number of people who could attend and so we planned to have a second reception in London, after our honeymoon. We were filled with excitement as we looked forward to whatever adventures our new life together might bring.

CHAPTER 8

A New Life

Our impending marriage meant that I had a pressing matter to sort out. I still had Sergio living with me, and I could not put my new bride through the ordeal of living with a schizophrenic friend, so I had to set about getting professional psychiatric help for Sergio. For a while he was hospitalized to receive treatment; then social workers helped him to begin receiving regular benefit payments and also found him a nice apartment to live in. They even provided furniture for him. Sadly, Sergio's problems persisted, as did his odd behaviour. I went to visit him one day and saw a coffin sitting in the middle of his living room. I asked why it was there and Sergio told me that this was his bed, and that every morning when he woke up and got out of it he was born again. He went on to explain how he thought that most Christians had failed to realize that they needed to be born again every single day and that sleeping in a coffin was the way to achieve this.

Meanwhile, parish life continued and it was a joy to spend time in fellowship with many other colourful characters. Dr Charles Bartley was a consultant physician at St Thomas' and had also attended St Mark's, Kennington. He had been my teacher for a while. His deeply spiritual and dynamic wife,

Madeline, led the church's prayer movement. Even though the relationship between Dr Bartley and me had changed now that I was no longer a medical student, I remained in awe of him.

Then there was an elderly Jamaican lady known as Sister Delilah Langley. She spoke in a wonderful deep, resonant voice with a strong West Indian accent and regularly cooked me rice, peas, and curried goat, which I loved. She had many wise sayings, such as, "Don't worry if you give God too much, because He will always give it back." It was a great quote, which I use to this day whenever I'm preaching on the subject of giving.

Friday was my day off and the day on which I pursued two passions from my former life. The first was that I would rise early and cycle to St Thomas' Hospital to work as a volunteer. This was not "normal" voluntary work, but working back in the operating theatre doing anaesthetics. I never did officially sign on with the hospital's volunteer bureau – I don't think they knew what to do with someone who wasn't there to make cups of tea or arrange flowers. It wasn't a "day off" as most people know it, but I thoroughly enjoyed keeping in contact with my old way of life.

The second was a continued involvement in Jewish–Christian relations. I was still chairing the young leadership section of the International Council of Christians and Jews. As a result, I regularly needed to travel to deal with various issues and, looking back, it must have seemed strange to the church members that their young curate was always whizzing around the world addressing international concerns, not least because I had developed a close relationship with Pope John Paul II and would, at times, pop over to the Vatican to see him. My relationship with the Pope had also developed out of my involvement in Jewish–Christian relations. When I was appointed chair of the young leadership section of the ICCJ,

I also became part of the International Council's main board. Serving on the board was the senior bishop at the Holy See responsible for Jewish–Christian relations. He was taken with the radical development of our work and was convinced that the Holy Father would be interested in it. It was only a matter of weeks before I went to see him for the first time. By then I had just been ordained and was at the beginning of my curacy.

I had several invitations to go and see the Holy Father. It always seemed strange to me to be making regular trips to the Vatican and staying in a private part of the palace where all the cardinals stayed. On one occasion the Holy Father said he wanted to meet our entire young leadership group from around the world. I managed to raise sufficient funds to bring a delegation of young leaders from five continents, both Jews and Christians. I continued to see him until just before his death, when he was old and frail. I may have started by taking our young leaders group to meet him but I finished by introducing to him the Alexandria Declaration Group of chief rabbis, bishops, and imams. How it distressed me to see his physical decline: once we would go walking together in the gardens of the Vatican but by the end he could no longer even walk into his audiences. People have often asked me who are the greatest people I have ever met, and I always say the Catholic and the Protestant popes, John Paul II and Dr Billy Graham.

My curacy was fairly strange!

AN UNUSUAL HONEYMOON

Lord Coggan was so helpful and strategic in the planning of our wedding. I recall his telling me very clearly that I was wrong in wanting to get married according to the 1662 Book of Common Prayer, which implied that marriage was mainly to do with overcoming the lusts of the flesh – at least, that is certainly what it implies. So Caroline and I allowed Lord Coggan to decide what service we would have, and what he chose was wonderful. It turned out that he wrote a lot of it himself.

We married on Easter Monday 1991. We had a great time and knew that the glory of the Lord was with us. Even though it was early spring, the weather could not have been better. One of my groomsmen, Bruce McKinnon, had been converted on the first Alpha Course I had ever led, and my best man was Richard Coombs, my great friend from Cambridge days who had chaired the controversial "Jews for Jesus" mission. At the wedding were also many Jewish friends from Cambridge, so the wedding itself was a symbol of reconciliation. At the reception there was kosher food on offer for all Orthodox Jewish guests.

Lord Coggan did a wonderful job, as did David Armstrong and Paul Perkin. The wedding reception was held in a grand marquee in the gardens right next to the chapel. Afterwards, according to tradition, the wedding guests were expecting a car to arrive to take us away for our honeymoon, but to everyone's surprise a helicopter appeared in the sky and landed to whisk us away for our first night in a country house before we left the next day for a trip abroad.

There was only one place we could go for our honeymoon as far as I was concerned, and that was to Israel – the place that had become so much more than my place of learning. It was my second home. I had decided that our first week together should be spent alone, so we went to the Golan Heights. It was an unusual honeymoon destination, I grant, given that it had been a war zone, but we spent our time up in the hills by rushing streams, overlooking the Sea of Galilee, and it was a wonderful, special place to begin our new life together.

From Galilee we headed up to Jerusalem. (Even though

Jerusalem is south of Galilee you only "go up" to Jerusalem, so up we went!) We stayed in a very special place called Mishkenot Sha'ananim, which in Hebrew means "peaceful habitation". It was a row of almshouses built in 1860 by Sir Moses Montefiore, a British Jewish banker and philanthropist who worked for the establishment of a Jewish homeland. One could stay there only with the approval of the government or municipality. We had a wonderful time in Jerusalem meeting lots of my old friends and colleagues and going around seeing the wonderful sights of that great city.

We had one truly remarkable evening at the prestigious Yemen Moshe restaurant, next to where we were staying. We held a small reception there and a wide variety of my friends attended. I was amazed when my unnamed Hasidic rabbi friend turned up – as was everyone else. Moshe, the restaurant owner, came over to tell me that in twenty years no Hasidic person had ever set foot in his restaurant. It truly was a great honour and so humbling to have so many friends come together for such an important occasion.

One of my great friends who was there that day was Benji. Benji is the managing director of Regina Tours, one of the finest tour companies in Jerusalem. On the day we were married, Benji's wife, Zhava, had given birth to their daughter, Roni. Now, in Jerusalem, I got to hold baby Roni. I loved her from the moment I laid eyes on her and I love her just as much today. In fact, apart from Caroline and my own children I have never loved anyone as much as I do her. To this day, whenever I am in Jerusalem I have to see my Roni first. The agreement is that she is my Roni and I am her Andrew.

Roni has grown into the most beautiful young lady and is one of the most talented pianists I have ever heard. I digress to tell a story about her. As with most young ladies, the time came for her to fall in love. She found a wonderful young man called Omer, who is also a musician. Until I had met Omer I was as worried about Roni as if she were my own daughter. Was he good enough for her? Would he care for her properly? Would he truly love her? When I finally met him, however, there was no doubt that he was the right person and I loved him too. They became engaged and I knew without doubt that it was right.

I often listened to Roni playing the piano and recorded her on my phone. When Roni plays it brings the presence of God, and I would regularly listen to her music, particularly when things were difficult. A few years ago, I was kidnapped while I was in Iraq. I was searching for some people who had been kidnapped when I was captured myself. I was thrown into a very dark room and left alone. I could hardly see anything. Amazingly, my captors had not discovered and taken away my phone, so I used its light to survey my surroundings. Terrifyingly, I could see amputated fingers and toes strewn over the floor of my cell, so I immediately began to listen to Roni's music on my phone and focused on the presence of God. It is amazing how God always knows and gives us what we need. I immediately felt as though I had been transported to heaven and I was later released without harm, calm and peaceful in the Lord's presence.

* * *

After our honeymoon, Caroline and I returned to Clapham. Whereas married life was great, I soon discovered that I was not the easiest person to live with! One of the more stupid things I did happened one evening when Caroline and I were preparing dinner. Caroline was chopping some carrots crossways and I told her that we wouldn't chop carrots like that in this house; we would cut them lengthways, that is the "proper" way. I soon discovered that this was not the kind of thing I should ever say.

In fact, in every marriage preparation course I can think of, this (or something very like it) is cited as a typical example of the sort of thing one should *not* say!

This was not the only mistake I would make; there were many others. In fact, I am still making them, still learning, and probably will be for ever. The most important thing I have learned over the years, however, is always to remember kindness. Part of remembering kindness is realizing how unkind we can be, especially to those we love the most. It took me a little while to realize that I was married to a real saint. Every day of my life I see what incredible sacrifices Caroline makes in order to allow me to do what I do. She never ceases to amaze me.

A NEW CHURCH PLANT

It was not long into our first year of married life that Paul Perkin decided that St Mark's needed to plant out to another church. There were painstaking discussions about which parish the church ought to graft itself onto, and a church on the other side of Clapham was eventually identified.

I wondered who might be brought in to lead this new offshoot, since I was too young to be a vicar and had not finished serving my curacy. Other than that, I didn't think very much about the initiative. That was, until the bishop called me in to see him. He was keen that I should lead this new church. By now I had heard one or two other names mentioned, so I felt a bit caught in the middle of these discussions, but in due course it was decided that I should at least be interviewed for the position, and I agreed.

I was interviewed by the PCC – a lovely group of people – and it went very well. They had about fifty in their congregation and the idea was that I would bring around fifty people with me, some from St Mark's and some from HTB. So it was that at the tender age of twenty-eight I became the youngest vicar in the country – a priest in charge of my own parish.

When the news was announced, people from St Mark's began to volunteer to come with us and soon we had a very good team around us. We decided to call this a church "transplant" rather than a plant, recognizing the pre-existence of the church. It may have been small and struggling, but it was certainly still alive. So the day came when Caroline and I moved from our small terraced house to a very large house right opposite the new church in Clapham.

CHAPTER 9

Several Landmarks

The vicarage of the Church of the Ascension, Balham Hill, was like no other vicarage I had ever seen. At the front of the house there was a large sundial, embossed with the words, "Watch and Pray, Time Flies Away", and near the wall at the side of the house there stood a large statue of Jesus. The house was huge and I must confess that I loved it. It had four large reception rooms, six bedrooms, and four further rooms on the top floor, out of which had been created a self-contained apartment that had its own external staircase. All this space meant that I could have a fantastic study. I chose a lovely large room which was over thirty feet long and it was wonderful having a place where I could house my many books.

My installation at the church was a memorable event, with people present from the Church of the Ascension, St Mark's, and also HTB, who saw this church as one of their first "grandchildren" along with the Oak Tree Anglican Fellowship which had been planted out of St Barnabas, Kensington. During my first few weeks there the church grew as new members were added – not just those from the parent churches, but also some from St Mark's, Kennington.

As I have already mentioned, all the time I was a curate I spent my day off going back into St Thomas' to volunteer, and

I continued to keep up this practice for a while. I worried at times that maybe I wasn't up to the job any more, but I was reassured by the number of consultants who continued to request my services. There were also a number of medical staff who required my presence at the hospital if they themselves needed to have surgery at some point, so occasionally I found myself back there during the week in a pastoral role, not just on my day off. I was able to do this now that I was in charge of my own parish.

The worship at the Church of the Ascension was wonderfully diverse. In the morning we would have a very traditional Anglican service and in the evening a more lively charismatic service. All of the services were great and we witnessed the congregation grow considerably. This in itself was a wonderful sign of the validity and reality of various types of worship, working together in harmony.

I immersed myself in community life and got involved with every aspect of the parish. I became a governor of the local school and the chairman of the local community centre. I also got involved with other ministries in the parish, despite their not being Anglican. What bound us together was our commitment to the love and worship of God and a common desire to see our community come into a real relationship with the Almighty.

Another area of involvement was local politics. I had been interested in politics since my teens and had, at one time, been a member of the Young Conservatives. The parish of Balham Hill, in which the Church of the Ascension was located, was part of the London Borough of Wandsworth – the most Conservative borough in the country. I got to know many of the local councillors and party meetings would regularly be held in our home.

It was not long before I was asked if I would be prepared to stand for election as a councillor for the Balham ward. Neither did it take long for me to decide to say yes, though I was keenly aware that this decision would not be popular with all of my congregation.

It was very interesting canvassing for the election, because I knew a large number of the people I met. When the day eventually came for the vote, I remember wondering whether this really was something I should be doing, or not. I simply put the matter in God's hands and prayed, "Lord, if it is right, let me be elected. If not, then don't let me."

I went along to the count at the town hall that night and watched my pile of votes getting bigger and bigger. I was elected with a large majority. Later, when the party decided who should take on which role in the borough, I was surprised that I was immediately given the position of deputy chairman of Social Services. My particular responsibility was children's and young people's services, which encompassed such important issues as adoption and overseeing social workers for children. It was a big responsibility and one that brought with it major challenges.

I soon realized how complex politics is and the amount of compromises one has to make. I had studied politics, but being a practitioner was totally different. At meetings I found myself embroiled in debates, discussing the intricacies of borough life until late into the night. It was a steep learning curve. It was, however, useful training for the future. Whether I am dealing with politicians in the UK, the US, Iraq or Israel, I am always aware of the two main issues that occupy political minds: the compromises they will have to make and the people they need to keep happy.

GROWTH OF INTERNATIONAL WORK

I continued my work for Jewish–Christian relations both in the UK and overseas with the International Council of Christians and Jews. Just as they had been at St Mark's, the parish council were a little surprised when I travelled abroad and met the Pope. But John Paul II was one of the finest people I had ever met and I loved spending time with him. I will never forget the occasion when I took Caroline with me to the Vatican. John Paul II looked quite shocked when I introduced her as my wife. Up to then, I don't think he had any idea that I was, in fact, an Anglican! He just knew that I was a young priest who was very involved in reconciliation between Jews and Christians. What variety of priest I was hadn't really mattered to him.

My parishioners were also beginning to realize that I was no normal parish priest. As well as my continuing involvement in Jewish–Christian relations, I was becoming more interested in the issue of persecuted Christians around the world. This meant a greater exposure to the Islamic world, particularly through a growing involvement with the Barnabas Fund, and I became one of their trustees. I was shocked by the immense suffering I began to see that was caused by religious intolerance, and it was not long before I began travelling to countries with a significant Muslim community – not just in the Middle East, but in African nations such as Kenya and Nigeria. I became particularly close to the Bishop of Kaduna, Josiah Idowu-Fearon, and stayed with him whenever I was in Nigeria. Although there was a Muslim majority in the nation, there was a significant Christian community, and it was a joy to join with them in worship. At the same time, there were major challenges regarding how to further the work of reconciliation in that nation.

Around this time I was approached by the Anglo-Israel Association to see if I was willing and able to lead a major delegation of church leaders to Israel. There would be a considerable budget allocated to the trip and I would have a lot of say in both the programme and the delegates. This seemed like far too good an opportunity to pass up, and I joyfully accepted it. The resulting delegation was very high-profile, including various senior bishops and other clergy. I shared the leadership of the tour with Lord Mackay of Clashfern, the former Lord Chancellor, and the Very Revd Dr James Harkness, the former Moderator of the Church of Scotland.

As well as enabling me to engage once again with many of the people I had grown to love in the Holy Land, this trip gave me the opportunity to connect with Israel at the highest level, from the president down. Back in London, I began to engage with both the British and Israeli governments on issues relating to Israel and the Palestinian Authority. Rather than treat this as something separate from my life as a parish priest, I sought to involve the people of the Church of the Ascension in what I was doing. On several occasions we had both Jewish and Christian delegations visit us from over thirty different countries. Bishops from Kenya came and Bishop Josiah from Nigeria was a regular visitor.

Despite my growing international focus, however, my parish had to be my first priority. I travelled around it on my bicycle so that I could stop and engage with whoever happened to be out on the streets. The local community was part and parcel of my daily life and most days I would have lunch with the senior citizens who frequented the local community centre.

A NEW ARRIVAL

In 1996, halfway through our time at Balham Hill, Caroline became pregnant. As far as I was concerned, there was no place she could be cared for other than St Thomas', and by my favourite obstetrician and friend Ian Fergusson – the surgeon who liked me for my big hands! Caroline and I went to see him together and he looked after her wonderfully.

The pregnancy went well and the day came when Caroline went into labour. Our good friend Laura Wallace, who lived two doors down, took Caroline to the hospital and I followed shortly after. On approaching the labour ward I spotted one of the consultant anaesthetists I had worked with, Dr Tessa Hunt. She was one of the top obstetric anaesthetists in the country. We had already decided that Caroline would have an epidural during the birth and so Tessa decided to accompany me to the ward and duly instructed me to set up for the epidural. It was just as if I were back in my old role! Tessa performed the epidural herself and though Caroline had a long, hard labour there was no pain, as the doctor had done an excellent job as usual.

Eventually our child was born and we named him Josiah Peter Bartholomew. In just a few weeks he would be baptized by the same person who had married Caroline and me, Donald, Lord Coggan. There we were with our Josiah in St Thomas' Hospital, overlooking the Thames, the Houses of Parliament, and the hospital gardens, the very place I'd been standing when God had called me to leave medicine and go to Cambridge to study theology. As I write this now, it is Josiah who is a student at Cambridge. I will never forget trying to persuade Josiah, whom I always call Yossi, to study Hebrew or Arabic. He told me clearly, "Daddy, you're from the past; I'm from the future. I'm doing Chinese!"

A TRAGEDY

A year later, into the midst of this happy, buzzing life came some tragic news. My brother, Mark, had been very unwell for a number of years and he had given up going to see the doctors at his local hospital because they had never been able to do anything for him. He still lived at home with my parents, but he hardly ever left the house and spent most of his time in bed. Then one day he suddenly went out, not telling my parents why or where he was going. He didn't return that evening as expected. My parents were extremely worried and next morning we informed the police. It wasn't easy convincing them that there was something serious about a young man in his twenties with a nondescript illness going missing for one night.

Two more nights passed and I awoke to the news of the tragic death of Diana, Princess of Wales. It was a Sunday morning and I had members of her family in our congregation. After the morning service we had a special service dedicated to her memory. It was an incredibly moving experience. While this special service was still under way, two policemen came into the church and indicated that they needed to speak with me. I waited until the next hymn began and then went over to talk to them. The news was not good. My dear brother's body had been found, washed up on the shore at Dover.

I returned to the podium and had to continue the service. At the very end, after the blessing, I told the congregation of the devastating news I had just received. People could not believe I had managed to continue with the service despite this tragic event. I asked our precious people to pray with me, and then I had the task of going to visit my parents to share this terrible news with them.

Mark had been ill for a long time, but, nevertheless, when

tragedy strikes it hurts so much and nothing can prepare you for this kind of emotional agony. I arrived at my parents' house and broke the news. I remember nothing of the event apart from all our tears and pain. The next few days were a blur, spent organizing his funeral. I wanted to take Mark's funeral service myself, even though I was worried that I would not make it to the end. But I was thankful to the Lord that He got me through it and the church was packed with our congregation and many of my friends, for which I was truly grateful.

CHAPTER 10

Sent to Coventry

Sitting in my study in Balham one day, I received a phone call, after which everything in my life changed. It was my diocesan bishop, Roy Williamson, a wonderful man whom I was honoured to serve under. We often chatted on the phone, but this conversation was very different. He told me he wanted to send me to Coventry. For international readers, this phrase has a double meaning in the UK, where "to send someone to Coventry" means to ostracize them and generally pretend that they don't exist! But Bishop Roy wanted me to apply for a highly significant and very senior role in the Church of England.

It was the position of Residentiary Canon of Coventry Cathedral, also working as Director of International Ministry and Director of the International Centre for Reconciliation. There was, however, no guarantee that I would be appointed, since it was such a senior role in the church and I was still relatively junior. It would also require a long selection procedure. Yet I felt that God was directing me to apply and it sounded so much in line with my growing involvement in reconciliation work. While filling in the numerous forms and updating my CV, I was struck by just how much diverse experience I had gained in the area of reconciliation.

I arrived in Coventry the day before my interview so that I could look round the cathedral and attend a service there. I found it a very moving experience. I had read much of the story of the destruction and rebuilding of Coventry Cathedral, but seeing it first-hand was totally different. The bombed-out ruins of the old cathedral standing side by side with the new, modern one formed a wonderful picture of death and resurrection.

It was the first service I'd experienced in a cathedral, worshipping with many other people. As the choir processed it was like hearing the singing of angels. I didn't know a great deal about the complexities of the job I was applying for, but I did know that I wanted to be here in this wonderful place. The opportunity to have a job in international reconciliation, at the same time rooted in the church, seemed too good to be true. I sat in awe in the cathedral, thinking about my interview the next day.

On the Monday morning I returned to the cathedral to face a large, impressive panel of people. I didn't know any of them, but they all seemed to be very high-powered individuals. The panel was led by the then Bishop of Coventry, Colin Bennetts, and the equally impressive Provost, John Petty. They questioned me long and hard! They seemed to be rather amazed that, at such a young age, I had acquired such a wealth of international experience. I mentioned to them that I had only really become aware of the breadth and depth of my experience as I had been completing the application form. The interview seemed to go as well as could be expected, and then I had to rush back to London to attend a Wandsworth Council election.

I was at something of a crossroads in my life. My interview in Coventry had dovetailed together with a vote for re-election to Wandsworth Council. Once again I put the matter in the Lord's hands.

"Lord," I prayed, "I want to be either re-elected or given the job in Coventry, but not both." Once again I saw my pile of votes getting bigger and eventually I was elected again with a large majority. With some disappointment I thought to myself, "OK, maybe I *am* supposed to stay here, then." I had had an amazing time in Coventry and it seemed like my dream job, but God knew best.

The next morning, however, Bishop Colin Bennetts called me from Coventry. He told me that the selection committee had unanimously decided that they wanted to appoint me as Canon Director of International Ministry and Director of the International Centre for Reconciliation. I was surprised, after having been re-elected in London, but clearly God had other plans. I assured the bishop that I would be honoured and delighted to accept the position.

There remained just one minor obstacle to my taking up this appointment. Officially, I was too young! The post of Residentiary Canon required one to be at least thirty-three years old. I was still thirty-two and my birthday was several months away, so I had some time to wait before I could be installed in this new position.

So much had happened in such a short time. I had a new position on my local council and a new job miles away in the Midlands. My agreement with the bishop was that I would not make any announcement regarding my appointment until the date had been set for my installation at Coventry Cathedral. The conversation at church the following Sunday therefore revolved around my re-election to Wandsworth Council. I realized the gravity of taking on such a role. If there were any problems with the borough's social services, it would be my fault and my responsibility to sort them out. I accepted this and was sure that I would do everything possible to ensure any issues were dealt with.

For a short while parish life continued as normal, but with

the added responsibility of running backwards and forwards to meetings in a variety of social services departments to discuss many different concerns.

Eventually I received news from the bishop regarding my installation at Coventry Cathedral. It meant that at last I could tell my dear congregation that I would be leaving them. When that moment came, it was much harder and more painful than I had anticipated. I had truly grown to love these people. I had seen the church grow to several hundred and I was involved in every aspect of parish life. As I broke the news, I burst into tears. To my total surprise, many of the congregation began to cry as well. I knew then, if not before, just how tight-knit a community we had become, living and worshipping together. The one consolation I had was that, although I would no longer be their vicar, I would still be their councillor. Exactly how the latter was going to work, with my being based in Coventry, I didn't really know.

Of course, there was one other implication of the move to Coventry to take up a demanding new role. It meant that my days off would no longer be spent volunteering at my beloved St Thomas' Hospital. On my last day there I said my goodbyes and left the hospital with a parting souvenir: my custom-made, size-sixteen, operating-theatre Wellington boots. I knew that this part of my life had finally come to an end.

Caroline was pregnant with our second child as we packed up our belongings and prepared to move to Coventry. It was hard work for both of us, but at the same time we were filled with eager anticipation about moving to a new place and settling in. Coventry would prove to be a shock to the system – a totally different social environment from anything we had known previously – but we greeted it with much excitement.

The day finally came for my installation at Coventry

Cathedral and I was deeply touched by the fact that hundreds of people made the effort to travel up from London for the event. Most of the church came in coaches, along with many members of Wandsworth Council, including the then mayor. It was a truly grand event and, looking back on it now, it marked the beginning of a completely different way of life for me – one in which I would never again be permanently based in the UK.

The very day after my installation, work began in earnest. I clearly had a huge amount to learn. My predecessor was the very well-known, left-wing Canon Paul Oestreicher, and here was I, a right-wing Tory councillor taking over his role. Paul was still based in Coventry and, despite our marked political differences, we got on very well. The fact that he was still around to consult meant that I could learn much from him, not least about Coventry's long historical involvement in reconciliation and its worldwide community, the Cross of Nails. This organization, which worked for reconciliation, had taken its name from Coventry's famous symbol of reconciliation – a cross wrought from three large nails that fell from the roof of the cathedral when it was bombed on 14 November 1940. Around the world, many places committed to reconciliation had become partners with Cross of Nails in the search for peace.

Parallel to my steep learning curve in the field of international reconciliation ran learning about the role and responsibilities of a cathedral canon. Being a canon had no similarities with being in a large parish church at all. Instead of sharing in the worship, I was now leading it, accompanied by the most exquisite choir. Besides that, there were many other different tasks that needed to be accomplished. I had, however, invited two of my most significant staff from London to move with me to Coventry and thankfully they had accepted, so we were already forming a good team.

From the beginning it was not easy to juggle my diverse responsibilities. I needed to travel down to London by train regularly on a Saturday morning to participate in council surgeries and also late at night during the week for council meetings. Aside from all the travel, my new council role presented me with great challenges. At one time I was forced to make some cuts in the social services budget, which was a highly unpopular move. Shortly after I arrived at the town hall one day, I was faced with a huge crowd of protestors baying for my blood. They were chanting, "Fire the Canon!" and had banners proclaiming "Cut church services not social services". I must admit that I went over to the protestors and told them how good I thought their slogans were!

FURTHER HEALTH CHALLENGES

As I settled into my role, it was clear that the scope of my ministry and calling would be different from the work that had gone on before. It was not going to be just a continuation of the involvement in the traditional places of Coventry's reconciliation efforts. God had called me to, and given me a special understanding of, the Middle East, so I was keen to expand the ministry in that direction.

I had not been at Coventry long, however, and had not made even a single overseas trip when I started having problems with my balance. Shortly after this began, I started losing some vision in my right eye. I went to see a local doctor and he referred me immediately to a neurologist.

The consultant neurologist was a very nice man who happened to be a Nigerian Muslim. The fact that I had spent a lot of time visiting Muslim areas of Nigeria was of considerable interest to him. He was obviously very concerned about my symptoms and said he wanted to admit me to hospital straight away for further tests. I took up residence on the neurological ward of the Walsgrave Hospital in Coventry. By now I was developing other symptoms and beginning to feel very ill.

A large number of tests followed, and the consultant made it clear to me that the symptoms could be very serious, pointing as they did to a condition such as multiple sclerosis. During my time at St Thomas' Hospital my one non-surgical allocation had been to the neurology department, so I did know a little about the subject. My stay in hospital proved to be longer than I had expected. I had been in there four weeks when they decided I needed a lumbar puncture to test my cerebral spinal fluid. I knew that this test could be definitive in the diagnosis of MS.

By this time Caroline was due to deliver our second child and she was scheduled to be in another hospital. I desperately wanted to be at the birth and we managed to get the location of delivery transferred to the same hospital that I was in. I had my lumbar puncture and felt very unwell afterwards, with the expected excruciating headaches and an inability to sit upright. It was all rather tough, but I knew it had to happen.

Just a few days after this Caroline went into labour and I received the news that she would shortly be on her way to the hospital. At the same time the neurology consultant was doing his ward round and I saw him making his way over to me. I could tell from the look on his face that he didn't have good news for me. He told me that they had found oligoclonal immunoglobulin bands in my cerebral spinal fluid. It was a conclusive sign that I did, in fact, have MS. I phoned Caroline, who had not yet left for the hospital, and told her my news, shedding many tears in the process. But my dear wife was in labour and about to come to the hospital herself, so I quickly changed my mindset from that of a patient to that of a husband whose wife was about to give birth.

I phoned John Petty, the provost at the cathedral, to tell him about my diagnosis. As ever, he spoke positively about the power of prayer for healing and was very reassuring.

Shortly after this, Caroline arrived on the labour ward and I was taken in a wheelchair to see her. She was doing very well, considering that she was about to give birth and she'd just been told that her husband had been diagnosed with an incurable disease.

In due course, a substantial ten-pound baby appeared, another boy. We had decided on the name Aaron, which pleased me as it reminded me of Rebbe Aaron the Great of Karlin, founder of the Karlin-Stolin Hasidic Jewish movement. The next day our elder son, Josiah, aged two and a half, came to the hospital to see me, his mummy, and the new baby. Josiah, though young, was so emotional about seeing Aaron that he called him his new sister. We assured him that Aaron was his brother, not his sister, but for a while he remained unconvinced, certain that he had a sister!

Two days later Caroline left hospital and I was allowed out the following weekend. Caroline and I had a big conversation about Aaron's name. In the end we both decided that we should change it to Jacob. I was pleased about this too, however, because Jacob/Jacobus was the name of the current Karliner Rebbe, who had influenced me very much when I was a student in Jerusalem. So Jacob it was. Josiah then had to come to terms with the fact that his sibling was a brother and not a sister, and that he was in fact called Jacob and not Aaron! Getting hold of this concept took a while, but eventually Josiah was happy with it.

Despite my diagnosis I was very soon back at work in the cathedral and even back on my pushbike. I was now planning my first overseas trip, which would be to Israel. This would turn out to be a good trip, during which I would be able to renew links with many of my old colleagues. Later that year I was also able to visit many of the centres with which Coventry had long-standing links, both in Germany and across America.

The next major change in my work and life would come in December 1998. Operation Desert Fox saw a combined US and UK military attack on Iraq with a major four-day bombing campaign from 16–19 December, designed to stem the rise of Saddam Hussein's military power. During those four days, much of Iraq was decimated. I was totally shocked by this radical military attack, knowing how it would affect the lives of ordinary people. I made my feelings known publicly to the media and our own government.

At the time Britain had no official diplomatic relationship with Iraq and therefore did not have an Iraqi embassy or ambassador. The only link was an Iraqi interest section at the Jordanian embassy, the head of which had become a friend of mine. I decided that I wanted to travel to Iraq to see if there was anything I could do to try to establish a relationship between Britain and Iraq. It was not, however, easy to get an invitation to visit Iraq. Every attempt I made failed and I was told emphatically, "We don't want you here. Just stop bombing us." It was hard to communicate the fact that it wasn't me personally who was doing the bombing.

In the end, I gathered my team together and we prayed about the matter. The very next day I was contacted with an invitation from Saddam Hussein's deputy, Tariq Aziz, to visit Iraq. After trying many different ways to try to get into Iraq, I had finally turned to prayer. That day I learned a very big lesson about how to conduct my work. Though I might try to use the routes of politics and diplomacy to get where I wanted, in the end, where I went and what I did was up to God. He was in charge, not me.

CHAPTER 11

To the Middle East

Following the miraculous provision of an invitation to visit Iraq, I began to prepare for the trip. I was surprised by the amount of interest shown by the national media in my going there. The BBC gave me a recorder to take with me so that I could make an in-depth radio programme. Many radio and TV interviews followed, such was the fascination with why a cleric had decided to visit what was probably the most dangerous country in the world for a Westerner at that time.

I arrived in Jordan and spent the night in Amman before setting off for Iraq at 4.30 the next morning. In those days there were no flights into the country, as they had been banned under radical international sanctions, so the only route in was via a very long drive, which I was not particularly looking forward to. I had with me a British Iraqi called Riad, who would be my driver. We set off and drove for some six hours to get to the Iraqi border. This was followed by a tortuous three-hour visa transfer process before we could be allowed into the country. The small border reception office was filthy. It had no phone connection, certainly no internet access, and there appeared to be very little organization. It was like entering another world. Eventually we were allowed into Iraq to begin the second leg of our journey.

The first thing that one noticed about Iraq was the state of the vehicles at the sides of the roads as we travelled away from the border. The vast majority of them had broken windows and many looked as if they would never run again. It was the first sign of the effect that the UN sanctions were having on the nation. After that we were faced with many hours of driving through nothing but flat, faceless desert. There was nothing of interest to look at until we got closer to Baghdad. There we saw the towns of Ramadi and Fallujah. Little did I know how significant those places would become in years to come.

Fifteen hours after leaving Jordan we arrived at a hotel in Baghdad that I would frequent regularly over the years. The Al Rasheed Hotel was owned by the Iraqi government. As you entered the foyer you couldn't fail to notice the marble floor, which had a huge mosaic of George Bush Sr embedded in it, proclaiming "Bush is criminal" in both English and Arabic. Upon arrival I was met by a delegation from the "Ministry of Protocol". I had never heard of this particular government department and felt convinced that they were Mukhabarat – the Iraqi secret police. In other words, spies who would be watching my every move and listening to every word. When I got to my room there was a Mukhabarat officer sitting outside, where he would remain around the clock. I presumed that my room was also bugged and there was evidence to support this. It was my first, uncomfortable, experience of being continually watched.

Breakfast the next morning was awful, consisting of some stale bread and grim-tasting tea. It was beginning to dawn on me that everything here was awful. Then it was time for another meeting with the people from the Ministry of Protocol to discuss my programme for the trip. It was made abundantly clear to me that there was no flexibility whatsoever in my schedule – everything I would do had already been decided on by the government. I would be visiting various ministries in the nation, but would begin by seeing a bombed air-raid shelter which had been attacked in the war of 1991. I was informed that this was to happen immediately, so within minutes I was on my way.

THE REALITY OF CONFLICT

What I was faced with when I arrived was quite unbelievable. On the walls of the shelter, which had been horrendously bombed, were pictures of everyone who had been killed. A lady showed me around and she paused in front of a picture of a group of ten children. They were all her children. She explained that the only reason she herself was alive was that she had risked her life to go out to find food for her children. The bombs had hit while she was gone.

This was heartbreaking, but one image will remain with me for ever. In the shelter there had been a lady standing up, holding her baby, when a bomb struck. The blast had etched her outline onto the shelter wall as it killed her and her child. This place was horrendous. Even here, at the beginning of my trip, it was clear to see that such tragic effects of the conflict were being used as propaganda.

The meetings that followed were with political and religious leaders. Each person had the same message: the serious effect that international sanctions were having on Iraq as a whole. Then I was taken to see the state of their hospitals, all of which were in serious disrepair. What was of particular concern was the number of children who were suffering from illnesses such as leukaemia and terrible congenital deformities. I was told that all these conditions were the result of the radioactive depleted uranium that covered many of the missiles dropped on the nation during the 1991 war. Sadly, research by many had confirmed that this was indeed the case. Through all of this I became convinced that a major priority of mine must be the fighting of sanctions and objecting to the use of radioactive materials in weapons.

Eventually, I was taken to a palace to meet Tariq Aziz – a man clearly revered by those who were watching and escorting me. In a short while I found myself in the presence of the man I had seen so many times on television. In that meeting I heard a repetition of the story I had been hearing over and over: how the sanctions were affecting the entire nation, and how the dispersal of depleted uranium had caused a massive health crisis. I was beginning to see that central to any reconciliation work was going to be the skill of building good relationships with people whose ideology was diametrically opposed to my own.

By culture, Aziz was considered a Christian, but I was convinced that no one could work so closely with Saddam Hussein for so many years without being affected by him. Our meeting got off to a good start, however, and I was hopeful that we could form a good relationship. Aziz could tell that I truly cared about his nation and the plight of ordinary Iraqis, and he told me that I was welcome to come back and visit at any time.

Before I left he asked me if there was any way that I could come back and bring a delegation of church leaders with me, so that they too could see what the situation was really like. I assured him that I would try my best to arrange this. I was beginning to get a glimpse of what it was that I could do regarding Iraq.

Fifteen years on I am typing this on my laptop in the back of a car driving through Baghdad. I am on my way to see Tariq Aziz again, not in his palace but in his prison cell. He is now an old man on death row.[6] Oh, how people's stories change.

There was one other memorable visit on this first trip – to the

---

6   See Afterword.

home of the Sisters of Charity. The Mother Teresa Sisters had established a wonderful home to care for children born after the war with major congenital deformities. I was so impressed by what these wonderful ladies were doing to look after these most vulnerable and needy little ones. I wanted to take some pictures, but I was told it was forbidden. I wondered why and was informed that they were concerned that others might use the pictures for fundraising efforts for the home. I thought this strange: wouldn't they want people to raise funds to keep the charity going? But one of the sisters told me, "God was great enough and big enough to make the whole world, so He can certainly make sure we have what we need to survive." I learned so much from them about relying on our Father to meet all our needs according to His riches in glory.

To this day the home is still there and I visit it every week when I am in Iraq, to see the children and the sisters, who have become dear friends. Fifteen years after my first visit it is an important part of my life. The children who are cared for there are still those who, in the main, have been abandoned to die, often without limbs, or with other major congenital problems.

I had one last visit to make in Iraq before the end of my trip, and that was to the single Anglican church in Baghdad, on Haifa Street. The church had been closed down and deregistered by the Iraqi government after the bombing by the US and UK in 1991. The congregation had been made up of expatriates. Now it was totally devoid of any community.

A caretaker, Hanna, had recently been appointed to look after the building by the Bishop of Cyprus and the Gulf, Clive Handford. Iraq was in his diocese, even though there was no functioning Anglican church there. Hanna took me inside. The building was utterly derelict and filthy. Since it had not been a functioning church for about fourteen years, the building had been totally looted and not a single pew remained. Many of the windows had been broken, the organ had been removed, and the only church fixture that remained was the solid marble font. The only sign of life there were the pigeons that lived inside the building.

I was dismayed that the church should be in such a terrible condition. Despite having a caretaker, it was not being cared for at all. I gave Hanna very clear instructions on how the place should be looked after. I made it plain that I would be back soon and that I would expect the church by then to be clean, tidy, and in a good state. I was assured it would be. I remember praying to God that one day the church would be alive and functioning again. I never dreamed that one day this would be *my* church; that it would become one of the largest, most vibrant churches in Iraq and the entire congregation would be Iraqi.

GROWING LINKS WITH PALESTINE

My driver, Riad, and I left to embark on the long drive back across the Iraqi border and into Jordan. I felt determined to begin this new process of relationship building and reconciliation work in Iraq. I would return here soon. Meanwhile, I had to complete my work on the radio programme for the BBC. In due course it was broadcast and received a very positive response. Coventry was seen as the City of Peace and now its man of peace had visited Iraq. Following on from this, I had a discussion with my bishop, Colin Bennetts, and others about the prospect of taking a delegation of church leaders out to Iraq. They all agreed it would be a good idea and were excited about the project.

In the meantime, I needed to visit Israel and Palestine to take forward the work I'd already begun there. Initially, my relationships had been mainly with the Jewish community, but increasingly I was forming links with the Palestinian community at every level. Some of these connections were especially politically significant. One such person was Imil Jarjoui, the owner of the Christmas Hotel in East Jerusalem. Dr Jarjoui would later be elected as a member of the Palestinian Legislative Council and the PLO Executive Committee. He was a key political player. As we talked about various peacemaking initiatives he told me unequivocally that one thing I must do, if I wanted to make any progress, was to go and meet President Yasser Arafat.

This, I must say, did not really please me. Having spent so much time with the Israelis for so long, I was not particularly favourable towards Arafat. I took Dr Jarjoui's advice, however, and asked to meet him. When this eventually happened, we had a long and positive meeting. While I was there I was reminded again that the task of reconciliation and peacemaking means meeting and forming relationships with those who are not your friends and may even be your enemies. But reconciliation is about how we apply grace in the midst of conflict for the sake of a greater cause.

This was the first of many meetings between me and Yasser Arafat. For years afterwards I would go and see him in Ramallah on the West Bank every time I visited Israel. We grew to be very good friends and remained close until his death in 2004. Through him I discovered what it was to love a person who, ideologically, was opposed to everything one believed in.

At the same time as developing connections with the Palestinians, I maintained close relationships with my Israeli Jewish friends and colleagues. This was the cause of some controversy. Interestingly, the people who were complaining about my befriending the Palestinians were not Israeli Jews, but pro-Israel Western Christians. Similarly, it was pro-Palestine

Western Christians who were offended by my befriending Israeli Jews. I realized for the first time that perhaps Christians in the West were another facet of the problem, as they were adding to the division rather than the reconciliation efforts. To this day I still say that what we must do is work towards loving both sets of people, Israeli and Palestinian alike.

CHAPTER 12

Return to Iraq

I had made progress with my plans to return to Iraq and had assembled a number of delegates for the trip. Along with me there would be my bishop, Colin Bennetts, and Peter Price, my former bishop in Kingston, responsible for much of south London. We had also arranged to take Clive Handford, Bishop of Cyprus and the Gulf, and the final member was Patrick Sookhdeo, then Director of the Barnabas Fund, whose main work was to support those in the suffering church.

We flew to Jordan and then began the long drive across the desert, the same boring route I'd travelled previously. This was to be the first of many such long journeys I would make with Bishop Colin, but I soon learned that they were a gift from God. Very few people ever have the opportunity to spend several hours with their bishop and Bishop Colin was a remarkable man. I loved him and grew to enjoy the arduous drive across the desert.

We arrived in Baghdad and checked into the same dirty hotel with its warning about George Bush Sr. We were even greeted by the same spies as last time and told that in the morning we would have a similar briefing regarding our itinerary for the trip.

The next morning our programme was explained to us. As

before, precisely when things would happen we would not know. The only certainty was that we would go first to the terrible air-raid shelter, before undertaking various meetings with political and religious leaders. Eventually, at some point, we would also meet Tariq Aziz.

Our delegation heard exactly the same stories that I had on my initial visit – of the suffering caused by sanctions and the physical effects that depleted uranium had had on the population. During these discussions, it began to dawn on me just how scared everyone was. People were afraid to speak freely about anything, for fear of reprisals from Saddam. Even when we sat down to talk with religious leaders, it was obvious that they were being scrutinized by our spies. Every word they said was written down and, if necessary, could be used against them later.

During our trip, Bishop Colin asked if it would be possible to visit a particular family he knew. Previously he had been the vicar of St Andrew's, Oxford and during his time there some Iraqis who were studying at the university had attended the church. Our minders duly granted this request and we got to meet this wonderful family. Hermes Hanna was a retired headmaster and his wife, Maria, a retired headmistress. They had a son, Gehad, who was a flight lieutenant in the Iraqi air force. After this initial meeting I would see Gehad on every subsequent visit to Iraq, and fifteen years later he is a fluent English speaker and a member of my staff in England. Eventually, after the 2003 war, he and his family were forced to flee Iraq because they were threatened over their links with the West. It may have seemed awful at the time, but we are grateful for God's protection and that this precious family are still with us.

Our trip continued and eventually we saw Tariq Aziz. It was a good meeting and at the end he made it clear that he wanted our relationship with Iraq to continue and become a long-term arrangement.

Before leaving Iraq we visited St George's Church. Hanna, the caretaker, had cleaned up the building as I had asked, and Bishop Clive celebrated Holy Communion there for us.

One final significant event occurred before we left to return home. I was introduced to a man who was a lay reader at a Presbyterian church in Baghdad. He was a retired air vice-marshal – having basically run the Iraqi air force – and his name was General Georges Sada. In time he would become my right-hand man in Iraq and be an immeasurable help to my work there. After the 2003 war he became famous for writing the book *Saddam's Secrets*,[7] in which he showed that Saddam did indeed possess chemical weapons, which he moved to Syria before the war.

* * *

On each subsequent visit to Iraq I built stronger relationships with various political and community leaders. As trust grew between me and the security services I was able to have more say in what I did, but I was never totally free of the secret police spies and never had the freedom to go around or do anything on my own. Georges Sada now accompanied me wherever I went, however, which made things considerably easier.

Each visit included a meeting with Tariq Aziz. On one occasion he said to me, "You have brought your religious leaders here to Iraq; can you now take ours to England and America?" I told him that I could certainly host an Iraqi religious delegation in the UK, but the US was a different matter.

"I don't know anyone who can make that happen," I told

---

7   Published by Thomas Nelson, 2009.

him. He simply turned to me and said, "Ask Billy Graham." This surprised me, but I went away and did exactly what he suggested. I certainly thought that it would help relations if I were to accompany a group of Iraqi religious leaders on trips to the UK and the US, so I began making plans for it to take place. The English side was easy enough and I contacted the office of Dr Billy Graham for assistance with the US side of things. It so happened that Iraq was one of his great concerns, and he was happy to help.

After much logistical work and planning we had a good programme organized for both the UK and the US. It would begin in the States with a meeting with Dr Graham himself. The Iraqi government had selected three of its most senior religious leaders to make up its delegation. Ayatollah Hussein Al-Sadr was a Grand Ayatollah from Baghdad and one of the key Shia leaders in Iraq. Then there was a senior Sunni, Sheikh Dr Abdul Latif Humayeem, who was not only the most senior Sunni sheikh but also the personal imam of Saddam Hussein. The final member was the Patriarch of the Chaldean Catholic Church, Raphael Bidawid.

The trip began with my flying to New York where I was to rendezvous with the Iraqi delegation before taking them to see Dr Graham. I found myself waiting at the airport for hours, eagerly watching flights arriving, but there was no sign of them. Eventually I received a phone call saying that they were all stuck in Jordan. They had planned to travel to America with a Jordanian airline, but the US had made it clear that, if they did, they would not be allowed entry into the country when they arrived. Even though I was certain we had obtained security clearance for them at every point of their journey, it didn't seem to be working. I then heard the rumour that the trip was being blocked by the CIA.

Eventually, I had to concede that I would be going to see Dr Billy Graham on my own. We had a wonderful meeting. I had met many high-profile people in my life so far, from archbishops to heads of state, but I had never met anyone like Dr Graham. He was a statesman of the church and had an incredible warmth and godly presence about him. To this day I have only ever met two people like this, whose very presence has an immediate effect upon one: Dr Graham and Pope John Paul II.

We talked at length about my work in Iraq. In those early days the ministry looked very different from how it looks today. We had no functioning church, no medical clinic, no school or relief programme – I was just working flat out trying to lay the foundations of reconciliation and deal with the effects of sanctions.

We soon got talking about what to do with the Iraqi delegation. Dr Graham had a very wise assistant, Dr John Ackers, who commented that it was clear we had done everything we possibly could and nothing had worked; therefore, the only thing we could do was to ask Dr Graham to call the president, Bill Clinton. At that time, Mr Clinton's affair with Monica Lewinsky had just been uncovered by the media. Dr Graham was reluctant to get in touch with him during this sensitive time, but he could also see that no other course of action would yield the desired result, so he called Bill Clinton and the process of getting the Iraqi leaders into the US had a sudden kick start. But even then it was not without its complications. The delegation had to endure a huge number of security procedures and owing to Dr Graham's schedule we had to move the location of the meeting from New York to Boston.

The meeting took place and we spent a very valuable time together. Afterwards there followed a series of meetings with many different politicians and representatives of the United

Nations. After a few days we flew to the UK to begin the second part of the trip.

The whole venture was an intensive learning process for me. I had no real understanding of the expectations of Middle Eastern religious leaders when it came to accommodation. Basically, I thought that during their stay we could provide for them in the same way that we would have provided for fellow British church leaders. For instance, we began the trip in Coventry, an industrial town in the Midlands. The city did not possess a Grand Hotel, so we had arranged a nice, clean, simple three-star hotel. It quickly became apparent that this was far from acceptable, but the fact was, there was nowhere better to stay – and it was certainly much better than the accommodation I'd had in Baghdad.

Nevertheless, we had a very good series of meetings in Coventry, based at the cathedral. After this we moved to London, where we'd arranged to stay in a very nice retreat house. Again, it was made clear that these men were not looking for functional comfort but for luxury, so at great expense we had to move them to a large, opulent hotel in central London while I boarded at a monastery! Finally our guests were happy and we could continue with our programme.

Just as on the US leg of our trip, our meetings were varied and diverse and included speaking to gatherings of both religious and political leaders. One of our main meetings was at Chatham House, otherwise known at the Royal Institute of International Affairs. The audience were very powerful people and included many diplomats. But the fact was the Iraqi leaders were not really free to say whatever they wanted, because, even though we were not in Iraq, the Mukhabarat had sent spies to monitor what they said and write down every word whenever they spoke in public. We spotted them wherever we went.

Ayatollah Hussein Al-Sadr was the main speaker at Chatham House and after he had finished, the audience was free to ask him questions. I immediately recognized one of the people who stood up from my medical days. Known to me as Dr Baker, the head of a London medical agency, his Iraqi name was Dr Mowaffak Baqer al-Rubaie. As he addressed the Ayatollah he was very emotional and said, "You were my closest friend and I have not seen you for over twenty years!" It was an emotional occasion as these old friends were reunited.

The next significant meeting was at Lambeth Palace, where we met the archbishop of Canterbury, Dr George Carey. I had previously met the archbishop only briefly, and had never had a substantial meeting with him, but this one turned out to be crucial and was the beginning of an important relationship that endures to this day. Later, in his last week as archbishop, he would chair the meeting that produced our historic "Alexandria Declaration" for peace in the Holy Land. Now retired, Lord Carey is central to my ministry and is patron of our Foundation for Relief and Reconciliation in the Middle East.

Altogether, the visit of the Iraqi religious leaders was highly significant in many ways, not least because it had a major impact on how our ministry of reconciliation was perceived by others.

* * *

As the years went by, my reconciliation work in the Middle East expanded to a number of other nations and I began working in Jordan, Lebanon, and also Egypt. Each of these was a host nation for various major, life-changing reconciliation projects.

One such initiative was the effort to facilitate a meeting between Israeli and Palestinian leaders. Throughout all of the Middle Eastern conflict there had never been any serious engagement between opposing sides at a religious level, but I wanted to see the rabbis, priests, and imams agreeing to work together for peace. Achieving this was, of course, an incredibly delicate, complex task. I therefore began visiting the leaders of the various communities to canvass their opinions on whether they thought such a meeting was essential. After a number of initial discussions it seemed clear that there was the collective will to meet and talk. I felt that if a meeting of such gravitas were to take place, we would need a highly respected major leader to chair it. Owing to the nature of the meeting it would ideally be someone who was a Christian, rather than a Jew or a Muslim. I could think of no better person than the Archbishop of Canterbury, Dr George Carey.

On my return to the UK I went to see the archbishop and asked him whether he would chair this important meeting of Israeli and Palestinian religious leaders. It was so encouraging to receive his positive response. I then returned to Israel and Palestine to take things further. I now needed to get the political leaders on board as well, as is usual in such initiatives.

The first person I went to see was Yasser Arafat. By now we had a very good relationship, had met regularly, and had discussed issues relating to the peace process on many occasions. I put the proposal to him in depth. Also in attendance was Saeb Erekat, the chief negotiator and head of the peace talks. It was clear that Yasser Arafat was totally behind the initiative and thought that it was just what was needed.

After this I needed to speak to the Israelis. It was decided that I should approach the Foreign Ministry to discuss the project, not least because the foreign minister himself was also a religious leader, Rabbi Michael Melchior. Not only did Rabbi Melchior support the initiative, but it was clear that he wanted to be actively involved in every aspect of the event.

My team and I therefore began to plan a series of meetings, out of which we would draft a joint statement from all the religious leaders. It was important that, as well as brokering a meeting between representatives of each side, we should make a tangible declaration of our collective commitment to peace and reconciliation. It was clear that we had broad Palestinian and Israeli support to do so.

In every aspect of our reconciliation work I have always sought to work closely with the British government, and so we wanted to work on the declaration in the British Embassy in Israel. Our British ambassador in Tel Aviv at the time was Sherard Cowper-Coles. He had not been in office very long when I went to see him to discuss the project. In the midst of our conversation he stopped me and said, "I know you, don't I?" I told him I didn't think we had met before, and then he said, "We have. I came to see you about a parking problem at our home in Clapham. You were a councillor, weren't you?" It was a strange introduction to a man who would become a close friend and colleague!

CHAPTER 13

The Road to Alexandria

Preparation for the meeting to bring together the religious leaders continued night and day. Having received positive commitments from leaders on both sides of the divide, my next task was to find the right venue. We could not meet in Israel or on Palestinian National Authority (PNA) land – we needed somewhere nearby that was neutral, where both sides would be allowed to go. That didn't leave many options.

One possibility was Egypt. Both Israelis and Palestinians were allowed in and I had recently become friends with a significant Egyptian leader, Dr Ali Al-Samman, a government advisor who was also the interreligious advisor to Sheikh Tantawi, the Grand Imam of the Al-Azhar Mosque in Cairo.

Dr Ali and I travelled around Egypt looking for an appropriate venue, beginning in Cairo. There we also met with and consulted the Anglican bishop, the Most Revd Dr Mouneer Hanna Anis, and Osama El-Baz, who was a senior advisor to President Mubarak. Through Osama El-Baz we were able to secure the support of the Egyptian government.

As usual, I also sought to liaise with the British embassy

in Egypt, so I contacted the British ambassador, Sir John Sawers. John was very supportive and became intimately involved with our work.

After consulting these different parties it was decided that it would be better to hold such an important meeting outside Cairo, so we travelled for several hours south to Alexandria to look at venues there. The consensus was that this would be a more suitable location. We quickly found the perfect place in the Montazah Palace Hotel, which provided all the facilities we would need in considerable luxury. Bishop Mouneer, Ambassador Sawers, and Dr Ali all agreed that it was the ideal venue.

I could see that this whole venture was going to be hugely expensive to facilitate. How does one raise that kind of money? I had always been good at raising funds for ministry work, but to bring together and accommodate all the key religious leaders from both Israel and Palestine was a venture on an entirely different scale. I was reliant on God for His help. I knew that I could accomplish such a task only with the help of the Almighty, but I believed that God would provide what I needed; He had consistently done so in the past. I therefore committed the venture to Him in prayer: "Jesus, I love you so much. Will you provide all the money I need? I thank you and praise you that you always provide what I need."

It was a very simple prayer, but then all my prayers are simple. I have never prayed long and complicated prayers in times of need, always simple ones, with faith. I believe in spending much time with God, but He is our Father and knows our needs before we ask Him. We don't need to have long, drawn-out times of pleading with the Lord to provide for our needs. It is good to remain childlike before Him, especially in times of need.

God had already shown me wonderful provision for

this venture in the shape of a gifted assistant who would be my "armour bearer" throughout the process. Tom Kay-Shuttleworth was a well-educated young man, having studied at Eton and Cambridge, and was a person of great character and integrity. His father was Lord Shuttleworth, a hereditary peer. While I provided the vision and personal contacts for this venture, Tom dealt diligently with all the details, in Israel and Palestine as well as Egypt.

Having the Archbishop of Canterbury present as chair of this historic meeting meant that we needed to secure the presence of equally senior Muslim and Jewish religious leaders. So my next task was to get the Grand Imam Tantawi on board. After several meetings and much discussion he agreed to attend, and this strengthened the importance of the meeting considerably. Following on from this I was able to secure the presence of the Sephardi Chief Rabbi of Israel, Eliyahu Bakshi-Doron. Things were looking very positive. When I eventually returned to Israel there was much joy among my colleagues that we had been able to secure the cooperation of Sheikh Tantawi and had found a suitable venue. The next difficult task would be to arrange a date that everyone could agree on.

It took a considerable time, amid his very busy schedule, to pin down a date that suited the Archbishop of Canterbury, but although he was incredibly busy, he made this a priority and I began to make the final arrangements for the big day.

* * *

Eventually the day came for us to travel to the Holy Land. We flew to Israel initially and the plane journey provided me with the perfect opportunity to brief the archbishop fully on each of the delegates. We arrived in Tel Aviv and were greeted on the runway by the British ambassador, Sherard Cowper-Coles, who guided us through the airport via the VIP route. This was a way into Israel that I had certainly not experienced before.

Once in Jerusalem we met some of the delegates who would be accompanying us and the British ambassador handed us over to Geoffrey Adams, Britain's consul-general in Jerusalem and the man responsible for Britain's relationship with the Palestinians. After a brief dinner together we were taken to Ramallah under heavy diplomatic escort to see Yasser Arafat, now a good friend of mine. This meeting was very productive, and Arafat made it clear what he expected to be achieved by our venture. No meeting remotely like this had occurred before, and he was keen to be a part of the initiative.

Early the next morning it was back to the Israeli side, to be accompanied by Sherard Cowper-Coles to a meeting with Israeli Prime Minister Ariel Sharon and Foreign Minister Shimon Peres. As we waited outside the prime minister's office, Tom Kay-Shuttleworth turned to me and said, "I am just about to enter probably the most important meeting of my life and I'm only twenty-three!" I was only just over ten years older myself, but I sensed this would be one of many such meetings in the future. This was the very thing that God had called me to do. It was a strange and different type of ministry – not the usual teaching- and preaching-based activity that most priests engage in – but I knew that the Lord's hand was guiding me.

THE DECLARATION

For our various meetings we had produced a draft statement – a declaration of our commitment to peace as a group of religious leaders working in cooperation. To cut a long story short, this took many hours of hard negotiation to achieve and it was not without its problems. At one point it looked as though the whole process would be derailed over one point. There was a request for a *hudna* – an Arabic word meaning "calm" or "quiet" – in other words, a ceasefire. This was viewed as merely a temporary measure by much of the Jewish delegation and so was opposed. Then, at the eleventh hour, just before we were due to have a press conference, Ambassador Sawers came to the rescue and we were able to replace the call for a *hudna* with the implementation of the "Mitchell and Tenet accords" – a set of recommendations outlined by Senator George Mitchell, champion of the peace process in Northern Ireland, and CIA Director George Tenet. We had finally completed the First Alexandria Declaration of the Religious Leaders of the Holy Land and this is how it read:

> *The First Alexandria Declaration of the Religious Leaders of the Holy Land*
> *In the Name of God who is Almighty, Merciful and Compassionate, we, who have gathered as religious leaders from the Muslim, Christian and Jewish communities, pray for true peace in Jerusalem and the Holy Land, and declare our commitment to ending the violence and bloodshed that denies the right to life and dignity.*
>
> *According to our faith traditions, killing innocents in the name of God is a desecration of his Holy Name, and defames religion in the world. The violence in the Holy Land is an evil which must be opposed by all people of good faith. We seek to live together as neighbours, respecting the integrity of each other's historical and religious inheritance. We call upon all to oppose incitement, hatred and the misrepresentation of the other.*
>
> *1. The Holy Land is Holy to all three of our faiths. Therefore, followers of the divine religions must respect its sanctity, and bloodshed must not be allowed to pollute it. The sanctity and integrity of the Holy Places must be preserved, and*

freedom of religious worship must be ensured for all.

2. Palestinians and Israelis must respect the divinely ordained purposes of the Creator by whose grace they live in the same land that is called Holy.

3. We call on the political leaders of both peoples to work for a just, secure and durable solution in the spirit of the words of the Almighty and the Prophets.

4. As a first step now, we call for a religiously sanctioned cease-fire, respected and observed on all sides, and for the implementation of the Mitchell and Tenet recommendations, including the lifting of restrictions and a return to negotiations.

5. We seek to help create an atmosphere where present and future generations will coexist with mutual respect and trust in the other. We call on all to refrain from incitement and demonization, and to educate our future generations accordingly.

6. As religious leaders, we pledge ourselves to continue a joint quest for a just peace that leads to reconciliation in Jerusalem and the Holy Land, for the common good of all our peoples.

7. We announce the establishment of a permanent joint committee to carry out the recommendations of this declaration, and to engage with our respective political leadership accordingly.

There was much joy that we had finally achieved our goal. Following our meeting with Ariel Sharon and Shimon Peres, there was one last thing I needed to do, and that was to secure Yasser Arafat's approval of the final document. It was afternoon by now, the time when Arafat had a regular sleep. A few days before this I had disturbed his nap to discuss an important issue with him and had promised never to do it again, but we were soon to go before the world's media with news of the declaration and we had not yet run it by the Palestinian leader. So once again I had to ask for Arafat to be woken from his sleep to see me. Fortunately, he approved the declaration.

It had been incredibly difficult to reach this point. The meetings had been tense and the discussions heated and controversial. The thing that kept us going was that we all knew we had to achieve *something* from these historic discussions. No one wanted to leave the table empty-handed. Our meetings had brought together senior Orthodox Jewish rabbis with senior Islamic leaders, including one of the founders of the Islamic militant movement Hamas. Achieving an accord had been nothing short of miraculous. You can read more about the meeting between the religious leaders in my book *The Vicar of Baghdad.*[8]

* * *

From Alexandria we returned via Cairo, where we stopped off to see President Mubarak. We showed him the final declaration and he expressed significant pleasure in what had been achieved. It was a hugely encouraging sign that there was hope for peace and that we were moving in the right direction. Then, as we arrived back in Israel and were approaching Jerusalem, a huge bomb exploded in the city. It was a reminder of the fact that there was still a huge amount of reconciliation work to do and that the situation remained very volatile.

It was decided that we would form the Permanent Committee for the Implementation of the Alexandria Declaration (PCIAD) and that at least once a month I would chair a group in Jerusalem. There was much work to do and the Second Intifada (Palestinian uprising against Israel) still continued in the background, so we were working against the backdrop of a real crisis. Despite all this we persevered, and kept looking for ways in which we could

---

8   See Part 1 of this volume.

practically demonstrate peace and support. We launched many initiatives to show that we were utterly committed to peace in action. Reconciliation was the only way forward.

CHAPTER 14

Relief and Reconciliation Go Hand in Hand

had had links with the Syrian Orthodox Christian community in Bethlehem since my student days. (While studying in Israel I'd lived in Old Jerusalem, opposite a tailor's shop run by Sami Barsoum, the lay leader of the whole Syrian Orthodox Community in Israel and the PNA, and I used to visit him to have my clothes specially made. I don't think there were too many of my contemporaries who had their own tailor!) I had a good friend called Joseph in Bethlehem, who was a carpenter by trade, just like another Joseph from Bethlehem a long time ago. Joseph had a young daughter, Despina, who suffered from a serious congenital illness called Marfan syndrome – a genetic disorder that affects the body's connective tissue. As a result she needed major spinal and other surgery.

There was no way that Joseph could find the thousands of dollars needed for this surgery, and the Lord gave me great compassion for him and his family. I therefore promised that somehow I would raise the necessary funds for them, which I did. It dawned on me then that the works of reconciliation and relief go together, hand in hand. A demonstration of practical love and care will often open the door to peacemaking. Despina had her surgery and recovered well. Twelve years later she is a close friend of mine and is about to graduate with a nursing degree from Bethlehem University.

Following this, I sought to establish a means of practical help for many other people – mainly Palestinians from very poor backgrounds. One day I asked Joseph if there was anything else that his community really needed, and his response was very clear – they were in desperate need of a school.

If I agreed to help this would, of course, be a major project, but I was very committed to doing whatever needed to be done. At this time I was still chairing one of the sections of the Barnabas Fund charity, providing help for suffering Christians. The Christians of Bethlehem could certainly be seen as a suffering minority who experienced a great deal of hardship, so I took the request to my colleagues at the Fund and they agreed to support the initiative, as did the churches of Coventry.

A major difficulty with any such project is that of finding an appropriate building. I spent a lot of time looking at many possible solutions, but it seemed that there were no premises available that would be usable immediately. We decided, therefore, that we must buy a building and adapt it to the unique needs of a school. Joseph and I travelled all around Bethlehem and the surrounding area and looked at many buildings. Eventually, in the next town, Beit Jala, we found a large, single-storey house with lots of potential and, importantly, room to expand. We bought the property and started making plans for its development.

The resulting school would belong to the Syrian Orthodox community and would be named the Mar Ephrem Christian School, after St Ephrem the Syrian, the fourth-century theologian. The purchase of the building heralded a time of great joy for the whole community.

An architect called Ghrassam, who lived in the community, was appointed to oversee the project and before long major development work commenced. The school began to take shape before our eyes, but not without difficulty. The Second Intifada continued and Beit Jala was far from being a peaceful place. I recall one day sitting on the school's roof, observing the work, when a bullet whipped past me. It was a sobering reminder of the dangerous conditions we were working in. Not long after that, Ghrassam himself was tragically killed in the violence. I was heartbroken. But even in the face of such desperate circumstances I was committed to completing the project, and before long work recommenced.

On one occasion I was leading a Holy Land pilgrimage group from Coventry and I took them to visit the school. Everyone was very enthusiastic about the project and they decided to form a committee to help support the school. To this day they are still going strong and are continuing to support what they call the "Bethlehem School Project".

Finally, with much celebration, the school was opened. It began with just fifteen pupils, but today has over 400. The very first pupils who arrived aged three are soon to graduate, now aged eighteen. The school is bursting at the seams and is now looking to expand to a new site on some land opposite the existing one. It is brilliant to see this dynamic institution going from strength to strength.

Serious reconciliation work must include helping those we are seeking to work with. If we can provide for their needs, the process of reconciliation can move forward more easily. In due course I would set up a foundation to support this type of ministry work and call it the Foundation for Relief and Reconciliation in the Middle East, because at the heart of our work in this region is simple provision for those in need.

AN URGENT SUMMONS

My life and work split between Coventry and the Holy Land continued. Having been diagnosed with MS three years earlier I had been managing well, but one day all my symptoms returned with a vengeance and my consultant decided that I needed to be admitted to hospital for a course of intravenous steroids.

As I lay in my hospital bed feeling terrible, my phone rang and on the other end was Yasser Arafat, telling me in a shuddering voice that he needed my help as his "church" had "been taken". It took me a while to understand what he was saying, but eventually I realized it was something to do with the Church of the Nativity in Bethlehem being under siege. I tried to explain to him that at that precise moment there was nothing I could do, as I was ill in hospital. I hung up, but then a few minutes later the phone rang again. This time it was Rabbi Michael Melchior.

Rabbi Michael's approach was typically direct, in true Israeli fashion: "I told you not to leave last week," he began. "We need you back, quickly!" I tried to tell him that I was ill in hospital, but he simply said, "Come back, now!" I hung up. Two minutes later my phone rang again. This time it was the Archbishop of Canterbury, who also urged me to get back to Israel. I saw no alternative but to discharge myself from hospital. Within minutes I was on my way out and within the hour had arranged to fly to Israel that night.

On arrival I tried to ascertain what was happening and what needed to be done. The situation was extremely complicated. A large group of terrorists had moved into Manger Square in the centre of Bethlehem. The Israeli army had tried to move them and they had ended up taking refuge in the Church of the Nativity. The army had surrounded the church, but did not want to go into it. Geoffrey Adams, the British Consul-General, told me that he wanted me to negotiate an end to the stand-off. It was clear that this would not be a straightforward process.

Both the Israelis and the Palestinians put forward negotiating teams and I was the only person allowed to be involved in both teams. We then spent several days discussing how the negotiations would be handled. It seemed clear that I was the only person both sides trusted. But the problem was far bigger than the present stand-off: the whole of Bethlehem had been placed under a curfew and that meant that, immediately, people were suffering from a lack of food and essential medical treatment. We needed to get food and medical supplies to those who needed it before we resolved our negotiations.

On this occasion I had with me my assistant, Alex, and my driver, Hanna. I decided that we needed to take immediate action about the food crisis and so we went shopping and bought a huge amount of food. We then had the potential problem of getting the food back through the checkpoint and into the neediest areas. But, as it happened, the commander in charge of Bethlehem at that time was a man with the wonderful name of Shmuley Hamburger. I knew him well and it was he who was manning the checkpoint. I explained the situation to him and we were allowed through. We then sought out the neediest people in the affected community – those who were struggling to survive. There was absolutely no one on the streets apart from Alex, Hanna, and myself.

Just as the local community was suffering, so were the priests who ran the Church of the Nativity complex. No supplies had been allowed in. With Shmuley Hamburger's help, I managed to get food to them. Shmuley and his troops delivered it themselves. I asked Shmuley if the priests had been happy with their food and he told me there had been a problem: I had forgotten to give them some lemons. I made a mental note that, if I ever distributed food to the people of the Middle East again, I would remember the lemons!

The negotiations were long and difficult. I was not the only expat in on them: there was another Englishman helping, also sent by the Consul-General. His name was Alistair and I was told he also worked for the Foreign and Commonwealth Office. Alistair quickly made it clear to me that he was not FCO staff but actually worked for MI6, and was one of their top hostage negotiators. We became great friends and I learned a lot from him. Hostage negotiation was something that would become a regular feature of my future reconciliation work, so, looking back now, I am grateful for Alistair's wisdom and insight.

A base for negotiations was set up in the home of the Palestinian Minister of Tourism in Beit Jala, next to Bethlehem. The negotiations involved detailed discussions about what would happen to those presently controlling the church. We had one man in the church with whom we were allowed to communicate, and then representatives of the Israeli military outside. The talks went on for days. The situation became seriously inflamed when we discovered that some of the hostages had been killed and their bodies stored in the Grotto of the Nativity. So then we had to negotiate to be allowed to retrieve the victims' bodies. Eventually this happened and then we resumed talks to get everyone freed.

One of the most difficult aspects of the whole operation was finding out the identities of the people inside the church. Once we discovered who they were, the Israeli army carried out a full intelligence briefing on each person. There were about 200 people in the complex, but around twenty of them were revealed to have significant terrorist histories. Of all the people inside, some would be allowed to return to their homes in the

West Bank and others would be expelled to Gaza, but these twenty or so would need to go to other nations. We were now faced with the immense challenge of finding countries willing to admit known terrorists as residents. As you can imagine, countries were not queuing up to take them in.

I did, however, have a close relationship with a man called Miguel Moratinos, who at that time was the European Union's representative in the Holy Land. I therefore started the process of working through Miguel to try to find some European nations willing to take in some terrorists. It was a challenge that drove me to prayer, because only with God are such things possible. As in so much of my work, supernatural intervention is needed to get things done. Things that, on the face of it, seem utterly impossible.

A few countries were found, such as Spain, Italy, and Ireland. It looked as if we were finally getting to the end of the negotiations. Thirty-eight days had gone by and the hostages were still being held in the church. Finally, arrangements were made for each group of people to be taken by coach to a specific destination. We were nearly there. The transportation was due to arrive in the early hours of the morning and had been arranged by the US embassy. We expected the handover to happen at about 2 a.m. We all stood waiting in Manger Square, but we were still there at 7 a.m. with no sign of anything happening, and had to give up.

Another day of negotiations took place to see what had gone wrong and what we could do now. Then in the early hours of the next morning we were back again, waiting for the hostages to come out. This time it happened as planned. After almost forty days the siege was over and the curfew was lifted. I could return to the UK.

Though it was wonderful to get back home to my family, I suddenly realized how traumatized I had been by this whole event. I had been immersed in this complex process for over a month and hadn't had time to process it for myself. Then, as I walked down the street in Coventry, I was stunned by the number of people who stopped to congratulate me on what I had achieved. I hadn't realized that the siege had been constantly in the media and had been very high-profile.

To my even greater surprise, a local boy told me that I must come to his house and see his bedroom. I went round to visit his family and saw that his bedroom walls were plastered with newspaper coverage of the event. I looked through the various reports and understood the magnitude and seriousness of what had taken place. I congratulated this young man on his spectacular collection, made my excuses, and left for home. As I walked back, I burst into tears and all my suppressed emotions came flooding out. I realized that from now on my life would be a bittersweet mixture of agony and ecstasy, of terrible lows as well as joyous highs. I wondered whether I could really live with such trauma.

My dear friend Bishop Colin Bennetts realized the enormity of what I had experienced. I confess that I went to see him unannounced, held him tight, and once again cried and cried. He understood the intensity of the pain I was feeling and provided great love and direction. He suggested that I go to see a professional counsellor in the diocese. I did, but to be honest they could not understand what I had experienced at all. This whole experience, however, helped me to see my own fallibility and vulnerability – and how much I must rely on God for His grace and power in my life. Apart from Him, I could do nothing.

CHAPTER 15

Back to Coventry

I spent a total of seven years in Coventry. It was a highly varied and always intense experience, during which I was privileged to travel the world and see things I never dreamed I'd see. But there was one challenge I faced that was perhaps greater than any other. It was not grasping incredibly complex political and religious relationships or even having to deal with terrorists. Rather, it was the challenge of travelling so much while my two boys grew up. Constantly being on the move is a wrench, but I accept the responsibilities of my role and so have to live with its consequences. Thankfully, my boys are blessed with an incredible mother in Caroline and whenever I am at home we always try to make the best of our time together. Both my boys are wonderful characters and there are numerous stories I could tell about them from this period of my life, but a few stand out in my mind.

My installation at Coventry Cathedral had brought together friends and family from far and wide. Caroline's wider family had historic links to the West Midlands, though we didn't know too much about them. But, as is inevitable at such events, people talked about their families and it wasn't long before we had discovered a lot about its many branches. Surprisingly, we had a historic connection to the Chamberlain family. Joseph Chamberlain was a well-respected politician and held the offices of both Chancellor of the Exchequer and Colonial Secretary. Less accepted was his son, Neville Chamberlain, prime minister before Winston Churchill. Neville Chamberlain was famous for declaring "Peace in our time" following the Munich Agreement of 1938, only for the nation to be thrust into war less than a year later.

I mention this because when my older boy, Josiah, was about seven years old, I asked him one day what he wanted to do when he grew up. He was very clear about his life plan: "I'm going to go to Cambridge and then I will leave and become prime minister." I enquired whether there would be a gap between his leaving Cambridge and starting work as prime minister, and he assured me there would not. Then he told me that since we'd never had a good prime minister in our family (referring to Chamberlain), he was going to be the first one! He had absorbed this information from the various conversations we'd had at my installation ceremony.

My boys have never known what it is like to have a father who does not travel all the time, so from the earliest age my frequent absence was completely normal for them. On one occasion I had been back home for about a week when Josiah observed, "Well, Daddy, it is time you went back to work now!" He had no concept of the fact that I could be working and still be in the country at the same time.

During the boys' early years I was still able to do most things that fathers do – such as participate in their children's sports days. I remember once taking part in a race where the fathers had to run carrying their sons. I was overjoyed when Josiah and I won. Sadly, it was to be the last sports-day race I would take part in.

When away, I would speak to Caroline and the boys every day and they would inform me about what they had been studying in school. One day Josiah told me that he had been learning about stamps and commented that the Queen's head appeared on every stamp. Next came the question: would I take him to meet the Queen one day? This is not the type of request that most fathers are able to consider, let alone grant, but I promised Josiah that if I ever had the chance to meet the Queen I would do my best to ensure that he came with me. It was nothing short of a miracle that the very next day I received an invitation from Buckingham Palace to attend a lunchtime reception with the Queen. I phoned to accept and asked if it was possible for me to bring my young son, rather than my wife. I was told that the Queen loved children and that would be fine.

Next I had to speak to Josiah's school and ask permission for him to have a day off to meet the Queen. It was a rather strange conversation that I'm sure the school staff didn't have every day, but permission was granted on one condition – that he go wearing his smart school uniform. So, when the day came, Josiah travelled into London with me, correctly dressed and very excited. For the previous two weeks he had been practising how to say "Good morning, Your Majesty" and shake hands correctly. Accompanying us on the trip would be the Cardinal Archbishop of Westminster, so Josiah had also practised saying, "Greetings, Your Eminence" – which was altogether trickier for a small boy to accomplish.

At the lunch, Josiah was very taken with the idea of being inside a palace and eventually the Queen came along to greet each of her guests. She spoke to me and then I introduced her to Josiah. He spoke to her beautifully, bowed, and shook her hand in the way he'd practised. Her Majesty was obviously impressed and told him that he was very good at shaking hands. She then said that her grandchildren were not as good at shaking hands with people and she had to tell them that people had sweets in their hands in order to persuade them to do it. Josiah assured her that he was not like that!

As we left Buckingham Palace after the wonderful lunch and meeting, Josiah shocked me by asking if we could go to McDonald's next. I told him he'd just had a very nice lunch with the Queen.

"I know, Daddy," he responded. "It was very nice going to the Palace, but they didn't have any chicken nuggets or chips." I realized that for a young boy, meeting the Queen was all very well, but if she couldn't provide chicken nuggets and chips…!

My younger boy, Jacob, grew up with a bizarre understanding of international affairs for someone his age. Even before he was five he had an awareness of the kind of issues his daddy was involved in. In particular, like me, Jacob was fascinated with the Middle East. I remember when it was just coming up to his fifth birthday. He had already been attending school for a year and I asked him who he would like to have come to his birthday party. He responded immediately by saying he wanted my "friend" to come. I asked him which particular friend he meant, though I had my suspicions, and he confirmed that it was Yasser Arafat, whom Jacob always referred to as "Yes Sir Arafat". Each night before bed, Jacob would say his prayers and, without fail, pray for, "Mummy, Daddy, and Yes Sir Arafat." I had to tell Jacob that it might be difficult for Yasser Arafat to come to his party at the moment, as he was locked up in his compound and could not go anywhere. But I said that Jacob should write Arafat a letter and I would give it to him the next week, when I was due to go back to the Holy Land.

The next week was a difficult one in the Middle East. The Second Intifada continued and most of the West Bank was off limits owing to increased violence. I was the only person allowed into Ramallah to visit Yasser Arafat. I typically met him for about an hour each week, but this day our meeting went on for much longer, covering a lot of political and religious ground. After three hours I was just about to leave when I suddenly remembered Jacob's letter, which was essentially an invitation to his party. I gave it to Arafat and relayed the story of how Jacob had so wanted him to come to his party, and how he prayed for him every single night.

Arafat was visibly moved by this and began to cry. "He really loves me," he said over and over, and I assured him that Jacob did indeed care deeply about him. Then Arafat called over one of his aides and sent him to fetch one of his *keffiyeh* – the distinctive patterned headdresses he always wore in public. He wrote on it in red pen, "To Jacob from Yasser Arafat".

I handed the *keffiyeh* to Jacob on his birthday and his eyes widened.

"This must be from Yes Sir Arafat," he exclaimed, and I confirmed it was. His other birthday present was a green army uniform, so he put on both items and looked just the part. However, the look wasn't quite satisfactory for Jacob. He clearly wanted to look *exactly* like Arafat, so he took the somewhat dramatic step of drawing a beard on his face with a thick marker pen! After this, the *keffiyeh* came out for successive Christmas nativity plays.

From this time forward, during my meetings with Yasser Arafat, he would frequently call Jacob for a chat. It was quite bizarre seeing this renowned international figure talking to a little boy in England. One Saturday evening, while I was back in England myself, Arafat phoned me at home. He said he wanted to have a chat with Jacob before he spoke with me. I called from my study, "Jacob, President Arafat's on the phone and wants to talk to you." Jacob shouted back, "Tell him I'm busy and I will call him later." He was watching *The Simpsons*.[9] Well, that's a child's perspective of what is important!

GROWTH OF THE INTERNATIONAL CENTRE FOR RECONCILIATION

Meanwhile, the work of the International Centre for Reconciliation (ICR) expanded in many different directions, meaning that my role as director grew ever more demanding. In order to cope with these demands, I increasingly leaned upon the Lord.

Whenever I was not travelling I shared in the running of one of Britain's most significant cathedrals and learned much from taking part in the daily liturgy, often accompanied by Coventry's outstanding choir. Some people think that sharing in such "professional" worship is far removed from a real encounter with the Almighty, but nothing could be further from the truth.

Time and again our Lord met with me in supernatural ways. He would speak to me and impart incredible wisdom for the situations I was involved in. I would be kneeling quietly in my stall, in the midst of exquisite worship, and God would tell me what He wanted to do in Iraq, Israel, Palestine, or northern Nigeria. The words from the Communion liturgy became my reality: "The Lord is here; His Spirit is with us." Today, writing this in Baghdad, I declare this truth several times a day. It is God's very presence that sustains us through the most difficult and challenging of circumstances.

Although the Middle East remained the central focus of my work for the ICR, other areas of the world opened up

---

9   *The Simpsons* is an American animated sitcom created by Matt Groening for the Fox Broadcasting Company.

that were also experiencing conflict. This was chiefly through the Community of the Cross of Nails (CCN), a worldwide community committed to reconciliation, established in 1940. In post-war years it was significant in healing the rifts between countries that had been in conflict, such as Britain and Germany. During my time in Coventry there were over 200 CCN centres around the world and some of my time was taken up visiting them.

Many of the European centres had either once been at war with the UK or caught up in the battles surrounding Communism. But other centres were being established in areas of new conflict, such as northern Nigeria – not least in the diocese of Kaduna, where my friend Josiah Idowu-Fearon was bishop.

Northern Nigeria was the scene of a growing conflict between Muslims and Christians. Our ICR team thought it wise for me to visit there to ascertain what might be done to establish a process of reconciliation. When I arrived, the situation was much more tense than I'd imagined. Hundreds were being killed on each side and both churches and mosques were being ransacked and destroyed.

I soon became friends with a Christian pastor called James, who was working closely with an imam called Ashafa. Together they had formed the Muslim–Christian Dialogue Forum to conduct talks between the conflicting groups and make an attempt at reconciliation. I was invited into this group and that was the beginning of a long, complex process within northern Nigeria.

On one of my early visits I was joined by a contact from my former Wandsworth Council days, fellow councillor Lola Ayorinde. Lola was a Nigerian Muslim and, since the days when we'd served together, had risen to the position of Mayor of Wandsworth. The fact that we were prepared to travel together into this place of conflict spoke loudly of our mutual commitment to peace. It also raised a considerable amount of interest among the locals – the fact that a Nigerian lady was the mayor of a part of London.

We stayed with Bishop Josiah. As was our practice, we divided our time between involvement in the serious political aspects of conflict negotiation and engaging with and supporting local churches. The churches were delighted to see us and were deeply concerned about the nature of the conflict. What was clear was that many Christians were involved in the conflict themselves and didn't intend to take lying down the aggression being shown towards them. There were as many who were prepared to fight back as there were committed to turning the other cheek.

Meetings between Muslim and Christian leaders were intense and inflammatory. Churches and mosques had been destroyed, religious seminaries burned to the ground, on both sides of the divide. We started from the ground up to try to establish how everyone might work together, to respect and learn from one another. The bridge that had been established by Pastor James and Imam Ashafa was a critical aspect of the discussions.

Over the following months I returned to Kaduna many times and we began working towards drafting a declaration for peace called the Kaduna Declaration. It was based on the Alexandria Declaration, but contextualized for northern Nigeria. In due course, after many meetings at both a local and a city-wide level, it was decided that the words of the declaration should be set in marble and stone and placed on the main roundabout at the entrance to the city. Several months after my first visit there, this symbol of reconciliation was unveiled by the state governor in an atmosphere of great joy.

* * *

While the ICR's reconciliation work became increasingly complex in different regions of the world, we began to think about how to marry up these different initiatives. Coventry did not have a partner diocese, so with Bishop Colin Bennetts' blessing it was decided that there should be formed a three-way partnership between the Diocese of Coventry, the Syrian Orthodox Diocese of Jerusalem and the Middle East, and the Diocese of Kaduna in Nigeria. These two dioceses were already Coventry's closest partners so it seemed appropriate, if all three bishops agreed, that a formal link be established.

After much discussion, everyone agreed that the official partnership should go ahead and a date and location were set for a celebration to mark the event. This would take place in St Mark's Syrian Orthodox Monastery Church in Jerusalem. St Mark's is the mother church of the Syrian Orthodox Church and the oldest church in the world. It stands on the ancient site of the house of Mary, mother of St Mark the Evangelist (Acts 12:12), according to a sixth-century inscription which was discovered in 1940, and it is traditionally held to be the place where the Last Supper took place in an upper room. That room is no longer above ground but underground, since the streets of first-century Jerusalem were at least twelve feet lower than they are today.

The ceremony eventually held there was a remarkable event. It was a hugely emotional moment when the Coventry cross of nails was placed on the altar in the ancient chapel of the upper room. To this day the cross of nails remains in this most hallowed site. When in Jerusalem I often just go and stand in this holy place and gaze at the cross, wrought from nails from the ruins of Coventry Cathedral, and in it see my whole life summed up.

As the work of the ICR became increasingly intense and hectic, it became clear that it was all too much for one person to handle. Bishop Colin was very happy with the way the work had developed, but thought that I needed another senior member of staff to work with me. Bishop Colin asked me if there was anyone in the diocese I would consider inviting on board as a co-director. There was one person I respected greatly, who had accompanied me on a previous trip to the Middle East – the vicar of Southam, Warwickshire, none other than Justin Welby, the present Archbishop of Canterbury. I could think of no one better suited to the role, and Bishop Colin agreed. In just a few weeks Justin had joined me as co-director of the ICR and it was wonderful having my friend share the work alongside me.

To start with, Justin travelled with me to visit all of our projects in Nigeria and the Middle East. Immediately he was at ease communicating with all the diverse groups we were working with, Jews, Arabs, and Nigerian Muslims and Christians, as well as our long-term colleagues in Europe and the US. After working together closely for a time, we knew that we must divide the work between us. It was clear that, owing to my historic and extensive connections in the Middle East, I should continue that work. In Nigeria the work was not as well established and Justin had already experienced working in Nigeria during his time in the oil industry, so it made sense for him to take the lead there.

Shortly after Justin came on board I felt it was time to take a long-overdue sabbatical. In truth, it wasn't a typical sabbatical – it was not to rest or do less work. Instead, I returned to my beloved Cambridge to take up residence as a visiting fellow at Clare College. I suppose it was a sabbatical in the sense that I was able to have a complete break from my usual work and focus on something different. It was wonderful to be back in the academic hothouse. I divided my time between teaching, studying, writing, and preaching. While there, I was able to write my first book about ministering in Iraq and my call to the ministry of reconciliation.

I remember one day standing up to give a lecture and looking out at the audience. I had been taught by the majority of the people I was about to address and I found it a very humbling experience. All I could think was, I am who I am today because of these great people.

CHAPTER 16

Brought Back to Life

After my first visit to Iraq, whenever I travelled there I made sure I paid a visit to St George's Anglican Church. I mentioned in Part 2, Chapter 11 that the church had been looted and was lying derelict. Not a pew remained in the building – it was empty apart from the heavy marble font. There was obviously no market for fonts in Iraq.

The church had formerly been an active place of worship, serving the expat community until the Iraqi invasion of Kuwait in 1991. After that, Saddam Hussein had shut it down, because it had always been known as "the English church". The church was indeed English: the land and property belonged to the British embassy, and therefore counted as a slice of British soil.

St George's was established in 1864 when missionaries from Christ Church, Jaffa Gate – the Anglican church located inside the Old City of Jerusalem – went to Baghdad. They began a ministry which eventually grew into St George's Church. It is significant to me that St George's came out of the ministry of Christ Church, Jaffa Gate, a church that is very important to me. Christ Church functions under the patronage of the Church's Ministry among Jewish People (CMJ), of which I happen to be vice-president. In so many ways my ministry began in Jerusalem and has ended up in Baghdad. I give the Lord thanks for the historical link between these two places that I love.

Clive Handford, the former Bishop of Cyprus and the Gulf, had put in place Hanna the caretaker to look after the building, and with the oversight of my aide in Iraq, Georges Sada, it was in much better shape by the time I visited it with a delegation of bishops. In a sense, St George's first official service took place on that trip with bishops Colin Bennetts, Peter Price, and Clive Handford. We celebrated Holy Communion and I prayed, "One day, Lord, may this church come alive again." So bleak was the situation for Christians in Iraq that essentially I was asking for the miracle of resurrection. But as we continued to pray I was struck again by that phrase from the Eucharistic Prayer, "The Lord is here; His Spirit is with us", and I thought, "Well, my God is rather good at resurrections!"

Justin Welby accompanied me to Iraq on my first visit there after the outbreak of war in 2003. I wanted to open St George's officially and felt strongly that somehow God would restore it to its former glory. We planned a service during which Justin would celebrate Communion and I would lead and preach. We invited Archbishop Mar Addi, leader of the Assyrian Church, to reconsecrate the church. We also invited John Sawers, British ambassador in the Coalition Provisional Authority, to read one of the lessons, along with one of the US Army generals. There were still no pews in the building, but we had managed to buy enough plastic garden chairs for everyone to be seated.

The reading that day was a hugely significant one, from Haggai 2:9 (KJV):

> *The glory of this latter house shall be greater than of the former,*
> *saith the LORD of hosts: and in this place will I give peace, saith*
> *the LORD of hosts.*

These words are inscribed on a tablet set into the face of the ruined tower of Coventry's old cathedral. Suddenly I could see their prophetic relevance in the place I was currently standing – St George's, ruined by war, just like Coventry, but with a more glorious future ahead. Was God telling me that St George's would be greater than it had ever been in the past? Greater than in the vibrant days of its foundation? I believed that was exactly what God was saying.

We held services for the following two weeks and people began to attend the church. Then the violence outside the secure Green Zone began to get worse, meaning that it was too risky for people to venture out to St George's to worship, and our numbers immediately diminished.

Determined to see the ministry of St George's resurrected, however, we moved our service to the chapel of the Republican Palace and into Saddam's former throne room. Interestingly, from that moment the local Iraqi Christians began to perceive that we were less affiliated with the Coalition than they had thought, and began to attend our services. The church grew quite rapidly from then on, multiplying by almost a hundred new people each week. After it had lain dormant for so long, suddenly we had a viable Iraqi church filled with people from every possible Iraqi denomination. There were no Anglicans, but there were Chaldeans, Assyrians, Armenians, Syrian Orthodox, Assyrian Catholics, and Presbyterians. At no time did we ever try to convert them to Anglicanism – we just made it clear to people that we were Christians and that we respected their immense spiritual heritage.

I had a great deal to learn about the Christian heritage of Iraq and it was a steep but exciting learning curve. I took our Anglican liturgy and contextualized it, taking account of Iraqi culture, so that it would be understandable to the average Iraqi.

The hugely significant words from the Eucharistic Prayer, "The Lord is here; His Spirit is with us", became, in Arabic, *Allahu ma'ana*: "the Lord is here". This was the beginning of our Iraqi church.

Meanwhile, I continued to establish the wider work of reconciliation in the nation. A huge help in this was the head of the British Mission to Baghdad, a wonderful, experienced diplomat called Christopher Segar. He headed up what was called the BOB House (British Office Baghdad), which in essence functioned as a British embassy. Christopher was a very helpful diplomatic colleague, but in due course also became a good friend. He would later become one of the trustees of my Foundation.

Christopher helped us immeasurably with our work in Iraq by always providing for us the right contacts at the right time. Although Georges Sada accompanied me constantly as I travelled around, I really needed another person with a diplomatic background who was able to translate for me. Christopher found me just the right person in Ambassador Sadoun al-Zubaydi. He had been Iraq's ambassador to Indonesia, had a PhD from Birmingham University in England, and was an expert in Shakespeare! Having studied in the Midlands, he knew Stratford-upon-Avon very well, which happened to be in the Diocese of Coventry. What I didn't know about Sadoun when I first met him was that he had also been the senior translator for Saddam Hussein – so Saddam's translator became my translator!

GROWTH OF ST GEORGE'S MINISTRY

I was aware that St George's was supposed to be an Anglican church, despite the fact that none of the congregation were actually Anglicans. I thought about the different aspects of ministry that characterized the Anglican Church around the world and how they related to the needs of ordinary people. I had experienced the full dynamism of the Anglican Church in both Kenya and Nigeria, and in each case the Mother's Union (MU) had been one of the most prevalent ministries. I was, of course, aware of the organization in the UK and had even been a member myself (yes, men are allowed to be members of the MU!), but it had a much more active ministry in Africa.

I decided that we needed to establish a branch of the MU in Baghdad, which we did, and one of our ladies, Nawal, led the project. Within days of its beginning, the Baghdad MU had over 2,000 signed-up members and they set to work, worshipping the Lord together and going out into the community to care for the poor and suffering. We created a link between our branch of the MU and their headquarters in London. Our ladies were very excited about being part of an international movement.

MEETING PRACTICAL NEEDS

One day, I was standing in the grounds of the church, having one of my regular conversations with the Lord, and I was telling Him that the needs of our church people were huge. I asked, "Lord, what do I need to provide for our people?" His answer came back very clearly: people needed food, adequate healthcare, and an education for their children.

Each was a big area of need, but it was relatively easy to start with food. The MU played a key role in distributing food to those who most needed it. All of our congregation were issued with photo ID cards and a "distribution area" was created, so that each week after the main Sunday service food could be properly allocated to those in need.

Healthcare and education needs were more difficult to meet – especially the former. Already, large numbers of people were looking to the church to help them with their health problems. As the need arose, we paid for people to see doctors, have tests done, and obtain medication. But this policy was not sustainable for the long term. It was clear that it would be better to establish our own health centre.

We had one place in the church grounds that could be turned into such a facility – the old church hall, where Hanna the caretaker lived with his family. We found a new home for Hanna and his family and started planning the creation of a new health centre with several aspects. We needed an area for general practitioners to function, and also a dental clinic. Eventually we would also have a pharmacy, a laboratory, and a clinic for autologous stem-cell treatment (transplants using the person's own stem cells). It was a huge project, which, fortunately, the US embassy agreed to both organize and fund. It was all overseen by Brigadier General David Greer, who today is the executive director of the US branch of my Foundation.

The clinic now treats over 150 people every day, and the treatments provided range from seeing the doctors and dentists to distributing medication from the pharmacy. Most of our patients are Muslims. In Iraq it is impossible to do any overt evangelism, but scores of people have joined St George's after receiving free treatment at our clinic. Our health centre is our biggest means of evangelism. The thing that distinguishes it from every other clinic in Baghdad is that it is completely free. The fact that it is located in the church complex follows the historical precedent set by the church throughout the ages, of offering a ministry of healing to all who need it.

Jesus is our model for all ministry and a key feature of His ministry was supernatural healing, so we not only aim to treat people with medicine, we also pray for everyone. Thus the ministry of the church is not restricted to the help that our clinic can supply; at its heart is the supernatural healing power of our Lord.

St George's has a very significant prayer ministry and people have a great expectation that, if they are prayed for, the Lord will meet with them and heal them. People regularly experience the reality of the Lord's power. The majority of the Muslims who visit our clinic hold the belief that if a priest anoints them with oil, they will be healed. Sadly, there is too much reliance on the ministry of the priest, instead of on a personal relationship with the Lord who supplies the power – and this is true of some of the Christians as well as the non-Christians.

Every Saturday afternoon, a group of our MU women go out visiting the poor and praying for those who are ill. They ask the Lord to heal everyone they meet. Each year at our diocesan synod, which meets in Cyprus, the bishop will bless the oil that all the churches in the diocese will use for anointing. We are given a fairly large bottle of oil. St George's is the only church in the world I know of that regularly runs out of oil – because we pray for so many people.

St George's is also the only church I know of where people regularly ask to take the sacraments away with them to minister to others. People ask for anointing oil, which is good because it means they are praying for healing for others. They also ask for Communion wafers for those who are too frail to come to church. They will take burnt-out candles, water from the font, and anything else they consider holy.

Some people may think this strange, yet every week I hear stories about what God has been doing in people's lives. There are stories of supernatural healing and of prayers for needs being miraculously answered. Then there are countless visions of Jesus, with people relaying to me what the Lord has said to them. It is truly remarkable what God is doing in the lives of ordinary Iraqis.

CHAPTER 17

An Oasis of Healing

Each Thursday evening at the church we meet to pray specifically for healing. Whenever I am there, people will expect to be anointed with oil. At these services we don't just pray for the people who are present; we keep a book listing the names of everyone who has requested prayer. This book is lifted up to the Lord in prayer with the assurance that He will indeed hear and answer these prayers. Each week after this meeting we hear more stories of how God has answered people's prayers, often with dramatic healing. We have seen people healed of heart disease and various cancers, and children healed of congenital illnesses. We have even seen the Lord raise people from the dead. Allow me to tell you about two such incidents.

One Saturday afternoon some ladies from our MU went to visit a pregnant lady who was ill in hospital. As they entered the ward, they saw another patient next to her crying hysterically. One of our ladies asked what was wrong with her and was told that her baby had just died and been taken down to the mortuary. Immediately our ladies asked if they could go there and see the baby. They were allowed to do this and were directed to the baby, who had been placed in one of the refrigerated units. One of the ladies took the lifeless child in her arms and they all began to pray that life would return to him. After a moment, the child opened his eyes and began to cry. They were able to carry the baby back to the ward and place him in the arms of his astonished and overjoyed mother. Now everyone was crying.

The next story is my favourite. Ahmed was a normal working man in Baghdad. He came to our clinic one day and pleaded with one of our doctors to treat his daughter. It turned out that his teenage daughter, Abouna, was seriously ill in Medical City, Iraq's main university hospital. He asked if our doctors would treat her because of the popular local belief that the so-called "English clinic" could cure anybody. Our doctors had to explain that, sadly, we could not treat someone who was already a patient of another hospital.

Ahmed was very distressed but there was nothing to be done, so one of our doctors suggested that he return to the hospital and visit his daughter. Before Ahmed left, however, I had the opportunity to speak to him and pray with him. As I did, I felt the Lord speak to me and I became utterly convinced that the Lord was going to heal this girl. I told Ahmed, "Go to the hospital now and pray for her. And, all the way there, just keep on saying "Yeshua, Yeshua, Yeshua', continuously." ("Yeshua" is the Aramaic name for Jesus.)

Ahmed arrived at the hospital only to be greeted with the tragic news that his daughter had died minutes earlier. In desperation and with many tears, he went to her bedside and wrapped his arms around her body, saying "Yeshua" over and over again, just as I'd instructed him. His daughter immediately breathed out, sat up, and said, "Baba (Daddy), I'm hungry. Can I have some food?" Later, when Ahmed came to see me and tell me what had happened, I said to him, "Don't worry; it has happened before..."

WHY NOT YOU?

As is so often the case in parts of the world where Christians are experiencing great hardship and persecution, or there is just great spiritual darkness, manifestations of the power and presence of God occur regularly. For us, here in Baghdad, we live daily with an awareness of the supernatural. One such manifestation is the appearance of angels. Western readers might find this hard to grasp, but here we see many angels.

One day, my adopted son, Dawood (you'll hear more about him in a later chapter), was trying to take some photos of me for one of my books, and he said, "Daddy, there are too many angels. They are getting in the way of the picture!" I told him to take the picture anyway and the result was extraordinary – I was clearly surrounded by what I would describe as glowing orbs of light.

Previously I was sceptical whenever I heard people talking about angelic encounters. Not that I didn't believe it could happen, but I like to check things out and make sure they are real. But now I have seen the angels for myself and I accept that, in a church where the miraculous is the norm and incredible healings take place, the presence of the Almighty and His angelic hosts is tangible, and sometimes even visible.

Whenever I travel and speak at different churches, I will usually mention some of these things, which frequently results in my being asked, "So why not you? Why have you not been healed?" I think this is a fair question: why am I still living with MS when God is obviously capable of healing me? With all my heart I believe that the Lord can heal me if He wants to, but at the same time I am acutely aware of how the Spirit of God has been with me constantly, miraculously enabling me to do everything I've ever needed to do.

I have known what it is to be so ill that I can hardly move, and yet here in Iraq, with its fairly primitive medical facilities compared with the Western world, at our own clinic in our own church the doctors have found a way of treating me with my own stem cells. Other people would travel around the world for such treatment, but I can walk down our church path. I was the first person to receive this treatment and it has totally transformed my life. We have since had people come from as far away as the USA to undergo similar treatment. Several thousand people have been treated and the condition of 80 per cent of them has radically improved. For this I so thank my God. Who would ever have thought that treatment for MS would be available at my church in Baghdad?

I give thanks for God's provision in this. At the same time, I feel great frustration at the bad counsel that has often been given to me by other Christians. People have told me that I haven't been healed because I've never really believed God enough for it – suggesting a deficiency in my faith. Others have told me that my view of God is too small, too limited – suggesting a deficiency in my understanding of the Almighty's power and sufficiency. I have heard these things time and time again. In addition, countless people have come to me saying that they are the one through whom I'll be healed. At least all of this has taught me how *not* to pray for people in need, and I have learned much about the never-failing love of God in our most difficult circumstances.

One thing I know for sure is that if God calls us to do something, He always enables us to do it, and He also gives joy in the doing. He who has called you will never fail you. I know without doubt the truths that, "my grace is sufficient for you, for my strength is made perfect in weakness" (2 Corinthians 12:9, NKJV) and "I can do all things through Christ who strengthens me" (Philippians 4:13, NKJV). The fact that God should use me and not someone who is a picture of good health to bring His healing to others is another sign of God's incredible grace. It's all about Him, not me.

GOD'S PRESENCE MANIFEST THROUGH OTHERS

There is so much need in this war-torn country of Iraq that we could not possibly carry on conducting this ministry without God's help – and so often that help is manifested through others. When we say, "The Lord is here; His Spirit is with us", we also think of so many friends around the world who support us in a multitude of ways. Like all churches in every land, the church here is not just about where the building is located.

One thing we do frequently in Iraq is to go and visit people in their homes – an experience that manages simultaneously to be both thrilling and devastating. Thrilling because the presence of God is always manifest and devastating because the people live in such extreme poverty. It is hard to describe the poor state of people's accommodation: damp, run-down buildings with peeling plaster, no proper floor surface, nothing to sit on, very little food – the list goes on and on. There is no such thing as a comfortable chair – most people just have to sit or lie on the floor, including some very disabled people. But, without exception, people are always delighted to see us and they say that when a priest visits them they are indeed visited by the Lord.

In our ministry to these people we are helped by so many other churches around the world that I must make mention of them. I realize that in mentioning some I may forget to mention others, and I hope that I don't offend anyone.

First of all, there is the "second" St George's – an extension of our main fellowship. Each Saturday I conduct a service based in the US embassy complex – a large site covering 100 acres that I refer to as the largest prison in the world, since it is surrounded by a twenty-four-foot wall topped with razor wire and punctuated by military watchtowers. It is impossible to get into or out of the place unless you have security clearance at the highest level.

I conduct two services there: first a general, interdenominational service, and then a more traditional Anglican service. The congregation are not all Americans; about half come from Kenya and Uganda. This means we enjoy some wonderful African-style worship, with great joy and rhythm. This embassy church also calls itself St George's, Baghdad because we are one, even though it is not possible for the whole church to gather together most of the time.

Once each year, however, at Christmastime, we do gather the church together as large numbers of our young people go to the embassy to receive toys from the US Marines as part of their "Toys for Tots" programme. Throughout the rest of the year our embassy congregation does what it can to support and provide help for the families we reach out to on a daily basis, enabling us to show them the love and care of God.

Then there are churches around the world that constantly support us. There are several in the US who, whenever I visit them, fuel my vision and courage for the work in Iraq. Pastor Kyle Horner is one such man, leader of Connect Church in Cherry Hill, New Jersey. I met Kyle not in America but in an Indian restaurant in Kent in the south of England. We were both preaching at the same conference and instantly clicked and became friends. Kyle and his wife Danielle's church is so alive and filled with the Spirit of God – they are a great inspiration to me.

I cannot think about churches in the US without thinking of the work of Bill and Beni Johnson at Bethel Church in Redding,

California. To me, this church is like no other and has such an incredible emphasis on abiding in God's presence.

Then there are numerous churches in the UK: Holy Trinity Brompton where I have many friends; Cornerstone Church at Sandown Racecourse in Epsom, Surrey, led by my dear friend Pastor Chris Demetriou. There is Kerith Church in Bracknell, Berkshire, with its pastor, Simon Benham. Pastor Phil Whitehead at Chiswick Christian Centre is someone who never fails to truly inspire me in my mission. Finally, there is LIFE Church, Bradford. I have only been to this church twice, but each time I found it inspiring. I can guarantee that once each day I will hear from someone from at least one of these churches, and this does so much to encourage me to keep going.

Someone once said to me that going from our church in the war zone of Baghdad to Bethel Church must be like going from heaven to hell. I replied, "No, it's like going from one form of heaven to another." Why? Because we are both pursuing the call of the kingdom as laid out in Isaiah 61:1–4 (NIV):

The Spirit of the Sovereign Lord is on me, because the Lord has anointed me to proclaim good news to the poor. He has sent me to bind up the broken-hearted, to proclaim freedom for the captives and release from darkness for the prisoners, to proclaim the year of the Lord's favour and the day of vengeance of our God, to comfort all who mourn, and provide for those who grieve in Zion – to bestow on them a crown of beauty instead of ashes, the oil of joy instead of mourning, and a garment of praise instead of a spirit of despair. They will be called oaks of righteousness, a planting of the Lord for the display of his splendour. They will rebuild the ancient ruins and restore the places long devastated; they will renew the ruined cities that have been devastated for generations.

These words describe the sum total of what we are doing in Baghdad and what the worldwide church as a whole should be doing. This is our mission – the same mission as that of Cornerstone Church in Cherry Hill and Bethel Church in Redding. We may be conducting our ministry in the midst of terror and the carnage of war, but we are still working together with the wider church, proclaiming good news to the poor, binding up the broken-hearted, and proclaiming freedom for the captives and release from darkness for the prisoners.

CHAPTER 18

Don't Take Care; Take Risks

President Jimmy Carter once said, "Go out on a limb – that's where the fruit is." I share his philosophy. I constantly say to people, "Don't take care; take risks." It has become my motto and the principle by which I live my life. Risk is inherent in most of my work. The fact is, if I weren't prepared to risk everything for the sake of peace, then very little would be achieved.

Recently, I was honoured to receive the William Wilberforce Award (given to individuals who "exemplify the passions and principles of Wilberforce as a witness of real Christianity in society"). When I arrived at the award ceremony, all the posters bore the words "Take Risks". People assumed those words came from me, but in fact they came from my great mentor, Donald, Lord Coggan.

Lord Coggan first uttered this statement to me as we were walking together in London. We had just come from a meeting of the Council of Jews and Christians and he gripped my arm tightly, looked me in the eye, and said, "You're a young curate. I want to give you just two words of advice for your ministry: take risks." The weight of those words stayed with me.

Just a few weeks later I was in Rome, visiting Pope John Paul II in my capacity as chairman of the young leadership section of the International Council of Christians and Jews. I went for a walk with the Pope through the Vatican and, similarly, he turned to me and said, "You are at an early stage of your ministry. You will go far if you always take risks." I replied, "Yes, Your Holiness, I promise I always will." And this is what I have done throughout my ministry.

I know for a fact that, whenever I have decided not to take a risk, I have limited the work of the Holy Spirit. So, whenever the Lord has brought this to my attention, I've repented and next time been bolder in stepping out and trusting Him.

What risks do I take? I will talk about them in this chapter, but it occurs to me that whereas these areas of risk apply to my peculiar context, we all face the same risks, regardless of our walk in life, because they deal with the two greatest facets of our humanity: our relationship with God (and the degree to which we trust Him) and our relationships with one another. I summarize these risks as follows:

- The risk of loving
- The risk of asking much from God
- The risk of seeking reconciliation
- The risk of engaging with our enemies
- The risk of trusting God to keep us safe.

THE RISK OF LOVING

To love is to risk

The act of demonstrating love to another is perhaps the greatest risk any of us will ever take, because it can be the most powerful thing, but is also fraught with danger. What if our love is rejected or misunderstood? What if our love is in vain or we have risked loving only to be used and then discarded?

At the start of this book I recalled how, from the earliest age, I was aware that Jesus loved me very much. So one of the first things I did was learn to love God back. Loving God is perhaps the only love without risk, because our Lord took all the risk upon Himself.

Loving other people, however, involves risk – yet God has called us to be people of love; to love others selflessly; to be the hands and feet of Jesus by showing practical love to those who need it. Of course, it is easier to love those who love us, but what about our enemies, those who despise us? This is the real risk of love: to love those who you know have no intention of loving you back. But still God commands us to love them, and His love is a powerful catalyst for change. The real risk in loving is to trust God that, as we simply love, He will take responsibility for the consequences.

Love involves pain

We know that love also involves pain. We choose to love someone, but they reject us. Someone we love deeply lets us down. The more we love someone, the more acutely we feel the pain when things go wrong. Perhaps the most difficult thing I have ever experienced in my ministry has been the pain of betrayal – loving people unconditionally only to have them turn on me or reject me.

But we have a choice in how we deal with the bitterness and anger that can arise from such pain. We can either build fences around ourselves, to prevent the situation from arising again, or risk loving once again and build a bridge, leaving a way open for that person to come back to us, should they choose to do so. We all know which choice we *should* make, with the Lord's help.

Love is a choice

Love itself is not just an emotion; it is an act of the will. Loving others is a choice. If we are real, practising Christians, we do not have the option of simply rejecting other people. If we do that, we are failing to practise our faith. I would dare to say that such an attitude brings us very close to no longer even *having* a faith. To turn on others in this way is no less than turning on God and rejecting Him. We can try to make excuses for our behaviour, but the truth is that we are commanded by God to love others as He has loved us.

THE RISK OF ASKING MUCH FROM GOD

I regularly hear people discussing what the most important thing was that they learned from their theological education. It may be a particular insight into some complex area of theology, such as the teleological argument for the existence of God, or some other aspect of doctrine. For me, the single most important aspect of my Cambridge education was learned from Dr Margaret Bowker, one of my lecturers – but not in a classroom, rather one-to-one. She was the lady who taught me how to pray.

Dr Bowker, a much-respected academic, was not a theologian

but a historian. She was married to the dean of Trinity College, Cambridge. At one time in her life she had suffered badly with a form of cancer and during that time she made a deal with God. She promised the Lord that if she was healed and restored she would dedicate her life to teaching others how to pray. I was one of the people who benefited from that deal.

Over many months I learned so much from Margaret, but one thing that stood out for me was the fact that she would always want to know what I had asked for in prayer and whether I'd received what I'd asked for. Fundamental to her prayer life was the belief that every day our prayers had to ask something of God. Ever since then I have always asked God for specific things when I pray.

This is also a risk. People worry about asking God for things in case it is not His will or in case, seemingly, the prayer goes unanswered. (I know that my prayers are always answered, even if it is not the answer I want.) Yes, prayer is a risk, but the greater risk is that of not asking at all.

There are times when I am acutely aware that what I am asking for is very big, but can anything we ask for be bigger than God Himself? Of course not. The fact is, the more seemingly impossible the thing we are asking for, the greater the opportunity for God to display His goodness and glory.

I am constantly faced with asking "big" owing to the nature of our ministry. It is not unusual for me to say to the Lord, "Father, I need $150,000 in the next three days." Naturally speaking, I cannot think how such a request can be answered, but God knows! More to the point, where there exists a need among His children, He always answers such prayers. We must be willing to ask much of God and not be afraid. He is not offended by the earnest requests of His children.

THE RISK OF SEEKING RECONCILIATION

My life of working for reconciliation has been one full of risk. It is a major risk to bring together people from opposite sides of a hostile debate in the hope of finding at least a tiny bit of common ground on which they can begin a dialogue. Bringing together Muslims and Christians, Israelis and Palestinians, Shia and Sunni – all such occasions carry huge risk as one side confronts those they consider "the others" – those whom they have hated, even wanted to wipe out. The first step in reconciliation is therefore making an attempt to know and love our enemies.

Nearly all the Iraqi leaders I have worked with have hated Israelis – not just the Muslims, but the Christians too. When I began working there, it soon came to my notice that, in Iraq, no religious leader would contemplate meeting with an Israeli and none of them had ever met a Jewish rabbi. So I had a fairly simple, but radical, idea about bringing Iraqi and Israeli religious leaders together. Never before had such a meeting taken place.

I began asking senior Iraqi leaders if they would be prepared to meet the Israelis. Most were not. I asked if they would be willing to meet some Israeli Arabs. They were sceptical about that – most had little concept that there was anyone other than Jews living in Israel. Then I approached Israeli and Palestinian leaders to see what their reaction was. Their perception was that the Iraqi Shias had close links with Israel's enemy, Iran, and at first they could not believe they were being asked to meet Iraqis. For their part, the Palestinians had no problem dialoguing with Israeli Jews, but similarly hated Shia Muslims, since their Muslims were all Sunni.

I spent a long time trying to persuade the Sunni leaders that the Shia could be their friends and not their enemies. I explained that my heart was to work towards peace for our broken land. I also explained how the leaders involved in the Alexandria Declaration, although from opposing sides, had actually become friends through the process. If Jews and Palestinians could become friends, then there was hope for Sunnis and Shias, who were both Muslim.

Eventually, leaders on all sides were persuaded that it was a good idea to meet and plans could begin to arrange a suitable venue. It was not going to be easy to find somewhere appropriate. The Iraqis could not travel to Israel and the Israelis could not visit most Muslim nations. It was decided that Cyprus could be a suitable neutral venue, and so we arranged to hold the meeting in Paphos in the south-west.

Paphos was part of the Anglican Diocese of Cyprus and the Gulf, of which we in Iraq were a part. This meant we immediately had the support of a large number of churches on the island, both Anglican and evangelical, who were totally behind the venture. The prayer support from local Christians was truly tangible and together the churches agreed that they would provide 24/7 prayer support for the meeting.

With regard to risk, the Iraqis involved were literally taking their lives in their hands by agreeing to the meeting and would almost certainly have been killed for attending. Their identities have been protected and their names don't appear anywhere in this book.

The meeting itself was incredible. The Iraqi delegation told me that they had come to the meeting hating the Jews and wanting them wiped off the face of the earth. "Now we have been together and looked in one another's eyes," one person said, "we love them." Similarly, the Jews said that they had lived in fear of the Shia, but that after three days together – as one person so wonderfully put it – fear had been "cancelled".

There is huge risk in reconciliation, but this is a good example of what happens when enemies come together and hear each other's stories. The same is true in our personal lives. It is so true that our enemies are often "friends whose stories we haven't heard yet".

I cannot mention the risk of reconciliation without recalling a man who has been one of my greatest heroes throughout all my years in Iraq. He is not an Iraqi or a religious leader, but a soldier, the American general David Petraeus. At one time, General Petraeus was the commanding officer of the Coalition forces in Baghdad. He took great risks and was instrumental in bringing opposing factions together to work towards peace. There are few people I've met in life whom I so admire. Despite what the press may say to the contrary, I know that he is a great child of God and I love him – not exactly what one expects to hear someone say about a general, but it's true. I often think that if he were still in Iraq, we would not be confronted with the level of crisis and tragedy we are now facing. I honour David Petraeus as a true risk-taker for reconciliation.

THE RISK OF ENGAGING WITH OUR ENEMIES

Part of the risk of reconciliation work is that of dealing with bad people. I have always said that peacemaking is not about dealing with nice people. The very fact that people are caught up in conflict means that at least some of them must have been the cause of it. Those who turn to violence in order to achieve their own ends are not usually good people. Most think that their aims and ideals justify their radical actions, but to others this is terrorist activity.

Often I find myself sitting with leaders of radical groups such as Hamas or the Islamic State of Iraq (ISIS) – groups who are both involved in extreme terrorist activity – but the only way one can bring about change is by working with them. Someone has to risk loving them so that change might be possible, from the inside out. Change can happen, but it takes time and requires perseverance.

This type of work does put me at risk. The very fact of meeting the leaders of such organizations, getting to know who they are and where to find them, means one has vital intelligence – and there are other people who want that intelligence. If such intelligence can be obtained about one's enemies, then it is possible to hunt them down and take them out. And what about the person who possesses that intelligence? The fact is, if you don't share it, then the lives of people close to you may be threatened. This is the kind of ethical dilemma I am constantly faced with in Iraq.

At least when one brings enemies together there is the hope that something can be done to reduce violence and help bring about peace. The very act of being willing to sit down and begin a dialogue, however tense it may be, is the first sign of hope for reconciliation. In such situations it is not my job to judge who is right and who is wrong, but to facilitate an honest, open dialogue, getting each side to listen to the other side's story.

Before our major meeting of religious leaders in 2002 we met in a secret location in Jerusalem. Often we would meet late at night and talk into the early hours of the morning. Slowly, week after week, sworn enemies heard each other's stories and began to see that they all had at least two things in common: firstly, they were all minorities, and, secondly, they had all suffered grave loss – a loss of liberty, property, territory, and, ultimately, power. Over time they found some common ground and began to appreciate each other's point of view. I witnessed enemies becoming friends.

It is interesting to see how people respond to friends who used to be their enemies. During the time when I brought the Israeli and Palestinian leaders to London, we attended a press conference and two of the representatives stood side by side – Rabbi Michael Melchior, then foreign minister of Israel, and Sheikh Talal Al-Sadr, a former Palestinian Authority minister. At one point, someone heckled from the audience, shouting loudly, asking the Sheikh why he was with this "evil Zionist leader". Sheikh Talal took Rabbi Melchior's hand and said, "Rabbi Melchior is my brother. We will walk the long and difficult road to reconciliation together."

THE RISK OF TRUSTING GOD TO KEEP US SAFE

I have heard it said that the essence of our walk with God is overcoming our "trust issues" with Him: trusting that He really will provide for us as He says; trusting that He really will protect us from danger if we take a risk on His behalf.

The majority of my life is lived in Baghdad, which is a very dangerous place. As I write, there have been three recent suicide bombings within walking distance of the church where I live and work. A number of people have been shot and killed today. One of them was the person who was supposed to drive me to the US embassy. Each day, I cannot know the risks that will have to be faced or what tragedies may occur.

This is my "norm". I appreciate that it is not normal for most people, but we can all relate to needing to trust our heavenly Father more – to becoming completely dependent on Him. We tend to cling on to things in our lives and we fear letting go, but it is only as we admit our need and vulnerability that the Lord can take control and protect and care for us.

I have never once worried about being in Iraq, because I

know that God has called me to be here – and when God calls us to be somewhere, we can be sure that He will provide for us. Don't take care; take risks. Nothing worthwhile was ever achieved that didn't involve an element of risk.

CHAPTER 19

A Normal Day

People often ask me to describe a "typical day" in my life. In truth, no day is very typical, but in this chapter and the next I will try to provide small and large snapshots of my life.

I wake up at 5.30 a.m. Today is Monday, so a normal day without services. I start the day with prayer and Bible reading. I always begin by asking the Lord what passage he would like me to speak on when I next preach and then, according to His answer, I read that passage and pray around it. I am due to speak at some GOD TV revival meetings this coming weekend. Romans 8:17–18 is coming to me loud and clear:

> *Now if we are children, then we are heirs – heirs of God and co-heirs with Christ, if indeed we share in his sufferings in order that we may also share in his glory. I consider that our present sufferings are not worth comparing with the glory that will be revealed in us.*
> (NIV)

God's answer has to be loud and clear because He knows I do not really want to speak on these verses. I've done so many times before and I find it difficult. Nevertheless, God has asked me to speak about suffering again, so I'll obey Him.

By 7.15 a.m. I have finished my prayers and reading for the day and it takes me about half an hour to get out of bed. I should mention that my one room in St George's is a multifunctional space. It is my office, study, meeting room, dining room, and bedroom! At 7.45 a.m. Dina, our housekeeper, brings me a cup of tea. This is the only sustenance I'll have until after dark today because it is Ramadan and we can't actually obtain any food until after sunset. With my tea, I go to my laptop to do some writing.

Politically, the challenges for us in Iraq are very great at the moment. Despite the fact that in 2014 a new prime minister was appointed, Haider al-Abadi, his government is not in control of much of the country, as a large part of it is now in the grip of the terrorist group ISIS. Uncertainty remains and nobody knows what will happen now in Iraq. I phone a few journalist friends to see if there is anything we need to touch base on today. Then I try to phone some of the other church leaders in the area, but as usual find it virtually impossible to get through. There is a lot of fear among everyone about what is happening in Baghdad, with the very real risk of ISIS storming the city and taking control. If that danger appears to be imminent then it will be too dangerous for Christians to remain, and we will need to get them out of the country, to the north, into Kurdistan. The decision whether to stay or flee balances on a knife edge.

After making these calls I venture out to visit our school and clinic. The school has over 100 children from kindergarten age up to seven. Our clinic has a variety of medical specialists, general practitioners, and dentists, as well as laboratory and pharmacy staff. I chat to all the staff and encourage them and thank them for their service. We give thanks to God that we are able to provide all of our treatment free to many needy people.

After this it is time to go out of our complex and pay a quick visit to one of my favourite places – the Home for Disabled Children. I have visited here regularly ever since my first trip to Iraq sixteen years ago. The home has existed for twenty years, set up by Mother Teresa to care for the disabled and abandoned children of Iraq, most of whom have severe deformities. The sisters who run the home are all from India and visiting them is always a cause for great joy. They speak English with wonderful Indian accents. We are very close to one another, like family, and I always aim to provide something nice for the children each time I visit.

After this, I return to my church HQ and Dr Sarah and Sally Multi arrive (I will speak more about them in a later chapter). Together we talk through the plans for the remainder of the day. Top of our list for action is my need to meet with a top Sunni sheikh. He is one of the most senior Sunnis involved in the fragmented Iraqi government. We phone his team and they agree to arrange a meeting for later in the day.

Now it is mid-morning and, as is normal, people begin arriving and asking to see me. They have various problems and requests for help. We promise to help those with medical problems through our clinic. Several people need particular medication, so I send them to our pharmacy. By 1 p.m. I have seen around half a dozen people, some of whom also needed financial help. We gave them as much as we could.

During the afternoon I take a call from my office in the UK. Someone wants me to contact an Iraqi Christian they met while on holiday in Turkey. I manage to track him down, make contact, and arrange to meet up with him. I invite him to come and worship with us. I put the phone down from this very positive conversation and immediately a huge boom shakes the building. There has been another explosion. It will have been another suicide bomber or a nearby car bomb.

At some point each day I will call to speak to my colleagues at the US Embassy. It is usually to receive a breakdown of the latest intelligence in the area, though this is becoming increasingly difficult as many people have left the embassy because of the danger. I chat to the one person I'm able to get hold of, but in reality they are more interested in the intelligence I can give them than vice versa. After all, they are cocooned in their vast razor-wired fortress and I am outside. I describe what is going on and repeat what we've heard people saying on the ground.

In general, things are not looking good. The embassy fears the breaking out of full-blown war in a matter of days. They are worried about my being stuck out in the Red Zone (the real Baghdad). I tell them I'll be leaving for England tomorrow, which reassures them. I don't tell them that I have every intention of returning in a few days.

This conversation suddenly reminds me – I am returning to England tomorrow and need to prepare! I will be travelling to Plymouth to speak at the GOD TV event there. I will also fit in a meeting with my old friend Justin Welby, the Archbishop of Canterbury. All of this means I need to run a quick errand – to the nearby Abu Afif's Chocolate Shop. It is totally bizarre that in the midst of the trauma of Baghdad you can find the most exquisite, luxurious chocolate you'll find anywhere in the world. Before I go back to England, I always pay a quick visit here to stock up. I can show people that there is at least one good thing in Baghdad!

After this I have a scheduled meeting with my curate, Faiz. He is the only Iraqi who has been ordained as an Anglican priest. We sit down and talk in depth about the major problems that we face. The extreme terrorist group ISIS, now simply called Islamic State, has taken over much of Iraq, setting up bases in Mosul and Nineveh. The traditional home of many of the Christians has been taken over by these Sunni terrorists. Over a million people have moved out of Mosul. We talk about the reality of what we as a church now face. ISIS say they will take Baghdad, and they are now only twenty miles away. The government assure us that they will prevent them from entering Baghdad, but after seeing the last encounter between ISIS and the Iraqi army we are not totally convinced.

We talk about what we should do. It is clear that we remain in great danger if we stay. We may perhaps have to move to Erbil – many of our people have already gone there and so there is a congregation waiting for us. What we do not have is any kind of base there – a church or a place to live. We discuss the painful possibility of having to leave our church complex, our clinic, our school. We pray and thank God that, despite this terrible crisis, we have had sufficient funds donated to cope with the tremendous needs that confront us.

After this, more visitors come to see me. A couple arrive, bringing their son to be prayed for. He is in his late teens and is totally unable to hear. As a result he has never been to school and is very depressed. I hug him to show him that I love him, and then I pray for him and anoint him with oil. I give him a cross and one of my books that has lots of pictures in it. Then I talk with his parents about other needs that the family have and I promise to help them regularly if I can.

By now sunset is fast approaching and I have eaten nothing all day. Dr Sarah, our Iraqi director, is my main assistant as well as being one of our dental surgeons. She goes off to get us some food and returns in due course with a kebab for me. Sally Multi joins us, as do two other honorary members of our family, Rita (ten) and George (eight). We sit, surrounded by food, and talk.

While finishing my kebab, by telephone I join in a meeting of my Foundation's US board. Most of the board have previously served in Baghdad; it is made up of individuals ranging from former military men to high-level diplomats. Among them is Ambassador Paul Bremer, one-time leader of the Coalition Provisional Authority. Our executive director is retired Brigadier General David Greer, also a member of my US embassy congregation in Baghdad. I officiated at David's wedding to Susan, a wonderful lady who was also a member of our embassy congregation. Not many Westerners can say they were married in Iraq's Green Zone against a backdrop of rocket fire. At least it was a truly memorable occasion.

Though it is after dark, my day is nowhere near finished yet. I still have the Sunni Sheikh to go and see. I am driven over to meet him and the meeting is short and to the point. Together we have a major meeting to plan. We discuss what is happening with the Iraqi government and also ISIS. I mention the fact that I have discovered that one of my friends, a Sunni tribal leader, has in fact joined Daash,[10] the Sunni terrorist group.

When I arrive back at the church and enter my room I return to writing about current events. It is now 11.30 p.m. Shortly I will have my evening prayers and then retire. It is the end of a fairly normal eighteen-hour day.

The next day I mention to Dr Sarah that yesterday I worked for eighteen hours. She assures me that I regularly do this, and more. I do. It is the reality of my calling and this life of service.

---

10 The name "Daash" is an acronym for "Dulat al-Islam fi al-Iraq wal-Sham" – "the Islamic State in Iraq and Greater Syria", and it is a Sunni Salafi organization.

CHAPTER 20

The Bigger Picture

My "normal" day gives a good insight into my daily life, but an overview of the events of a couple of weeks helps explain the bigger picture.

As I write, I am on a plane from London to Israel, having completed my weekend speaking engagement for GOD TV. On this trip I once again had the help of my friend Terry Jones, a retired police officer whom I got to know during my time in Coventry. Terry is a dynamic guy who is able to make things happen, and so is the perfect companion for me. He is always there for me when I need him.

On this trip I also met my old friend and colleague Justin Welby. Seeing him is always such a pleasure. We had a comprehensive talk about major issues concerning Israel and Palestine, and then discussed the matters affecting the Christians in Mosul and Nineveh who have been forced out of their homes and churches.

I arrive in Israel at a time of all-out war between Israel and Gaza. Hamas militants in Gaza have been continually shelling Israel and Israel has responded with fierce attacks. Everyone is frightened on both sides. Everyone feels marginalized by the media. Each side is convinced that they are the ones who are in the right. Once again, the story of my life is repeating itself. My task is to try to show both sides the pain that the other is suffering and work with them to seek peace.

I stay in the Jerusalem Hills Inn, run by my great friends Chaim and Ruti Singerman, which is located in the Arab town of Abu Ghosh on the outskirts of Jerusalem. They have seven wonderful children. I confess that two of their children are very special to me. First there is Sarah, their eldest daughter, who is nineteen and currently completing her military service, working in communications. She is a wonderful worship leader and, when she sings, the presence of God comes.

Then there is Josiah, aged ten, also known as Yoshi, just like my oldest son. When I see him I give him a big hug and he holds on tight to me. Like my Yoshi back in England he has the most amazing grasp of politics, and we talk about the most difficult issues. Today we chat about the political situation in the Middle East and Yoshi has very clear ideas on what the regional political leaders should do. The following day I will see former government minister Rabbi Michael Melchior and he will say, almost word for word, what Yoshi has said.

A few months earlier Ruti gave birth to another baby girl, called Sheri. Yoshi is upset because now there are more girls than boys in the family. I chat to him and wonder what we can do to rectify this situation. It so happens that I have some honorary adopted children in Iraq. One of them, Amar, is a boy the same age as Yoshi, and Amar is an only child – he has always wanted a brother. I suggest that Yoshi and Amar become "brothers" and in due course they do! Now, every time I visit Israel I set up a phone call so that they can chat with each other. It is not possible to telephone Israel from Iraq, but we can do it this way round.

After staying with the Singermans I move into Jerusalem and

stay at Christ Church in the Old City, which houses the Israeli headquarters of the Church's Ministry among Jewish People, of which I am vice-president. I love meeting with David Pillegi, the rector, and the church is centrally located, so perfect for getting to a wide variety of meetings. I am not very good at keeping secrets, but much of my work in this area is confidential, so I can't write about it.

I have one meeting that I can mention, with the foreign minister. We discuss the Israel–Gaza crisis and how to deal with it. I make it clear that there are significant things we *could* do but are prevented from doing by the fact that no Israelis are allowed into Gaza at present. Despite this difficulty we will keep doing what we can to achieve peace. I also speak with the minister about the rise of Arab militants in the region and their threat to Israel. It is a grave threat and it is not clear how this situation will play out.

From Israel I fly back to England for several more speaking events. First I go to speak at my old parish church in Clapham. I have been invited back because they have just heard about my winning this year's Wilberforce Award. It is wonderful to visit there and meet so many of my old congregation.

I spend the night in London with my colleagues before going to preach at Chiswick Christian Centre the next morning. I love this church – a lovely group of people to worship and spend time with. Then, in the evening, I speak at another great church in Guildford, the town where Josiah attended school. Present is one of his former teachers.

Before I return to Iraq my main office is contacted by the office of HRH Prince Charles. The Prince's private secretary would like to meet me. It is so encouraging to realize that we are not forgotten here in Iraq.

The next day I begin the journey back to Iraq via Jordan.

When I finally arrive in Baghdad I am greeted by my security team. After travelling around the south of England suddenly I am confronted with the harsh reality of Iraq. As I travel back to St George's my armoured vehicle is surrounded by a large number of similar trucks full of armed soldiers whose weapons are pointing in every direction. The size of this moving shield and the amount of firepower seem utterly disproportionate, but the security risk in Baghdad is the greatest I have ever experienced.

People here are gripped with fear about what is happening with ISIS. Many of the people I meet have relatives in Mosul or Nineveh. ISIS has not yet entered Baghdad, but there have been random attacks on people and an increase in the number of kidnappings. People continue to flee the area in their masses, but the sad fact is, things remain dire even for those who have left. Most have gone to Turkey, but they have been told it will take several years to obtain an interview with the UNHCR to see whether they are eligible to be resettled as refugees. Until then they will live in awful limbo.

We continue to hope in the Lord despite the fierce sectarian division that exists. We may be attacked from outside by Sunni terrorists, but here the Sunnis are already being attacked by Shia militia. Today several Sunnis were killed and their bodies hung up in the street on public display. This is the reality of how bad things are. I always used to say to our congregation, "Don't you leave me, because I'm not leaving you." Now all I can say is, "I'm not leaving you." How can I expect our congregation to stay when things are so awful?

After this dreadful news, the next day I receive some joyous news. Dawood, my adopted son, and his wife, Sandy, have had a baby boy. Dawood and Sandy fled the country to go to Canada. Their baby will be called "Andrew Dawood Andrew".

According to Iraqi tradition, the child's chosen name is followed first by his father's name and then by his grandfather's name – hence my name appears twice. I miss them all so much and wish they could be here with me, but, of course, it is not safe. Dawood had to flee the country when spies discovered he was planning a meeting for me between Iraqi and Israeli leaders. As a result, his life was in danger.

Later I receive a visit from our archdeacon, the Venerable Bill Schwartz, who oversees the Anglican Church in the entire Gulf region, which includes Iraq and Yemen. There is much we need to discuss, not least the long-term future of the church. In truth, we don't know what the long-term prospects are. We don't know what will be happening in one month's time, let alone a year or more. Will there even be an Iraq as we know it? One thing is certain: it will be a very different Iraq from what it is now.

The next major event in my diary is a trip to Israel to participate in a GOD TV programme on the Middle East, broadcast from Jerusalem. Most of the interview is about the immense suffering that our people are going through. So much of my life is spent dealing with journalists, being interviewed, going to radio/TV studios, or being followed by a camera crew. To be honest, there are days when I wish I'd never have to do another interview again, but life doesn't really work like that. Our people often tell me that they feel forgotten. The most horrendous crimes in recent history are happening in our midst and the story is not being told. This is why I continue to do interviews and write books – so that the story may be heard.

There are some in the media, however, who are committed to getting our story told. A short while ago, Jane Arraf, a well-known journalist who has worked with CNN and is now with Al Jazeera, arrived with a team to cover what is happening to us in

Iraq. They were with us for a long weekend – Friday to Monday – and filmed everything they could, apart from our service in the US embassy, which was, of course, off limits. In due course her programme will be aired in the US on the PBS channel.

The Friday-evening youth meeting was as good as ever, with great worship and praise in the midst of our adversity. There was obvious fear among our young people, but worshipping together gives them hope. Jane enjoyed being with our youth and was struck by the light that exists in the midst of such darkness. Afterwards, as is our custom, we all had dinner together.

The next day is Saturday and we have our service at the embassy. A much smaller group of people attend because all non-essential staff have been removed from the embassy owing to the onslaught of ISIS. Nevertheless, we have a good service in this little space, cocooned inside the real world outside. There is still a strong sense that these people are "our people" and the love shared between us is tangible.

I return to our compound for a continuous stream of phone interviews with different radio and TV stations. In the evening the BBC decide they want me for a live TV interview. We are only one mile away from the studio that will host this, but getting there is a nightmare as we need to pass through endless security checkpoints. It takes over an hour to travel the one mile and the interview is short, but it will be broadcast on the BBC World News, so I know that the message will travel around the world.

The following morning is Sunday and this usually begins with my speaking live on several Christian radio programmes based in England. When there is a crisis it's not unusual for me to have spoken with ten different stations before going to conduct our church service. Today, however, I am scheduled to do an interview with Fox News and they have insisted it must be live, so I am up at 2.00 a.m. this Sunday morning to speak to them via Skype.

After speaking to someone I am effectively put on hold for a whole hour, since news has broken of a famous actor dying. I am still waiting at 3.30 a.m., when I give up. Once again I find the media frustrating, but Dr Sarah reminds me that there is no one else to tell our story.

The crisis in Iraq continues to get worse, and though we plan as best we can, often our plans turn out to be futile. Erbil is no longer the safe haven it was and access to it has been banned. Thousands of Christians and other minorities have taken refuge there. We have been feeding thousands of people in the area and supporting various Christian leaders who, in turn, are trying to support their people. So our main work has become supporting those who have fled the evil actions of ISIS, who are still causing havoc in Iraq but have not yet got into Baghdad.

At the moment our work here is very intensive. I have just been informed that some terrorists have kidnapped a number of Christian girls and have put them up "for sale". We are seeing if it is possible for us to buy them back. What a horrendous situation. This is the nature of the crisis we are in. What can we do? In all things we continue to pray and ask God for His help and, somehow, His supernatural presence continues to sustain us.

CHAPTER 21

My Choice

People often ask me why I choose to live my life in the way that I do. First of all, I have to acknowledge that I did indeed choose it. No one forced me to do what I do, or to live and work in one of the most dangerous places in the world. God called me to do it and yet He never forced me to go. He never violates His children's free will. I still had a choice. I chose to follow where He led me.

But I do love my life. I appreciate that most people could not live the way I do, but since my youth I have always loved adventure, excitement, and risk taking. It takes a certain type of person to be a member of a hospital crash team, just as it takes a certain type of person to live in a war zone. I have never wanted a quiet life. I have never wanted to conform to the norm.

Nothing was more exciting for me than to step in and help save the life of a patient with a ruptured aortic aneurism – a life-or-death situation in which one has to respond radically and quickly. Years later, as a priest, I had no desire to settle down in a nice, suburban parish, drinking tea and eating cucumber sandwiches! I feel more at home in an active war zone, where danger and crises go with the territory.

That is not to say that I like what is happening around me.

I don't like the fact that Baghdad is caught up in a war, just as I didn't like it when major medical emergencies occurred at St Thomas' Hospital. But the fact is, I like to respond to a crisis. When God calls us to something, He always provides us with the skills and wisdom we need to get the job done. He made me to thrive in an emergency.

Not only does God give us the skills we need, He also gives us joy in the performance of our ministry. People find it difficult to understand how I can be joyful in the midst of such dire, tragic circumstances in Iraq, and when I go to speak at a church the people are nearly always surprised that I am a joyful person, not grim-faced and sombre. As I go about my daily work in Baghdad I am very rarely sad; I am mostly joyful. When you feel as though you are doing what you're called to do in life, and therefore have the best job in the world, surely that is a reason to be happy.

Naturally, I am very sad when people I know and love in Iraq are killed, but one lesson I have learned through this ministry is that when I am knocked down I must get back up again. I don't get knocked down very often, but when I do, I make sure that I get up and carry on quickly. Why? Because there are still so many people in need and no one else is going to help them.

SUSTAINED BY LOVE

Despite the difficulties of this job and the constant danger that I face, I am overwhelmed by the continual love and support of others. God's love surrounds me and I am so aware of His manifest presence. His love is also demonstrated through the love of so many others. When I think about how many people express their love and care for me, it is so immense that I find it deeply humbling and often ask myself, "Why?" I recall days or years gone by when I didn't seem to have any real friends, and now I have so many.

As I write this chapter I am at home in the UK, ill with hepatitis. I remember from my medical days how we all lived in fear of this illness. I have to accept the fact that I probably contracted it because of the terrible hygiene of my living conditions in Baghdad. I knew that I might be attacked physically, kidnapped and tortured, or blown up, but the fact that I might get a serious infectious illness never occurred to me. It is at difficult times like this that one has to put into practice the reality of living in hope. As the words of Edward Mote's 1834 hymn say, "My hope is built on nothing less than Jesus' blood and righteousness."

As I look back over all that God has done in my life so far, I am amazed by how His plan and purpose for me has unfolded. I had an inkling of my destiny as a small boy, and I can only do what I do now because of the journey on which God has led me. The most thrilling aspect of this to me is the fact that no part of my training has been left behind. Nothing God led me to do has been wasted.

Who would ever have thought that a priest with a medical background would be running a church in a war zone with its own clinic, treating over 150 patients each day? I still think it is strange that the doctors come to me for assistance when they are having difficulty putting in intravenous lines – there aren't too many priests who can assist with that!

Then there is our pioneering stem-cell treatment. People travel to us from all over the world to be treated and, as I mentioned earlier, it has been vital in treating my MS. So our little church in the midst of tragedy and devastation has become an oasis of healing.

I could never have guessed that God's training and equipping would lead me to be involved in all of this, in an increasingly radical Shia Islamic state in the Middle East. Yet, as I survey the situation around me, there is nowhere I would rather be. I see it all as the work of the Almighty.

HE IS EXTRAORDINARY; I AM NOT

This morning, despite being unwell at the moment, I spoke on a London radio station. They introduced me in quite a bizarre way, calling me a "bold, heroic individual". I was there to speak about the really important subject of the terrorist activity of the Islamic State, but instead I spent the first two minutes explaining why I am not a hero. I don't think I won the argument, but I tried.

I find it difficult when people treat me as some kind of great or mystical figure. This week alone has provided two examples. The first was the aforementioned radio presenter; then the next day I was contacted by a senior member of the Conservative Party, who wanted to know if I was prepared to stand for the position of Mayor of London. He told me that they needed a dynamic, charismatic individual and that I met all the requirements. I simply said, sorry, that is not my desire or my calling. Such flattery led to a split second of temptation, but then I thought of the apostle Peter and of how, having been called from the commercial fishing business to be a fisher of men, he could never return to his former work. I was reminded once again that my calling is to the Middle East. I cannot leave until the Lord tells me to.

MY "THORN"

My health has been and continues to be a major challenge in my life. As is evident in my story, I have always had serious health problems. Yet, even now, I do not think of myself as being "ill" – it is just something that I've had to learn to live with. It is another source of humility for me, that I need to rely on the help of others to do certain basic things that other people take for granted – and that this help is given with such love and care.

I always need to have someone travelling with me to help me, for instance, owing to my limited mobility. Something as simple as carrying a cup of tea from one room to the next is impossible for me without an accident. My balance is so bad that I cannot bend down to pick up something from the floor. I can sit in a room and negotiate with world leaders, but I can't tie my own shoelaces.

Whenever I am on the BBC they make a point of telling their listeners when they introduce me that I have MS, because it affects my voice. I find this difficult to hear – it's not easy for me to accept that my diction is often flawed. But Caroline assures me that it is a good thing, because in the past people have written or phoned in to complain about the "drunk vicar" they heard on the radio!

Something else that has bothered me in recent times is the fact that I have had to sit down while preaching. I don't like doing this and there are some times, such as when lecturing at Cambridge, for instance, when I just refuse to do so, and continue to stand despite its making me feel very ill. Instead of giving in to illness, I choose to pray that God will help me to function as I should.

For me, the thorn in the flesh of Paul seems an obvious comparison. Our Lord allowed one of the greatest preachers, teachers, and pastors of all time to put up with a certain degree of suffering throughout his entire ministry, though we are not told exactly what it was. Why was this? We are given no explanation, but it gives me hope: one does not have to be in perfect shape to be a minister of the gospel. As the saying goes, God uses flawed, frail human beings to do His work, because they are the only type of humans available.

There is a claim from some sections of the church (often referred to as "the prosperity gospel") that doing God's will and following Jesus will be rewarded by good health and wealth. My personal experience doesn't include either of those, yet I can testify to the faithfulness of God in keeping His promises. I have never been wealthy, but God has always provided for all my needs and I have never gone without. God has also provided for the needs of many poor people through me, and in ways that, naturally speaking, seemed impossible.

At the heart of every ministry is the principle of servanthood. We are called to be God's servants in every aspect of life and ministry. It doesn't matter to me whether I am dealing with the poor people of Baghdad, diplomats, or heads of state – to me it is all the work of Jesus. So whether I find myself in the West or the Middle East, I seek to reflect the likeness of Jesus to everyone I meet. What greater calling can there be?

CHAPTER 22

Very Special People

In the previous chapter I spoke about being sustained by the love of God and God's love expressed through others. The Lord has been incredibly gracious to me in surrounding me with some utterly amazing people. I want to pay tribute to them in this chapter.

MY CHILDREN

I began this book by talking about the dream I had as a young boy – to be an anaesthetist and a priest. I was told that doing both was impossible, but with God all things are possible, and the course of my life was set before I was ten years old. Then I had other dreams that God has miraculously answered…

I dreamed of having a beautiful, clever wife, and God graciously gave me Caroline. Then I dreamed of having children and I have been blessed beyond measure with my two boys, Jacob and Josiah. I hoped and prayed that they would both be brilliant – and they are.

Everything was perfect, but if there was one more thing I could have wished for, it was a daughter. In due course,

God would bless me with more children – adopted ones – including some daughters!

At St George's there are many children who refer to me as "Daddy" – an affectionate term of respect. But I came to have a special connection with four children: Dawood, Lina, Fulla, and Amar. Sadly, I am not allowed to write about Lina here, owing to family circumstances, but I will speak about the others.

Dawood's story is the easiest to remember and explain. I found him living in the back of a US army tank following the Iraq war in 2003. He was twelve years old and had no one to look after him. I took him home with me and he learned to speak English in just three weeks. As he grew into a young man, he never left my side until he was forced to flee the country a short time ago. Like all boys, Dawood has had his good and bad moments, but he has been unswervingly loyal and has literally saved my life on more than one occasion.

In Iraqi Christian culture there is a particular method by which one gets married. They have no concept of a boy and girl going out, or "courting", to use the old-fashioned term; one just gets engaged and then the relationship begins. It is traditional for a child to present their intended to their parents, to receive their blessing for getting engaged. When he was of an appropriate age, Dawood would regularly bring me girls that he said he wanted to marry, but I could tell that they were not suitable for one reason or another. In all, Dawood brought thirteen girls to see me and I said no thirteen times in not very subtle ways! Then one day he turned up with a fourteenth.

This girl, Sandy, was different. I could tell that she was a godly woman who loved Jesus and instantly I knew she was perfect for Dawood. I gave them my blessing inside two minutes.

We had a wonderful engagement party for Dawood and Sandy. In Iraq, this event is almost on the same scale as a wedding. It is here that the rings are blessed and exchanged. Then we set about planning the wedding. Dawood reminded me that he'd always said he would get married on my birthday, and that is what happened. When the day came, and we were all at the wedding, Dawood brought out a huge birthday cake for me, which was wonderful and very moving.

In due course, Sandy began working for me and I came to love her like one of my own children – so God gave me a daughter. We were family together and it was one of the happiest times of my life. Dawood occasionally complains to me that I love Sandy more than him! I love them both, of course.

Fulla is not an officially adopted child, but several families asked me if I would take on looking after their children when they felt they could not, and this is what I do with Fulla. She was with me in Iraq until she moved to the US, where I still care for her financially, paying her college fees and for healthcare. Although I miss having her with me in Baghdad, she has become my unofficial assistant whenever I travel to America – which means that I still see her quite often. She also comes to visit me in Baghdad and holds the honour of being probably the only person in the world who goes to Iraq on holiday! But Iraq is her home and, if it were safe to do so, she would return to be with her people.

Then there is Amar, who is several years younger than all my other children. I met him when one of the ladies in our church came to ask me to baptize her son. It was known that one of Saddam Hussein's ministers had forced her into a marriage and Amar was the result of that marriage. The father disappeared after the war, but this lady brought her son up as a Christian and longed for him to be baptized one day. It was too great a risk to baptize anyone in public, so I took Amar into the Green Zone to do it.

It was a wonderful, emotional little service, after which Amar threw his arms around me, held me very tight, and said to me, "*Abouna*, will you be my daddy now?" (*Abouna* means "father" and is used to address a priest.) I assured Amar that I would be his daddy, and so I got a new adopted son. Even though I am no longer in Iraq, Amar and I speak regularly by phone and I love him and provide for all his needs from a distance.

All my children are the inspiration of my life and give me so much joy and a reason to persevere with the mission God has given me. They have all spent time with one another on various occasions and have no doubt that they are all brothers and sisters.

Back in England, Josiah is a quiet, studious person, whereas Jacob is loud, outrageous, and more like me! As I wrote this it was approaching Christmas, and I was thinking about presents. Jacob is easy to buy for, because he wants anything and everything. It is more difficult to buy something for Josiah. Eventually Josiah told me that he would really like me to buy him some points for a credit union account, to pay for short-term loans for people in the developing world. It is something I would never have thought of, and I think it is truly wonderful that he has a heart for others in far-flung corners of the world. Both my boys make me immensely proud to be their father.

MORE SPECIAL PEOPLE

I got to know Sally Multi when I met her family, who live in a very poor area of the city called Baghdad al-Jadida, or "New Baghdad". It is essentially a slum. I loved visiting there and often saw this family and the delightful Sally. We became very close and that is why I refer to her as Sally Multi (which means "my Sally"). Sally left school at seventeen and came to work for me at the church. Although I haven't officially adopted her, she too is like a daughter to me.

DR SARAH

There are many special people who, over the years, have made it possible for me to live my life as I do, but one of the closest and most vital members of my team is Dr Sarah Ahmed, my Director of Operations. This is how we met:

Every two years the Tanenbaum Center for Interreligious Understanding has a conference that brings together all the people who have been awarded its Peace Makers in Action award, of which I am one. I consider it a great honour to be a member of this incredible fraternity. One year, while attending the conference, I heard that another conference was taking place in the same convention centre – to bring together young Jews and Muslims.

One day the delegates from each conference were mixing and chatting and someone drew it to my attention that one of the young Muslim participants in the other conference was an Iraqi. I found it difficult to believe that any Iraqi would choose to attend a conference with Jewish people, knowing the extent of the Iraqis' dislike of the Jews, so I asked to be introduced to her. In due course I met Sarah and we began talking. I soon realized that here was a quite amazing person.

I discovered that Sarah was an Iraqi dentist who was passionate about peacemaking. I listened to what she had to say and, as she was still talking, God spoke clearly to me about her: "Take her to work with you." I recall thinking, "Lord, she's a Muslim; how can she come to work with me?" But then I thought, "Who am I to argue with God?" So I told Sarah that I had a church, a clinic, two dental surgeries, and a major ministry that was working towards reconciliation in Baghdad. I followed that up by saying, "I want you to come and work for me."

Sarah certainly didn't jump at the opportunity. Instead, she told me that she didn't want to come and work with me! She later told me that, following our chat, she went away to do some research on the internet to find out exactly who this strange man was. I thought that was that, but a short while later she got in touch with me to say that she would come and work with me on a short-term trial basis.

So eventually Sarah arrived and we began working together. She divided her time between the dental clinic and my office. At the time I'd just lost some key office staff, so after a few days I asked her if she would consider becoming my personal assistant. She agreed, and it was not long before I discovered my life had changed for the better. Sarah transformed my working environment and I realized that here was someone who could be a real partner in every aspect of my work.

In the clinic she established herself as one of the most sophisticated and talented dentists. If there was a difficult case, it would be Sarah who was asked to deal with it. Within a short while, the patients were saying that they only wanted to see Dr Sarah.

The dental clinic was not the only place where she earned rapid respect. Although the Christian community knew that she was a Muslim, the parish quickly embraced her. She became my translator at our midweek services and events. She had the greatest impact in our Friday-night youth meeting, because not only is she an outstanding interpreter, but she also has a vibrant, engaging personality and the young people love her.

Sarah has since become deeply involved in the comprehensive relief work of the church, as we seek to meet a wide variety of needs in the community. On one occasion I took her with me into Baghdad al-Jadida, which was an unusual event in itself, since upper-middle-class Iraqis never venture into the slum area of the city and Sarah had never set foot there. While there, I thought it strange that there were sheep wandering around the streets, since there is not a blade of grass to be seen. I wondered out loud, "What on earth do these sheep eat?" and Sarah replied, "Garbage." I'm afraid she was right – I never saw them do anything other than rummage for food amid the rubbish that lies strewn across the streets.

On all of our visits, Sarah would always examine the teeth of every person in every house we visited. Iraq's standard of dental hygiene is among the worst in the world. There is no culture of visiting the dentist for a check-up – people go only when they are in agony and need a tooth removed. But, with Sarah, in addition to the food we distributed, there would also be toothbrushes and toothpaste to give out. The people thought this was wonderful.

Sarah also assists me in my reconciliation work. You may guess that it is not generally acceptable for a woman to play a role in engaging with major Islamic leaders, but Dr Sarah is different. She is able to grasp and interpret the most complex religious discussions and communicate them in such a way as to move things forward. Nowadays, religious leaders don't ask when I am next coming to see them; they ask when Dr Sarah is coming! She continues to play a major role in our international reconciliation meetings.

Sarah is like one of my family now, and has had an impact not only on my work life but on my home life too. She rapidly developed a very close friendship with Caroline and I think it is true to say that they never disagree on anything. In fact, if Caroline ever finds it difficult to persuade me to do something, she just asks Sarah to get me to do it!

Sarah has also become great friends with Jacob and Josiah. On a recent trip to Los Angeles, she took the boys to see the LA Clippers basketball team play when I wasn't well enough to do so. They had a fantastic time and the fact is, I think that Sarah gets along with them so well because she is more than capable of joining in with their boyish pranks!

OTHER SUPPORT STAFF

Sarah is one of four people who effectively run my life. There is Caroline, of course, and then also Lesley Kent, my PA in the UK, and Terry Jones, whom I mentioned in the previous chapter, who travels with me.

Lesley is amazing. She is in her sixties, but rides a Harley Davidson motorcycle to the office and has no plans to stop doing so! Lesley works from my home office in Hampshire, UK, and manages all my speaking engagements in both the UK and overseas. She also arranges all my travel and so virtually every day speaks to a young man named Stuart at our travel agency. We constantly tease her about her relationship with Stuart! People often ask me where exactly I live and I tell them it is Seat 1D on an aeroplane, so I suppose Stuart must be my landlord!

Retired police officer Terry Jones is sixty-seven but says he is nineteen in his head, and as far as I can see this is true. Two years ago he began travelling with me to various parts of the Middle East and he is now my right-hand man. He is central to my work, as I don't know how I could function without him. What's more, he has passed the test of our ministry: he has an equal love for both Jews and Arabs. This may sound like a light thing, but it is not – so many people struggle with despising one or the other group.

I have a great team who also help to run my UK office. There is Fiona, our office manager, David, our financial manager, Daniel, our project officer, and Gehad, whom I mentioned earlier in this book, who is an Iraqi Christian and functions as our Arabic translator and IT consultant. Then there are three further part-timers, Angela, Caroline, and Michael, working in admin and finance.

Last but not least, there is Phillip, who acts as my special assistant and driver. Like Lesley, he has been with me for several years and helps me to be in the right place at the right time. The story of how I met him is rather interesting. He often used to come and babysit for the boys when they were small. One day Jacob came up to me and said that I must give Phillip a job. He was rather persistent, so I thought I should at least meet him and see what he could do, if indeed he was inclined to work with us. After a week's trial it was clear that Phillip was a multi-talented individual who fitted very well into my personal management team. So he came to work for me and, in my absence, instantly fell into the role of surrogate father to Jacob and Josiah.

* * *

I have written about my wonderful wife, Caroline, and inspirational sons, Jacob and Josiah, and mentioned my adopted children. Now, at the close of this book, I want to mention the other people whom I love so much and who are like the fire in my bones – my godchildren. There are rather a lot of them!

Leilani Locket Bliss Haney: her grandmother is an African American who worked with me in my operating-theatre days. Leilani is now also a mother of two children.

Mark and Oliver Roberts: these twin boys were born seriously premature in London and spent many days in the neonatal intensive care unit at Hammersmith Hospital, where I baptized them both.

Alexander Muir: he is the son of Maria Muir, one of my closest friends from our student days at St Thomas' Hospital. It was Maria who persuaded me to go to Cambridge and not Oxford.

Alice Cross: Alice is the daughter of friends of ours from the first parish I worked in, St Mark's, Battersea Rise, in London. Her father is an organist and played the organ at my wedding.

Sasha Watson: Sasha is the daughter of two of my former St Thomas' colleagues and I also married her parents. She too was born very prematurely and I remember the hours I spent praying by her side in the special care baby unit at the hospital.

Isaac Hart: Isaac is the son and grandson of two sets of great friends. His grandparents are Lord and Lady Reading. Lord Reading was a close colleague when he was an active member of the House of Lords. His daughter, Natasha, came to work with me for a while and married a student, David Hart, whom I met and became friends with while in residence at Clare College, Cambridge. I eventually had the joy of officiating at their wedding.

Hannah-Rivkah: the final godchild I mention is my Hannah-Rivkah, the closest to me of all my beloved godchildren. We often discuss why we are so close and can only conclude that it must be because of God. She was born in Israel on the highway before her father was able to get her mother to hospital. I dedicated her underneath a lemon tree in the courtyard of Christ Church, Jaffa Gate, in the Old City of Jerusalem.

Sadly, her parents soon separated and her early life was very difficult, but she has a profound faith in and love for Jesus. Hannah-Rivkah went on to study Arabic at London University and is now taking a year out in Jordan – a place I pass through regularly, so we get to see each other quite frequently and we talk most days by phone. Not so long ago I was able to take her with me to Israel. It was the first time she had been there since she was a baby and we prayed together underneath the lemon tree where I dedicated her. She is another of the great gifts God has given me.

Thank you, dear reader, for indulging me as I have mentioned so many people who are special in my life. I could not have written a book about my life without mentioning them, because my life would not be what it is without them. Every day I thank God that He has been gracious enough to allow these wonderful people to make up the rich fabric of my existence. With them and our Lord, I can do everything.

A Reflection: Tariq Aziz

Today should be the funeral of one of the people closest to Saddam Hussein, his deputy, Tariq Aziz. Coming from a Christian background, he was both revered and feared and yet there were many who respected him. For me it is a very personal story. At the moment the Iraqi government won't allow his body to leave Iraq for Jordan, where his family all are. We are working on it.

The fact is that if it were not for him I would not be where I am today. It was in fact he who in 1998 first got me into Iraq. Over seventeen years I would see him in so many different places. From Baghdad's Ba'ath Party offices, to grand palaces, to a prison cell in a maximum security prison.

I could write a book just on my discussions with him; indeed, I have in fact written much about him in many of my books. Every time I visited him I took him something. In all the years of our acquaintance he only ever asked for two things: first, he wanted brown sauce and, second, he wanted magazines and journals. You could say he wanted both the taste of freedom and the news of freedom.

I knew that, historically speaking, he was not a good man. I knew he had brought fear and death to many of the families I know and love, and yet I have to confess that I loved him. The most essential gift that the Lord has given me in my job is to be able to love my enemies, and that is what I do all the time. Enemies are not usually very nice to you. I got into the practice of inviting enemies to dinner, because I knew that enemies were people whose story you had not yet heard. The last enemy I invited to dinner – from ISIS – made it very clear that if he came he would chop my head off. So different from my experience, work, and life with Mr Aziz. The reality was that he was my friend. I will never forget two of the most important things he asked me to do. First, he wanted me to bring some of the religious leaders from Britain to Iraq and, second, he wanted me to take the religious leaders from Iraq to England and America.

Regarding England, I told him there would be no problem, the then Archbishop of Canterbury, George Carey, would help me do that, but as for America I did not know how to make it happen.

"Don't worry," he said. "Ask Billy Graham." As I have described earlier Dr Graham enlisted the help of President Bill Clinton, and the whole highly complex initiative eventually bore fruit. For me it was not only the beginning of a substantive relationship with Dr Graham but it was the beginning of an amazing relationship with the religious leaders, which has lasted to this day.

Yes, there are those who do not like my saying positive things about Tariq Aziz. I know people were very badly hurt by the Saddam regime. I know from my last meeting with him in prison that he never changed in his attitude. He made it clear to me that Iraq now was far worse than it had ever been before, and I could not disagree with him: indeed it was. Yes, I am sorry I will not see him again, and I just pray that before the end our Lord revealed Himself to him and had mercy on him.

Epilogue: Late Fragment

At the end of this book, I want to give readers an insight into the current state of our ministry in the Middle East.

PRESENT DANGER

It is a particularly difficult time as, recently, Islamic State terrorists nearly entered Baghdad. The people here are full of fear and this morning I noticed that the normally hectic local streets are deserted – no one has ventured out. News from our friends in the areas surrounding Baghdad is bleak: the terrorists are poised outside the city. No one knows precisely what is happening, but we know that civilians have been killed in air strikes and there are huge battles between ISIS and the Iraqi army.

We also know that our army is not very efficient. This morning I spoke to one of the soldiers assigned by the government to protect me. I asked him what he would do if he saw ISIS invading the city. He told me he would take off his uniform and run. I asked him if he took seriously his role as a soldier in fighting to protect his people. He replied that, no, he did not – he did it only because he needed the money.

CONCERNS FOR MY SECURITY

At 2.40 this morning I received a call from one of the security chiefs at the US embassy. The embassy had been contacted by a congressman from Washington, DC, Trent Franks, who was very concerned about my security. Mr Franks had, in turn, been contacted by one of our US Foundation's board members. Security is a constant topic of discussion. I am no longer allowed a badge to get into Baghdad's Green Zone. I am allowed access to the US and British embassies, but I cannot get to them without passing through the Green Zone, so this is a constant source of frustration.

The news this morning is that the advance of ISIS towards Baghdad has been halted. Information about how far away from the city ISIS are varies depending on whom one asks, but we live in hope.

Later I went to see Frank Baker, the new British Ambassador to Iraq. To my surprise we were from exactly the same town in the UK, went to the same school, and had a lot in common. We talked at length about the situation here and about issues of security generally and my security in particular. He was happy with the security arrangements we had in place and assured me there would be additional help if I needed it.

I returned to St George's to be greeted by messages from my US board saying that they felt it was too dangerous for me to remain in Iraq and that I needed to get out quickly. They insisted that I leave immediately and travel to Israel. As I have already stated, I accept the risks as part and parcel of my ministry here, and so am naturally resistant to the idea of leaving my people.

But pressure on me to leave began to mount from a number of different sources. Among the members of the UK Foreign Office and US Congress there seemed to be equal concern. It was not long before these people were expressing their concerns in the strongest terms to the Archbishop of Canterbury. Then my own Bishop of Cyprus and the Gulf was in contact with me about his discussions with the Archbishop.

It was clear that they had decided it was now just too dangerous for me to be in Iraq – and not just in Baghdad, but also Kurdistan and other areas where I could have engaged in relief work. In the end I spoke at length to my friend Justin Welby and he told me that I was more use to my people alive than dead. I could not deny this: we were providing food, clothing, healthcare, and much more for them.

I must confess that I was so depressed by the thought of not being in Iraq that for a brief moment I considered whether I should resign from the church and continue my work here regardless, as part of a humanitarian organization. But I could not do this – I am a man under authority and I cannot just do whatever I want. It was a very hard decision to leave, but one which pleased Caroline.

LATE FRAGMENT

People often ask me how they can pray for or help the believers in Baghdad. I say to them, "You can both pray for peace and pay for peace." We are extremely grateful for the prayers of other believers, but we also need practical aid to provide relief for those in dire need, so financial contributions are equally welcome.

Recently, I travelled to the US to visit a number of different places and meet some church leaders who really care about and support our mission. One of the highlights of the trip was a visit to a Christian school in Seattle. As I was being shown around, a little boy called Sean came up to me and gave me $1, telling me

Our wedding day in 1991. From left to right: my parents Maurice and Pauline White; our best man, the Revd Richard Coombs; and Caroline's parents Peter and Mary Spreckley.

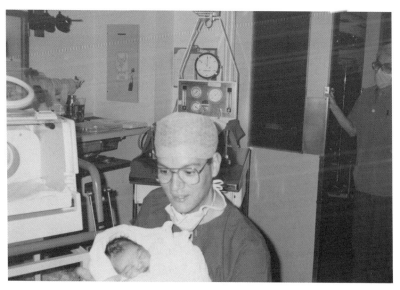

1986, during my medical career: I had just helped deliver this baby by caesarean section.

Punting the boys down the Cam beside Queen's College, Cambridge. Twelve years later Josiah is now a student at Queen's.

Introducing Caroline to Pope John Paul II in 1993.

The signing of the historic Alexandria Declaration. Seated: the then Grand Imam of the Al-Azhar Mosque, Mohammed Sayed Tantawi, and to his right the then Sephardi Chief Rabbi Bakshi-Doron. Standing behind them, from left to right: Sheikh Talal Sider, founder of Hamas; Chief Rabbi Michael Melchior, then deputy Foreign Minister of Israel; the assistant to the Chief Rabbi; the Most Revd George Carey, Archbishop of Canterbury; and Andrew White.

Standing amid the ruins of Coventry Cathedral: the first time the Iraqi religious leaders visited us at Coventry in 1999. From left to right: Fr Philip, a Chaldean priest; the Grand Ayatollah Hussein Al-Sadr; the late Chaldean Patriarch Raphael Bidawid; Andrew White; Sheikh Abdul Latif Humayem, formally Saddam Hussein's imam, now the head of the Sunni Wakf, and still a very close colleague.

Caroline and me with Prime Minister John Major.

With George Carey, Archbishop of Canterbury, and Prime Minister Tony Blair.

Presenting a bottle of HP sauce to Tariq Aziz, Deputy Prime Minister under Saddam Hussein, who first got me into Iraq.

I gave the Coventry
Cross of Nails to
Archbishop Desmond
Tutu during a visit to
the Holy Land in 2000.

With Sir Richard Branson at
Coventry Cathedral, 2001. He
worked closely with us on various
reconciliation projects.

Above: He used to be my enemy, but he became a close friend: President Yasser Arafat, the
leader of the Palestinian National Authority until 2005. One of my regular meetings with
him along with my then project officer at Coventry Cathedral, Oliver Scutt.

Left: With my then co-director of the International Centre for Reconciliation at Coventry Cathedral, Justin Welby, now the Archbishop of Canterbury, on the day we reopened St George's Baghdad after the war in 2003. With us are the caretaker of St George's, Hanna Toma, and his daughter.

Right: Caroline and me at the launch of the Foundation for Relief and Reconciliation in the Middle East (FRRME) at the House of Lords in 2003.

Below: The Hasidic Rabbi Shimon Naftalis is very dear to me: he was my teacher when I was at Yeshiva, and is still my friend and colleague.

Right: Hundreds stand in line to receive food relief after church in 2005 at St George's, Baghdad.

Left: Dr Sara Ahmed is our inspirational director of operations. She has left her work in our clinic in Baghdad and is personally heading up all of our work amongst Internally Displaced People, the IDPs, in Northern Iraq. She herself is a Muslim, but is caring for the Christians and other minorities who have lost everything. True reconciliation in practice.

Below: J.John, Killy John, Caroline, Josiah, Jacob, and me together on their first and only visit to Erbil in what I call "pretend Iraq": Kurdistan, 2012.

Top: Two of the most important people in my life: my elder son Josiah with my dearest goddaughter Hannah-Rivkah, before I baptized her in the River Jordan.

Right: A normal day in war-torn Baghdad. On my rounds, wearing my body armour.

Left: For many of the Iraqi refugee children in Jordan, this is their first Christmas away from home. With help from our supporters, we made sure they had presents to open on Christmas Day.

Right: Iraqi refugee children may have lost their homes but they have not lost their faith in Yesua. Here they are at our school in Marka singing the Lord's Prayer in Aramaic, which they do three times a day.

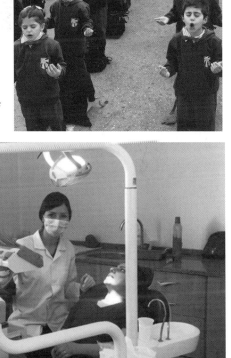

Above: Our health clinic in Jordan (complete with dentist's chair) provides essential medical care to five hundred Iraqi refugee families. Our dentist Lina (masked) is one of my closest friends.

Above: Our school for Iraqi refugees in Marka had humble beginnings but now the children have their own school uniform, complete with logo. I baptised Marion, above, in Baghdad. Her older sister Mabel (left, holding a handbag) has worked with us for years.

I am no longer Chaplain of St George's Church in Baghdad but I still minister to our Iraqi brothers and sisters in Christ living in Jordan.

Much of our work in Iraq is overseen by Dr Sarah Ahmed, FRRME's Director of Operations in the Middle East. She trained as a dentist but now works on the front line just miles from the Islamic State, distributing food and medical supplies to thousands of displaced Iraqis.

Top: Mario and Mariam

Right: Father Khalil

Above: Chief Rabbi Michael Melchior at Christ Church, Jaffa Gate, Jerusalem.

Gideon Ariel

Rav Ariel Cohen

Nisreen and Hanna Ishaq

Top: The Singerman family

Left: Sheikh Imad Falouji, one of the founders of Hamas, who became a radical peacemaker.

Below: Myself, my son Josiah, Rabbi Shimon Naftalis, and Hanna Ishaq.

Left: Michael Kerem

Below: Norman and
Lola Cohen

Above: Shibly Kandoor, brother-in-law of Hanna Ishaq, standing in front of one of the
pots in which the Dead Sea Scrolls were found.

Left: Sheila and Zvi Raviv. Zvi was chief of staff to Ehud Barak, former Prime Minister of Israel.

Below: David Pileggi, Rector of Christ Church, Jaffa Gate, Jerusalem.

Above: Ambassador Daniel Taub, former Israeli ambassador to England.

Christine Darg

Myself, Lidiia Nagirnie, and Peter Christenson

it was for the children in Iraq. It was a hugely moving moment and, to me, a true symbol of the widow's mite.

A few days later I was visiting the school that is based in Bethel Church, Redding, California, and I told the story of Sean's $1 gift and how I saw it as a sign of God's goodness and provision. I said that the Lord can use anyone to meet our needs and this little boy wanted to help his brothers and sisters on the other side of the world, many of whose families would have been dispersed or even killed. As I told the story, the students began to get up and come to me, each handing me their $1 or more.

For the remainder of my trip, wherever I went I told people about Sean and the response was always the same. By the end of my trip, that $1 had turned into an incredible $25,000! For me this is the perfect illustration of how God is able to take a "small" act of faith and multiply it into something amazing. That little boy had no idea of the blessing his $1 would trigger; he simply sowed a seed and left the rest in God's hands.

Back in Israel and Palestine, my story continues. My work is varied and intensive. During the last few days I have given lectures to major Israeli audiences, appeared on radio and TV, and spoken at a church in Bethlehem. Recently I became friends with a lady called Roma and her husband, Mark Burnett. I don't watch much TV, but one show I do watch with Jacob is *The Apprentice* – one of the programmes devised by Mark.[11] Mark has a heart to support the beleaguered Christians of Iraq. Before too long I will visit their home in Malibu and take Jacob with me. Suddenly I have become a hero in his eyes because I'm taking him to meet the creator of *The Apprentice*, which is far

---

11 *The Apprentice*, which began in 2005, is a British reality TV show in which a group of aspiring businessmen and -women compete for the chance to work with the business magnate Lord Alan Sugar.

more important to me than being seen as a hero by the media!

As I look back at my journey so far, I am simply overwhelmed by the greatness and the magnificence of God in my life. I am stunned by all that He has achieved through me; amazed by how He has enabled me to survive the most horrendous situations. Above all, I am overwhelmed by God's love for me. In the end, to know the love of God and to love others truly is all we can hope for. I came across this poem by the American poet Raymond Carver called "Late Fragment".[12] I think it says everything:

> *And did you get what*
> *you wanted from this life, even so?*
> *I did.*
> *And what did you want?*
> *To call myself beloved, to feel myself*
> *beloved on the earth.*

This is my story so far. What will happen next, who knows? Only my Lord and my Creator: He knows!

---

12 "Late Fragment" is the final poem in Raymond Carver's (1938–1988) last published work, *A New Path to the Waterfall*, a collection written while he was dying of cancer.

Afterword

My journey has not yet finished: it has only just begun. Since I stopped being based in Baghdad, my journey has moved to a whole new level. I gave up saying a long time ago that it could not get worse, or better, because it has become both worse *and* better.

I always used to say to my people in Iraq, "Don't you leave me, and I won't leave you."

However, as things got worse in Baghdad, people did start to leave. Many went north, to the traditional Iraqi Christian area of Nineveh/Mosul. For a short while there was such freedom and liberty there, but it was only a matter of months before things began to change. In Anbar Province a group had formed that became known as Daesh, or ISIS: a group of radical Sunni extremists who wanted to root out not only the Shia majority but also the Christian minority. It was not long before this group moved towards the Nineveh area. As they did, many fled with just the clothes on their backs.

ISIS went through the town painting the Arabic *Nu* sign on each Christian home to indicate that these people were Nazarenes, that is, that they followed Jesus of Nazareth. These homes were then ransacked and destroyed. Many of the people were killed and others fled north to the safety of Kurdistan. Though still in Iraq, Kurdistan is an autonomous, self-controlled region and has been for a considerable time – in fact, since the UN established a no-fly zone in the area in the 1990s.

Many of those who had fled to Kurdistan soon travelled on to Jordan. In Jordan they did not receive any financial support; they were simply registered by the UN as people seeking to obtain refugee status and move on to other countries. They often arrived very depressed, not knowing what the future would hold or how they would survive.

One of my old friends, a Baptist pastor called Hanna, from Gaza, shifted his ministry to Jordan as he focused on helping the Iraqi refugees.

I went to see one family who had recently fled to Jordan. The father had been a taxi driver, but one day he had been taken by a group, suspected to have been ISIS, and was never seen again. We asked how we could help the family. The children, Mario (a ten-year-old boy) and Mariam (his twelve-year-old sister), just wanted their daddy back. Their mother, Ban, was about to be evicted from their terrible apartment and had no money to get even simple basic food. So I immediately took care of these matters. Each time we returned to them we would ensure they were given the supplies they needed.

Mario became very close to me, and one day I took him in my arms and said to him, "Mario, you know I cannot get your daddy back, but is there anything else we can get you?"

Mario took my hand and said, "Abouna, will you be my daddy, and can I go to school?" I assured him that I would be his daddy and that somehow we would get him to school. The first was easy, but the second was very difficult, as no Iraqi children were allowed to go to school in Jordan.

We investigated what Christian schools there might be in Jordan. All the schools were private, and very expensive. There was one Catholic school outside Amman, in a poor area called

Macca, where many of the refugees lived. I discussed with the headmaster, a wonderful priest called Father Khalil, whether there was any chance of the school taking in at least fifty refugee children, whom FRRME (Foundation for Relief and Reconciliation in the Middle East) would pay for. It was obvious that these children would not fit into the day school that Father Khalil and his team were running. Therefore, it was decided that we would start an afternoon school, geared towards our refugee children.

This school would be Christian and Iraqi. Our Iraqi Christians did not, however, speak Arabic as their mother tongue: they spoke the ancient language of Aramaic, the language Jesus used. Among our Iraqi refugees we discovered that we actually had enough qualified teachers to staff the school.

Within three weeks we had everything in place to establish the school. Our American and British foundation offered to pay most of the costs of running the school, from buses, to teachers, to food. In addition to basic food for children at the school, we also faced the major challenge of providing food for their families. Meeting all these needs was a huge operation, and we were very aware of God's gracious provision. Through the help of many Jews and Christians we were indeed able to find the necessary resources. To this day we meet these needs, not just providing food but also covering housing costs. This new ministry has developed not just to meet the needs of the schoolchildren's families, but also to provide for many other Iraqi refugee families.

It soon became clear that, in addition to providing education, relief, and housing, we also had to meet another major need, health care. So a further major partnership was formed, this time with a Greek Orthodox clinic that provides a comprehensive general practice service including cardiology, general medicine, and paediatrics. This clinic also runs a comprehensive dental service, and all the treatment and prescriptions are made available free of charge. I go into the clinic most weeks, and am immediately asked to pray for and anoint all the patients. This is a perfect example of how spiritual and physical healing can go together. Surely this is how our Lord meant His Kingdom to be manifested.

Meanwhile, across the River Jordan, in the Land of the Holy One, our work continues to go from strength to strength.

Here we are looking after members of all the monotheistic faiths: Jews, Christians, and Muslims. The heart of this ministry is to provide for those in need, especially among the Palestinian community, but there are also many Israelis who need our help. As in Jordan and Iraq, we are deeply blessed to be working with many godly partners who are fostering reconciliation and bringing broken communities together.

These daily tragedies and their resolution – the cycle of agony and ecstasy – form the very foundations of our work. Looking back, the groundwork for this ministry had been laid much earlier: it was dealing with the tragedy of the siege of the Church of the Nativity that really proved to be the starting point. That event led to my being seen as a public figure, and thus enabled me to play an active role in resolving so many high-profile conflict situations.

***

POSTSCRIPT

Sometimes my illness flares up. At such times I find the following passage from Psalm 139 of great comfort:

> *Where can I go from your Spirit?*
> > *Where can I flee from your presence?*
> *If I go up to the heavens, you are there;*
> > *if I make my bed in the depths, you are there.*
> *If I rise on the wings of the dawn,*
> > *if I settle on the far side of the sea,*
> *even there your hand will guide me,*
> > *your right hand will hold me fast.*
> *If I say, "Surely the darkness will hide me*
> > *and the light become night around me,"*
> *even the darkness will not be dark to you;*
> > *the night will shine like the day,*
> > *for darkness is as light to you.*
> (Psalm 139:7–12, NIV)

As I sat in the doctor's surgery this morning, after a traumatic week, all I could do was think of the words of Psalm 139:7: "Where can I flee from your presence?" There were times this week when I felt so ill I could not even pray. I could only lie there suffering, aware of the presence of the Almighty. Yet in the presence of this darkness I was so aware, as it says in verse 12, that "even the darkness will not be dark to you; the night will shine like the day, for darkness is as light to you".

The thousands of prayers of my Facebook friends have made me realize that I am being prayed for by my family. Yes, a family on Facebook, but you are all my brothers and sisters and I love you so much. One of my friends pointed out that through my suffering people are drawn to prayer, and drawn together in a new relationship with God.

Suddenly I realized that this has indeed been the story of my life. Tragedy after tragedy, and people drawn together in unity, praying for me out of the crisis. Whether in the critical health crisis of my youth, or the terrorists' threats of recent years, or MS problems in the past two decades, I have been constantly sustained by the glorious presence of the Almighty and the prayers of His people, my friends.

This is my story. Where can I go from your presence, O Lord?

SPEAKING ENGAGEMENTS

Every week, invitations arrive from around the world. I am glad to receive them, because they allow me to share what I see each day of the grace of God in action in the Middle East, and also to present the needs of the people there. I can accept only a small percentage of the invitations I receive, sadly, but I do my best to respond.

If you would like to invite me to speak, or to obtain information about the work of FRRME, or to offer prayer or financial support, please see the page 378 about FRRME.

APPENDIX 1

Who's Who

Abdel Latif Humayem, Sheikh Dr

In effect Saddam Hussein's personal imam, who wields great influence among the Sunna in Iraq. He visited America and Britain in 1999. After the war, he took refuge in Jordan, where he still lives. He returned briefly to Iraq in 2004 (and was greeted with great warmth by Ayatollah al-Sadr) but fled again when the National De-Ba'thification Committee seized all his wealth. In 2007, he introduced me to a member of al-Qa'ida in Amman. A delightful man, and one of the four authors of the Sunni/Shia fatwa against violence in 2008.

Abdel Qadir al-Ani, Sheikh Dr

The principal lieutenant in Iraq of Sheikh Dr al-Kubaisi, until he was obliged to flee to Jordan in 2004 after he was accused of being a traitor and his house was bombed. An important early ally.

Abu Ragif, Ayatollah Ammar

A senior lieutenant of Grand Ayatollah al-Sistani, who is also close to two of Iraq's four other grand ayatollahs. He has been a crucial ally – and a friend of Sheikh Dr Abdel Latif – since he joined us in Cairo in 2007. One of the four authors of the Sunni/Shia fatwa against violence in 2008.

Alfatlawi, Fadel

A member of my team in Baghdad immediately after the war, whom I first met as an exile in Coventry. In 2004 he succeeded Georges as secretary general of the Iraqi Institute of Peace, but he had to quit (and flee to Jordan) at the end of 2005 when the price on his head became too great.

al-Kubaisi, Sheikh Dr Ahmed

The most senior of Iraq's Sunna. He lives in Dubai, where he fled after falling out with Saddam many years ago, but exerts great influence in Iraq through his televised sermons. He joined us in Cairo in 2007, and was one of the four authors of the Sunni/Shia fatwa against violence in 2008.

al-Maliki, Nuri

The leader of the (Shia) Da'wa Party, who became Prime Minister of Iraq in May 2007. He is a strong supporter of our work.

al-Sadooni, Samir Raheem

The former lawyer who was my driver in Baghdad immediately after the war and went on to become my right-hand man in

Iraq, first for the International Centre for Reconciliation in Coventry and then as the FRRME's director of Iraq. He also interprets for me.

al-Sadr, Ayatollah Hussein

The most senior Shia in Baghdad, an old friend of Dr Mowaffak and my closest spiritual ally in Iraq. He visited America and Britain in 1999, when I learned how his family had been decimated by the Ba'thists; but I found out only later how cruelly he himself had been tortured. A man of great holiness and wisdom, he was the "father" of the Baghdad Religious Accord in 2004 and showed great warmth to Sheikh Dr Abdel Latif on his return to Iraq.

al-Sistani, Grand Ayatollah Ali

The most senior of Iraq's five grand ayatollahs, and the most powerful man in the country – his lieutenants told one of my colleagues, "We are the government." He lives in the holy city of Najaf and does not meet foreigners, but is said to approve strongly of our work. He endorsed the so-called Mecca Document in 2006, and his senior lieutenant Ayatollah Abu Ragif co-authored the Sunni/Shia fatwa against violence in 2008.

al-Ubaidi, Sheikh Salah

The chief spokesman of Muqtada al-Sadr, he joined us in Cairo in 2008 and has since been a key ally, although he was not a signatory of the subsequent Sunni/Shia fatwa against violence.

al-Zuhairi, Sheikh Abdelhalim Jawad Kadhum

The chair of the gathering of Sunni and Shia scholars who signed the so-called Mecca Document in 2006 and chief religious adviser to Nuri al-Maliki since he became Prime Minister, who has worked with us since 2007. One of the four authors of the Sunni/Shia fatwa against violence in 2008.

Ariel, Gideon

Gideon, a visionary and pioneer in Jewish–Christian relations, is the founder and CEO of the organization called Root Source. Gideon made Aliyah (that is, he was a Jew from the diaspora who returned to Israel) from the USA when he was fourteen, and spent close to a decade in advanced Jewish institutes of learning (yeshivas), and in the Israel Defense Forces (IDF). After spending over twenty years in the Armoured Tank Corps, Gideon now serves in the IDF reserves as a captain in the military spokesperson's office. Raised an Orthodox Jew, he has observed Jewish traditions his entire life, and is a seasoned Hebrew and Judaism instructor. He has been working with Christian organizations in Israel, the USA, and internationally since 2005.

Aziz, Tariq

Deputy Prime Minister of Iraq under Saddam, who first invited me to his country in 1999.

Aziz Mohamed, Mrs Samia

The (Shia) Faili Kurd who chaired the IIP's working party on women, religion and democracy and herself became an MP.

Benham, Ammal

Ammal is the headmistress of Mar Ephrem Syrian Orthodox School in Beit Jala, close to Bethlehem. I have been involved with the school from the day that Joseph the carpenter first decided a school was needed back in the year 2000. Nowadays, Mar Ephrem is the most academically proficient school in the whole Palestinian Authority. The building has grown and the school, which began as a kindergarten, now offers education through to high-school level.

Bremer, Paul

The American administrator (or "king") of Iraq from May 2003 to June 2004.

Carey, Dr George (later Lord)

The Archbishop of Canterbury from 1991 to 2002, when he was ennobled. He co-chaired the summit that produced the Alexandria Declaration in 2002, having called all the delegates together, and sent me to Bethlehem later that year to try to help to resolve the siege of the Church of the Nativity. A kind and wise man, he became a very close friend and ally and was first chair and then patron of the Foundation for Relief and Reconciliation in the Middle East.

Coalition Provisional Authority (CPA)

The international (but overwhelmingly American) administration that ran Iraq from May 2003 until the handover of sovereignty in June 2004.

Cohen, Rav Ariel

Rav Ariel is an ultra-Orthodox (and wonderfully eccentric) rabbi whose passion is to see Jesus accepted in Israeli society. Rav Ariel is regarded as highly controversial by many other rabbis. His inspiration comes very much from the ultra-Orthodox and Kabbalistic traditions. While Kabbalah may be viewed as verging on the occult by many in the Christian tradition, it is clearly very mystical and can really be understood only within the context of ultra-Orthodox Judaism by someone who is steeped in Torah and Talmudic studies. Even within these traditions it is not seen as permissible to begin to study Kabbalah before the age of forty, by which point one should already have a solid grounding in the Torah.

Cohen, Norman and Lola

Norman and Lola are also part of our Jerusalem family. Norman is in his nineties and was one of the first people to reach the beach in the D-Day landings. His wife Lola is almost a decade younger. They are both from Coventry, where I used to work. They contacted me after seeing me on TV in the Bethlehem siege. Lola and Norman made Aliyah over thirty years ago, and live in Gilo, between Jerusalem and Bethlehem. Lola is the only person I know in the whole of the Middle East who provides perfect English afternoon tea, with scones, cream, and the best home-made shortbread I have ever tasted. Norman became a writer in his old age and wrote the inspirational book *The Torah on One Foot*. This provides an insight into the weekly Torah portion known as the Parsha. They know all my UK family and my boys used to love visiting them when they were young, as Norman's retirement job was volunteering at the Jerusalem Zoo and he and Lola always took the boys to see behind the scenes there. We will never forget the story of one newborn elephant, which became known to us all as the "pink elephant".

Darg, Christine

Christine is an inspirational leader. Like me, she does not live solely in Jerusalem but is also based in England, though she stays in the Middle East much of the time. She also moves around the world. Like me, she passionately loves both the Jews and the Arabs and is also friends with many of the people mentioned here and has an online Jerusalem TV programme. She is simply a legend you should all follow. Here is the online link to one of her programmes: it is really worth viewing: http://jerusalemchannel.tv/video/latestvideo-countdown-pentecost-mystery-omer/

Falouji, Sheikh Imad

Central to our work among the Palestinians has been one Palestinian who is an avid peace activist and a member of the peace-making coalition. Sheikh Falouji was a former member of the Palestinian Authority government and a minister in Yasser Arafat's administration. He teaches at the Jerusalem International School for Reconciliation. He has not always been a "Peacenik", though. He is known for being one of the founders of the terrorist group Hamas. He is one of the people who have moved with us from darkness to light, from war-making to peace-making. He is one of the heroes of our work.

Heflin, Sister Ruth

The most forceful person I have ever met, who ran a charismatic church in Jerusalem and prophesied that my calling in life was to "seek the peace of Jerusalem and the Middle East'.

Heldt, Dr Petra

Petra is the person I have known longest in Israel. I met her on my very first trip there, in 1988. She has lived in Israel for many years but comes from Germany and is an ordained Lutheran minister. A highly respected academic of international renown, and an expert in the early history of Christianity and Jewish–Christian relations, she is the executive director of the Ecumenical Theological Research Fraternity. Several years ago she was seriously injured in a terrorist bombing in the centre of Jerusalem. After many months in hospital she recovered well and is back in action.

Hoyt, Colonel Mike

The most senior of the US Army chaplains in Iraq from 2006 to 2007 and a colleague in the Pentagon funded work of the Iraqi Inter-Religious Congress.

Iraqi Institute of Peace (IIP)

The final name of the organization established by the Baghdad Religious Accord in 2004 to pursue peace and reconciliation in Iraq.

Ishaq, Hanna and Nisreen

Hanna has worked for me, and with me, longer than anyone else. Initially he was my driver, but eventually he became my right-hand man and the coordinator of much of my work in Israel and the Palestinian Authority. Without Hanna, nothing happens. Whether it is organizing the release of hostages from Gaza or dealing with complicated negotiations with Yasser Arafat, Hanna has always been there in the lead. He and his dear wife, Nisreen, have three children, Maria, Katrina, and Anton. I am also very close to his children. Nisreen works at the American consulate.

We have had many memorable experiences over the years, but Hanna will always say that for him the highlight of the job was in 2002 when we were negotiating during the siege at the Church of the Nativity, and providing relief for the people of Bethlehem. On one occasion we had a crash with a tank, and Hanna asked the tank commander if he had insurance. Central to my whole work is the fact that close to me is the one man who will always take risks with me and who will never say we can't do something, because one of his core beliefs is that we can always make things happen.

Hanna is Aramaic, from the Syrian Orthodox community, and an active deacon in the Syrian Orthodox Church. He is also one of the leaders of the Syrian Orthodox scout movement, which is famous for its marching band and bagpipe players.

Kandoor, Shibly

My dear friend Shibly is something else. He is married to Hanna's sister and has surely the most outstanding souvenir shop in Bethlehem, the Kandoor Store. Not only does he have the most amazing olive-wood souvenirs, many made by Joseph the carpenter, but he also has one of the original vessels that the Dead Sea Scrolls were found in. Shibly is a dear friend who, despite not being involved in our work, is a major part of our life in Jerusalem, as we visit him on every trip.

Kerem, Michael

Michael works out of Christ Church, Jaffa Gate, and is essential in heading up the Isaiah 19 Highway Ministry. This is a ministry that takes its vision from the Isaiah 19 prophecy that talks about the link between Assyria, Egypt, and Israel. This prophecy forms the basis and inspiration for our whole ministry:

> *In that day there will be a highway from Egypt to Assyria. The Assyrians will go to Egypt and the Egyptians to Assyria. The Egyptians and Assyrians will worship together. In that day Israel will be the third, along with Egypt and Assyria, a blessing on the earth. The Lord Almighty will bless them, saying, "Blessed be Egypt my people, Assyria my handiwork, and Israel my inheritance."*
> **Isaiah 19:23–25, NIV**

Michael self-identifies as a Messianic Jew. His wife is a Turkish Armenian, so somebody else whose family has a history of suffering. His daughter Nava also worked for me at one stage. She served as a gun commander in the IDF (and is a very good shot!).

Maki, Peter

The young American who was the FRRME's director of operations from 2005 to 2007.

Mandeans

Adherents of a religion derived from the followers of John the Baptist.

Melchior, Rabbi Michael

The Deputy Foreign Minister of Israel from 2001 to 2002 and also (as it happens) the Chief Rabbi of Norway. One of my closest friends and co-workers for peace, whom I first met in 2001, when he suggested what was to become the Alexandria Process. An Orthodox Jew, he led the Jewish delegation in Alexandria and forged a crucial alliance – and friendship – with Sheikh Talal, with whom he shared the Coventry International Prize for Peace and Reconciliation with Patriarch Sabbah in 2002.

Mowaffak al-Rubaie, Dr

An old friend of Ayatollah al-Sadr whom I first met in 1999 in London, where he was living in exile and working as a neurologist. After the war, Paul Bremer appointed him to the Iraqi Governing Council and then gave him a five-year contract as Iraq's National Security Adviser. He is my principal adviser and one of my closest friends and allies in Iraq, and is the first chair of the Iraqi Institute of Peace. In 2008, he was awarded the FRRME's Prize for Peace in the Middle East.

Mukhabarat

The Arabic word for "intelligence", and hence the name of Saddam's intelligence service.

Muqtada al-Sadr

The fiery young son of a grand ayatollah who was assassinated in 1999 by Saddam's agents, and the nephew of my dear friend Ayatollah al-Sadr. He commands Iraq's largest militia, the Shia Mehdi Army, which is a powerful opponent of both the multinational forces and al-Qa'ida in Iraq. His chief spokesman, Sheikh al-Ubaidi, joined us in Cairo in 2008 and has become a key ally.

Naftalis, Rabbi Shimon

Vital to my involvement with the ultra-Orthodox Hasidic community is Rav Shimon Naftalis. An ultra-Orthodox Hasidic rabbi, he was the one who first got me involved with the Hasidic community, and got me into a yeshiva. He was at the party that Caroline and I had in Jerusalem during our honeymoon, and every week that I am in Jerusalem we will go and have dinner together in the glatt kosher13 ultra-Orthodox Chinese Restaurant.[13] I remember so well the very first time that we met in the late 1980s. I was still a student at Cambridge at the time, and doing some research on the role of Israel in Christian theology. Since that day, Shimon has been a great friend, colleague, and teacher. He was the person who first introduced me to Ruth Heflin, the great pastor of Jerusalem until she passed to glory in September 2000 at the age of just sixty. It was she who first told me that my life would be spent working for peace, not just in Israel but in the Middle East, and so it has proved.

Nagirnie, Lidiia

Lidiia was originally a volunteer working at Christ Church, Jaffa Gate, in the Old City of Jerusalem. She is from Ukraine and is a brilliant pianist. I got to know her when I asked her to play the piano at a last-minute wedding I was taking at Christ Church one day. She had also grown up in a place of intense conflict

---

13 "Glatt kosher" means meat from animals with smooth or defect-free lungs, but today the term is often used informally to imply that a product was processed under a stricter standard of *kashrut*, or Jewish religious dietary laws.

and had a fairly traumatic upbringing. We became very good
friends and she told me I was like a true father figure to her.
The relationship was very similar to the one I had with my six
unofficial adopted children in Iraq. It was not long before she
started calling me "Poppa", and she has increasingly supported
me in my work. So she, like Hanna, has become not only part
of my team but part of my family.

Petraeus, General David

The American commander of the multinational forces in Iraq
from January 2007 to September 2008, when he directed the
so-called surge.

Pileggi, David

Another deeply inspirational person who is very much part of
Jerusalem life, David was for many years the leader of Shoresh
Tours, part of the CMJ ministries (The Church's Ministry
among Jewish People), but became the rector of Christ Church,
Jaffa Gate several years ago. He is one of the most inspiring
guides in Israel and people are still desperate for him to do
guided tours. As he is the rector of the key church in the Israel
Trust of the Anglican Church, many presume that he is simply
a friend and lover of Israel. He is not: he is a passionate lover
of Jews and Arabs alike, and thus a real friend to all the people
of the land. At his very heart he is a man of reconciliation. He
is a great support to us in our work, and hosts our Jerusalem
International School of Reconciliation.

Raviv, Sheila and Zvi

Sheila and Zvi are also part of our Jerusalem family. Sheila is originally Welsh, while Zvi was born in Israel. Zvi was chief of staff to Ehud Olmert when he was mayor of Jerusalem, before he became prime minister. Zvi is the only person I know who has the same size feet as me (sixteen English / fifty European). Sheila regularly welcomes me for lunch or dinner and serves me my favourite classic Jewish dish, gefilte fish.[14] In all the years I have been taking people for dinner there I have never found one other person who likes this dish, but for me it is the taste of Shabbat.

Sabbah, Michel

The Latin Patriarch of Jerusalem, an Israeli Arab who led the Christian delegation in Alexandria. With Rabbi Melchior and Sheikh Talal, he was awarded the Coventry International Prize for Peace and Reconciliation in 2002.

Sada, Georges

A former air vice-marshal in the Iraqi air force and a passionate Christian, whom I first met in Baghdad in 1999. He was my right-hand man in Iraq until he was headhunted to run its new Ministry of Defence in 2005. He was the first secretary general of the Iraqi Institute of Peace.

---

14 An Ashkenazi Jewish dish made from a poached mixture of ground, deboned fish, such as carp, whitefish, or pike, which is typically eaten as an appetizer.

Sawers, John

The British diplomat who as ambassador to Egypt in 2002 played a crucial part in the Alexandria Process. I worked with him again in 2003 when he was Britain's "special representative" in Iraq. He is now Britain's ambassador to the United Nations.

Shehan, Josef

Josef is known to me and many of my colleagues simply as "Joseph the carpenter". He is an expert olive-wood craftsman and his skills are highly prized. Once again, he is somebody whom I have had a close working relationship with for over twenty-five years. Initially, I was helping support the funding for his daughter Despina's treatment. She suffers from the congenital condition Marfan syndrome. This caused serious scoliosis and she required major surgery to correct this problem. The family are Syrian Orthodox and live in Bethlehem, so are not entitled to free medical treatment

Singerman, Haim and Ruti

Haim and Ruti are dear friends who run the Jerusalem Hills Inn in Abu Ghosh, a small, mainly Arab town between Jerusalem and Tel Aviv. This town is famous for always having been proud of being Israeli. Their family consists of seven children between the ages of three and twenty-two. Once again, I have a very close relationship with the whole family. I am especially close to their eldest daughter, Sarah, and youngest son, Yoshi. I will regularly celebrate Erev Shabbat with them if I am in Jerusalem for Shabbat. Haim and young Yoshi both came to Cyprus with me when we had our first meeting between the Israelis and Iraqis, and helped provide the continual prayer cover.

Talal Sidr, Sheikh

A minister in the Palestinian Authority (though he had been one of the founders of Hamas) who was the inspirational leader of the Muslim delegation in Alexandria. He forged a crucial alliance – and friendship – with Rabbi Melchior, and shared the Coventry International Prize for Peace and Reconciliation with him and Patriarch Sabbah in 2002. He died in 2007.

Tamari, Salah

The former PLO commander, then a member of the Palestinian Legislative Assembly, who led the first Palestinian negotiating team during the siege of the Church of the Nativity. He is now governor of Bethlehem.

Tantawi, Sheikh Muhammad Sayed

The Grand Imam of al-Azhar in Cairo, and as such the highest authority in Sunni Islam. He was the co-chair of the summit that produced the Alexandria Declaration in 2002.

Taub, Ambassador Daniel

Daniel served as the Israeli ambassador to the Court of St James (UK) from 2011 to 2015. As he is British-born, he had the very strange privilege of serving as ambassador to the country of his birth, a fact that the Queen famously commented on when he was presented to her. He is an Oxford graduate, a lawyer, and a former combat medical technician in the Israel Defense Forces. He has a wonderful family, with six children. Now back in Israel working at the Foreign Ministry, he is a seasoned diplomat who was previously a speechwriter for President Herzog. He is exceptionally articulate and one of the most outstanding speakers at the Jerusalem Reconciliation School.

Wijdan Michael Salim, Mrs

An outstanding member of the Iraqi government who is currently Minister for Human Rights. A Chaldean Catholic who has become a very good friend of mine.

Wilson, Connie and Bill

Connie and Bill are essential to my life and work in both Jerusalem and Washington, DC. They live in both places and I stay with them in both! They truly do live in two of the most outstanding locations in the world. They have an incredible apartment in Jerusalem, in the King David apartments next door to the King David Hotel, with a stunning view over the Kidron Valley and the Old City of Jerusalem. How we came to get together is almost like a biblical story itself, and to me they are a gift of the Almighty. We were even married on the same day in 1991.

Yazidi

Members of an ancient community concentrated in northern Iraq who revere an angel sometimes called Shaytan and hence are often (wrongly) regarded by Muslims as Devil worshippers. In 2007, almost 800 were killed by suicide bombers in two co-ordinated attacks.

The Foundation for Relief and Reconciliation in the Middle East

FRRME is a non-profit organization and a registered UK charity supporting the unique work of Canon Andrew White, the Emeritus Vicar of Baghdad, who led St George's Church in Baghdad until November 2014.

FRRME promotes conflict resolution in the Middle East, specializing in conflicts with a religious component to the violence. It also provides humanitarian relief and economic rejuvenation in areas where conflict has caused poverty and hardship. This work is primarily conducted in Iraq, Jordan, and Israel/Palestine.

FRRME provides vital relief – food, medicine, and shelter – to Iraqi Christian refugees who have fled the sectarian violence in Iraq.

Currently, FRRME runs a church, school, and health clinic in Amman, Jordan, where many Iraqi Christian refugees are now based. FRRME also provides relief for Iraqi Christians who are categorized as Internally Displaced People (IDP), many of whom have fled to the semi-autonomous region of Iraqi Kurdistan.

For his reconciliation work, Canon Andrew White has been awarded numerous international prizes, including the 2014 Anne Frank Special Recognition Award for Religious Tolerance and Reconciliation, as well as the 2014 William Wilberforce Award.

As part of our reconciliation work, FRRME founded the High Council of Religious Leaders in Iraq (HCRLI) which exists to bridge religious divides, enabling faith leaders to use their considerable influence to persuade people to refrain from violence, to engage politically, and to support the rule of law. It includes senior religious leaders from across Iraq's faith and ethnic groups that hold greatest political sway – Sadrists, Kurds, Sunni, Shia, and Christians.

To find out more about FRRME's work, please visit: www.frrme.org, or get in touch at: office@frrme.org.